7/60

‖‖‖ ‖‖ ‖ ‖‖‖‖‖ ‖‖ ‖‖‖ ‖‖‖
◁ **P9-DTA-897**

The Middle Ages
An Illustrated History

The Middle Ages

An Illustrated History

Barbara A. Hanawalt

Oxford University Press

New York • Oxford

Oxford University Press

Oxford   New York
Athens Auckland Bangkok Bogotá Buenos Aires Calcutta
Cape Town Chennai Dar es Salaam Delhi Florence
Hong Kong Istanbul Karachi Kuala Lumpur Madrid
Melbourne Mexico City Mumbai Nairobi
Paris São Paulo Singapore Taipei Tokyo
Toronto Warsaw

and associated companies in
Berlin Ibadan

Copyright ©1998 by Barbara A. Hanawalt
Published by Oxford University Press, Inc.,
198 Madison Avenue, New York, New York 10016

Design: Sandy Kaufman
Layout: Loraine Machlin
Picture research: Lisa Kirchner

Library of Congress Cataloging-in-Publication Data
Hanawalt, Barbara.
The Middle Ages: an illustrated history / Barbara A. Hanawalt.
          p. cm.
Includes bibliographical references and index.
1. Middle Ages—History—Juvenile literature. [1. Middle Ages.]
I. Title.
D117.H26   1998
909.07—dc21

ISBN 0-19-510359-9

1 3 5 7 9 8 6 4 2

Printed in Hong Kong
on acid-free paper

Frontispiece: Image of knight praying on 14th century
stained glass window, Kreuzenstein Armory,
Kreuzenstein, Austria

Contents

Introduction

The terms "Middle Ages" and "medieval" were first used by Italian Renaissance historians of the 15th and 16th centuries. They regarded their culture as similar to that of the classical world of ancient Greece and Rome, but very different from the period between the fall of Rome and their own enlightened time. To Renaissance scholars that long interval was a period of superstition, ignorance, and barbarism, which they also called "the Dark Ages."

The scholars recording history during the Middle Ages, however, perceived the period very differently. Their chronicles show that they saw history as a continuous procession of events from the Biblical creation down to their own time. Augustine of Hippo (354–430), one of the early writers on Christianity, explained in *The City of God* that events such as wars and the formation of empires and kingdoms were not significant divisions in history. He instead maintained that human history progressed continuously from the creation to the end of the world. Like Augustine, people living in the Middle Ages did not discern a chronological break from the Roman period to their own.

Modern scholars of the medieval period, or medievalists, often struggle with the question of when the Middle Ages began and ended. The question is not easy to answer, because for the most part change takes place gradually and periods form their characteristics over centuries. But generally the medieval period is considered to stretch from the fifth to the 15th century, or from about 400 to 1500.

Another artificial boundary imposed on the Middle Ages is geographical. Medieval scholars did not use terms such as "western Europe" and "eastern Europe" or names for nation-states such as France, Greece, Germany, Turkey, and Italy. They were more inclined to draw boundaries along religious lines, by which they could distinguish their Roman Catholic culture and beliefs from those of Islam or of the Greek Christian (Orthodox) Church. By the end of the Middle Ages, people began to develop national identities—a sense, for example, of being French as opposed to English. But most people would have had a very local identity, defining themselves first by their father's or mother's name, then by their village or town of origin, and perhaps then by their overlord, their king or queen (if they had one), and their religion.

Before the 1970s, books on medieval history would deal exclusively with emperors, kings, battles, crusades, feudalism, manorialism, the rise of towns, the growth of parliament, universities, and the Church. In the past several decades, however, historians have been researching how average people experienced life in the Middle Ages. Histories of the period now contain information about Jews, women, children, peasants, heretics, mystics, and criminals. Such histories include a skeleton of traditional historical narrative fleshed out with stories about the ordinary as well as extraordinary people who lived through the events of the Middle Ages.

Medieval maps of the world were always round and showed Jerusalem, the place of Jesus's resurrection, in the center. The top of the map is east so that the sun rises where Jesus stands, flanked by two angels. Africa is the land mass on the right side (south), Europe is at the bottom (west) and extends almost to the nine o'clock position (north). The Mediterranean Sea separates Africa and Europe. Asia is to the left of Jesus.

Chapter 1
The Three Cultures That Made the Middle Ages

Two of the early "Doctors of the Church"—prominent interpreters of Christianity—were Augustine of Hippo (left) and Ambrose of Milan. Bishop Ambrose's sermons were in part responsible for Augustine's conversion. Augustine went on to write his Confessions, *an autobiographical account of his spiritual life, and* The City of God.

Because Augustine of Hippo (354–430) wrote the first autobiography, his *Confessions,* we know more about his personal life than we do about almost any other medieval figure. Augustine came from one of the most prominent Roman provincial families of North Africa. His father, Patricius, was a Roman noble who accepted the Greco-Roman pantheon of gods and thus worshipped Jupiter, Venus, and Mars. But Augustine's mother, Monica, was a Christian, and urged him to worship only the Judeo-Christian God.

Otherwise, Augustine's early life was typical of boys of the upper class. He learned Latin and Greek; read stories of the exploits of the gods, goddesses, and heroes such as Hercules and Odysseus; studied histories of the founding of Rome; and memorized the speeches of great Roman orators such as Cicero. His parents expected that he would go on to take a position in the Roman imperial government and sent him to Carthage for further education when he was in his teens. Augustine's training included the study of Greek and Latin rhetoric (the art of making convincing arguments) and literature, geometry, and philosophy. He read

Homer, Plato, Aristotle, Pythagoras, Virgil, and Cicero, among other authors. The study of rhetoric was considered useful for the political and administrative role he would one day play. (This education—with the exception of the study of Greek language—would become the model for medieval scholars and universities.)

Away from home, he pursued interests then typical of a teenager. He took a mistress at the age of 18 and eventually had a son by her. He also came into contact with new philosophies that questioned the old order of the gods and instead addressed moral issues, including questions about the nature of good and evil behavior.

Moving on to Milan in Italy, Augustine continued his preparation for a career in keeping with his upbringing. He became engaged to a wealthy young woman of his own class and cast aside his mistress and their son. But he also attended the sermons of a persuasive Christian orator, Bishop Ambrose of Milan. Christianity made Augustine feel increasingly guilty about his life of pleasure and his ambitions to play a major role in Roman politics. A friend furthered his anxiety by telling him the story of two young

To pay for the extensive public services that Rome provided, including paved roads, fresh water supplies for cities, and the administration of justice, the empire had to tax its citizens heavily. The people paid coins (they did not have paper money) directly to the tax collector.

upper-class men who had given up their engagements and careers to become Christian monks. Torn between the traditions of his Roman heritage and the new Christian ideals espoused by his mother and Bishop Ambrose, Augustine retreated to his garden to meditate on his beliefs. In tears, he heard the voice of a small child repeating over and over: "Take it and read, take it and read." He returned to his house and opened his copy of St. Paul's Epistles to the Romans, in which he read Paul's exhortation that Romans should abandon their lusts and accept Jesus Christ as their protector. Augustine later wrote in his autobiography: "As I finished the sentence, as though the light of peace had been poured into my heart, all the shadows of doubt dispersed." He converted to Christianity and returned to Hippo, in North Africa. There he established an order of monks and eventually became the bishop of Hippo. From that town, he observed the incursion of barbarian tribes, who sacked the city of Rome and destroyed the way of life that he knew.

Rather than looking upon the changes in his world negatively, he wrote in another book, *The City of God,* that the world of the spirit was more important than that of the empire. Ironically, he died a few months before the Vandals, one of the invading tribes, captured Hippo.

Three cultures—Roman, Christian, and barbarian—strongly influenced Augustine's life and pulled him emotionally in three directions. In the end, these three cultures were all instrumental in shaping the Middle Ages. As Augustine's life shows, living through the fourth and fifth centuries was not easy. People had to struggle with conflicting ideas about spiritual values, reconcile different forms of government, learn new languages, and cope with major changes in their daily lives.

The Roman Empire initially controlled only the city of Rome and the surrounding countryside, known as Latinium. Through gradual conquests, its control extended over a vast area surrounding the Mediterranean Sea. Eventually portions of the continents of Europe, Africa, and Asia were included in its borders. The populations that Rome dominated included Celts in the territory of modern Britain, France, and Spain; Berbers and Egyptians in North Africa; Germanic tribes in modern Germany; and Greeks, Syrians, Jews, and Arabs in the eastern Mediterranean. In Europe Roman control extended into Britain, across the Rhine River into Germany, down the Danube River to the Black Sea, along a fringe around that sea, and deep into the Middle East. From east to west the empire extended 3,000 miles, approximately the distance between New York and San Francisco.

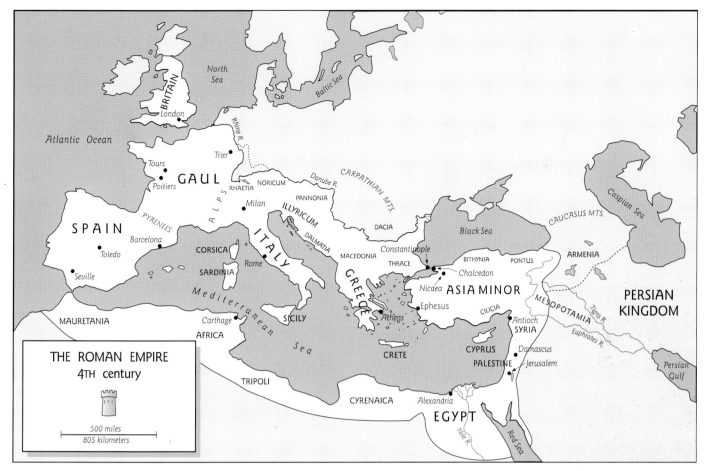

The map shows:

THE ROMAN EMPIRE
4TH century

500 miles
805 kilometers

North Sea, Baltic Sea, Atlantic Ocean, BRITAIN, London, Rhine R., Trier, Tours, GAUL, Poitiers, NORICUM, Danube R., CARPATHIAN MTS., ALPS, RHAETIA, PANNONIA, DACIA, Caspian Sea, Milan, ILLYRICUM, SPAIN, PYRENEES, ITALY, DALMATIA, MACEDONIA, Black Sea, CAUCASUS MTS., Barcelona, Rome, Constantinople, THRACE, BITHYNIA, PONTUS, ARMENIA, Toledo, CORSICA, SARDINIA, Chalcedon, Seville, Mediterranean, Nicaea, ASIA MINOR, PERSIAN KINGDOM, MESOPOTAMIA, Tigris R., MAURETANIA, Carthage, SICILY, GREECE, Ephesus, CILICIA, Antioch, SYRIA, Euphrates R., AFRICA, Sea, Athens, CRETE, CYPRUS, Damascus, Persian Gulf, PALESTINE, Jerusalem, TRIPOLI, CYRENAICA, Alexandria, EGYPT, Nile R., Red Sea

The Roman government began as a republic governed by a senate that represented wealthy established families and an assembly that represented the plebeians, or ordinary free citizens. As the territory expanded, this representative form of government no longer worked, and an emperor became the titular head of Rome and the large land mass it had acquired. Some aspects of the older form of government were retained. The senators, for instance, still served as generals in the army and governors in the provinces. They also oversaw a highly sophisticated bureaucracy that administered laws and public services and collected taxes. (In his youth, Augustine had been grooming himself to become just such an imperial administrator.) A common language for administration (Latin), a system of paved roads that made it possible to send mail and move troops rapidly, and Roman law held together this vast geographic area with its diverse ethnic groups. The peace that the Roman Empire secured for its conquered peoples was called the "Pax Romana," or the peace of Rome.

The physical remains of the remarkable Roman culture still exist throughout Europe, Asia, and Africa. In all parts of the former empire, portions of the Roman roads used during the Middle Ages can still be seen today. In Britain, the remnants of Hadrian's Wall (a stone barrier erected to keep out the Picts, or natives of Scotland) still stand; in Trier, Germany, a large Roman gate (Porta Nigra) is the focus of the town; and in Syria and Egypt the ruins of major Roman buildings are a common feature of the landscape. Still standing in other areas of the Romans' vast territory are the remains of country villas (often with only their magnificent mosaic floors intact), aqueducts for carrying fresh spring water to the heart of the cities, theaters and coliseums (public stadiums) for races and gladiator fights, forums for political debate and markets, public baths, and temples for the worship of the gods and goddesses.

The most remarkable ruins are found in Pompeii, a city that was buried under a layer of volcanic ash in A.D. 79. Here a whole city is preserved—from the corpses of those

The Roman Empire was a large land mass stretching from Britain down into Egypt. Its trade and administration focused on the Mediterranean. Its borders in Europe were exposed to Germanic tribes to the North; in Asia the Persian Kingdom to the east posed a threat. In the fifth century the Germanic tribes flooded across the border.

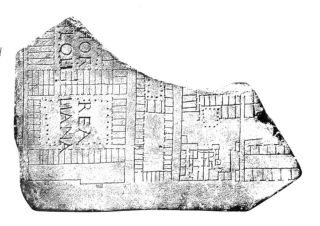

A fragment carved in stone of the street plan of Rome in A.D. 203–211 shows that the city was planned in a grid with buildings facing the street and a garden area behind the buildings. The grid pattern was adopted widely in 18th- and 19th-century urban planning.

This amphitheater in Arles, France, was built in the late first century A.D. in imitation of the Coliseum in Rome. The people of Roman cities came to see chariot races, wild beast hunts, and gladiatorial games. During the persecution of Christians in the early third century, the imperial authorities had wild beasts kill Christians in the amphitheaters as entertainment.

killed in the disaster, positioned just as they were when caught unawares in their houses or streets, to the wall paintings in villas and even the graffiti in alleys. The remains of Pompeii reveal that the houses of the rich were brilliantly painted and had glittering mosaic floors. Although the furniture was sparse, statuary was common. Indoor plumbing added to the comfort of these private houses.

Booty and slaves from conquests further enhanced the wealth that the upper classes received from their vast country estates (*latifundia*). Unfortunately for most people, however, only members of the upper classes—the senatorial families, well-paid bureaucrats, and others with considerable wealth—enjoyed such a high standard of living. The Roman Empire did not provide such comforts for ordinary people, and ill-fed and over-worked slaves and laborers made up 80 to 90 percent of the population. Many slaves were highly educated Greeks who tutored young patrician boys such as Augustine. Others were skilled artisans, and still others from conquered tribes were fit only for fieldwork, the army, or fighting as gladiators. As slaves, they suffered violent removal from their language and culture, disruption of family life, sexual exploitation, brutality, and other abuses. Under the empire, plebeians no longer served in the army, but they continued to have political influence. To keep this restive group from rebelling against the senators and emperors, they received public support in the form of "bread and circuses," that is, free grain and sporting events.

An empire composed of diverse and hostile populations is difficult to hold together, but more severe problems arose from the chaos in the central government of the Roman Empire. By the third century, generals were declaring themselves emperors and leading armies of professional soldiers (mercenaries, or non-citizen soldiers paid to fight) against each other. Of the more than 20 emperors who served during one 50-year period, only one died of natural causes. The taxes levied to pay the mercenary soldiers became so burdensome that bureaucrats, retired soldiers, and others of the middle class fled to the countryside to avoid them. Added to the internal

stresses and strains on the empire were external threats. The Persians began invading the empire's extreme eastern frontier and a series of barbarian tribes were beginning to move across its western borders. By 407 Rome had already abandoned control of England.

The general disorder and the invasions led to a major reorganization under Emperor Diocletian (245–316; reigned 284–305). He was not a member of the traditional Roman senatorial class but rather a career soldier who came from the Balkan peninsula. He favored the eastern half of the empire, which he knew best. There Greek was spoken, and it was wealthier and easier to defend than the west, where the invading tribes were already settling within the empire's borders.

In 330, the Emperor Constantine (c. 280s–337; reigned 306–337) moved the capital from Rome to Byzantium, a small Greek city on the Bosporus channel, and renamed the city for himself—Constantinople. He moved many treasures and sculptures from Rome to Constantinople and encouraged the senators and patrician class to join him in the new capital. This eastern empire, which has become known as the Byzantine Empire, survived in diminishing form until 1453. To people in the Middle Ages, it remained the Roman Empire and its ruler was the Roman emperor. In medieval chronicles, however, its people were always referred to as Greeks because they spoke the Greek language.

Yet another source of turmoil added to the imperial officials' sense of unrest—Christians. Rome did not impose a religion on its conquered subjects. Although its official religion was based on its pantheon of gods, it allowed local groups to worship the gods of their ancestors. Among these groups several mystery religions (religions based on divine revelation) had also grown up, including the worship of Mythras, the god of the sun. The mystery cults offered their followers the assurance that the cults' founders were resurrected after death, a code of ethics, and the promise of an eternal afterlife. For soldiers, slaves, and even some patricians, Mythrasism was a comforting religion that they could practice while also worshipping Roman gods and goddesses. Christianity, a new religion with some of the characteristics of the mystery cults, posed more of a threat to Roman traditions, however. As an offshoot of Judaism, it was monotheistic (recognizing only one god rather than numerous gods) and denied its adherents worship of the official pantheon.

The story of Jesus recorded by his early biographers in the four Gospels—Matthew, Mark, Luke, and John—spoke not only of his message of salvation, peace, love, and compassion, but also of his disruptive relationship with his fellow Jews and eventual

Christians used a variety of symbols as metaphors for their religion. Stone carvings on sarcophagi, such as this one from the fourth century, include fish to represent converts, an anchor to signify hope, and a shepherd to symbolize Christ caring for his flock.

execution by Roman officials. Of the historic Jesus of Nazareth little is known aside from what is told in the Gospels. He was Jewish and probably born sometime between 8 B.C. and 4 B.C., rather than the traditional date of A.D. 1. He was an itinerant preacher who attracted followers. The period in which he preached was one of unrest in Palestine. Jews were hoping for the advent of a messiah who would deliver them from Roman rule. Where Jesus fell afoul of the Jewish population, however, was his claim that he was a spiritual messiah, seeking religious renewal rather than war. (Christ is the Greek translation of the word messiah.)

Christianity spread through the preaching of the first apostles and the efforts of an early convert, Paul. Speaking in the marketplaces, the apostles and other missionaries encouraged people to convert to the Christian faith. Baptism—a ceremony in which

water is used to wash away the original sin of Adam and Eve—distinguished membership in the sect. Baptism and the Eucharist (Greek for "thanksgiving")—the commemoration of the last supper Jesus had with the apostles, which is also known as communion—were the religion's chief sacraments. Soon Christians were meeting in small groups under the leadership of bishops. Paul gave advice on issues of worship through letters to these communities, and these were preserved in the New Testament as the Epistles of Paul. Although Christianity was most popular in the eastern part of the Roman Empire, the disciples traveled all over the empire, and Christian tradition maintains that Jesus' chief disciple, Peter, was martyred in Rome.

As the religion spread, Roman officials became suspicious of its followers. After all, the sect worshipped a man who reportedly was executed by crucifixion—a common Roman punishment for criminals that entailed either binding or nailing their hands and feet to crossed pieces of wood and leaving them to die. The organization of the religion into congregations under a bishop and the possibility that it would cause uprisings in the Jewish communities also suggested that it was a politically dangerous movement. Furthermore, Christianity's message was finding acceptance among the urban poor, slaves, women, and even soldiers. For the downtrodden, its promises of the forgiveness of sins and eternal salvation for those who suffered in this world had a strong appeal.

In the early fourth century, Diocletian issued an edict against Christians and their worship. It called for the confiscation of

The Byzantines closely associated Constantine (wearing crown) with Christianity and called him "the equal of the apostles." Pictures represented him as the religious leader of all Christians.

copies of the Gospels and Epistles of Paul and the execution of Christians who would not renounce their faith. The response of Christians to this repression is recorded in both official documents and the traditions of the Church. Some turned over their religious books and abandoned Christianity, but others chose to become martyrs for their religion. The atrocities they suffered—including crucifixions, flayings, fatal confrontations with wild animals in amphitheaters, and being forced into prostitution—gave Christian culture powerful stories of the martyrs' devotion to their religion.

One well-known story is that of Androcles and the lion. Androcles was a Christian slave who had run away into the wilderness, where he met a lion with a thorn stuck in its paw. Overcoming his fear of the beast, he extracted the thorn. Shortly afterwards, Androcles was captured and taken to a coliseum to be executed. He was thrown into the arena with a lion, which by chance happened to be the same animal he had helped. Recognizing his savior, the lion would not kill Androcles.

The writings of Vibia Perpetua, who died in an arena in Carthage on March 7, 302, provides a moving personal account of martyrdom. Although her father was a high-ranking Roman official who believed in the pantheon of gods, Perpetua refused to renounce her Christianity. Educated in Latin and Greek, she wrote an account of her arrest, her father's anguish, how she cared for her infant son in prison, and her visions of deliverance into heaven after her impending martyrdom. The person who wrote the end of her story recorded that the

The Four Gospels as Mythical Beasts

In medieval illustrations and sculpture, the four Gospel writers, or the Evangelists—Matthew, Mark, Luke, and John—were represented symbolically as beasts. This symbolism was drawn from the book of Revelations (Rev. 4:6-10).

The beasts used to symbolize each of the Evangelists reflected both the way in which they began their Gospels and an aspect of the life of Christ. Matthew was represented as a winged man because his gospel starts with the human genealogy of Christ. The human figure also represents Christ's Incarnation or birth. Mark was represented as a lion. His Gospel begins dramatically with the preaching of John the Baptist, described as a "voice crying in the wilderness" like the roar of a lion. The lion also stood for Christ's resurrection. In the Middle Ages lion cubs were thought to be stillborn and roared into life by their mother. An ox or calf was the symbol of Luke, whose Gospel opens with an account of Zacharias making sacrifices in the temple. Sacrificial animals such as oxen and calves are also used to represent Christ as the atoning sacrifice for human sin. Lastly, John was symbolized by an eagle. His gospel begins with Christ as the Word of God, existing in heaven before the Incarnation. The eagle also represents Christ's ascension into heaven.

In this 10th-century manuscript, Christ is enthroned in the center; the four evangelists in the corners, with their allegorical symbols in the adjacent circles.

Calendars: Regulators of Life

Calendars group days to regulate religious observance, business, agriculture, government, and daily life. Calendars were developed according to both solar and lunar cycles. A solar calendar calculates a year as a complete round of seasons, or one revolution of the earth around the sun (roughly 365.25 days). A lunar calendar relies on moon cycles (from one new moon to the next). A lunar year of 12 moon cycles has only about 354.33 days. In order to keep a lunar calendar from becoming out-of-step with the seasons, extra days have to be added.

By the time of Julius Caesar, the Roman lunar calendar was about three months out of sync with the sun's equinoxes, or seasons. In 45 B.C. he reformed the calendar on the advice of Sosigenes of Alexandria. The resulting solar calendar became known as the Julian Calendar after the emperor. The old lunar calendar was abandoned. In use during the Middle Ages, the Julian Calendar has

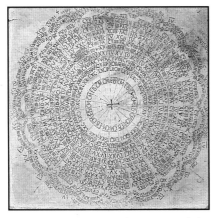

The Julian calendar, based on the seasons and the sun, was the basic calendar from Roman times thorough the Middle Ages.

365 days with a leap (366-day) year every four years.

Because the year is actually a little shorter than 365.25 days, discrepancies continued to appear. In 1582 Pope Gregory XIII revised the calendar yet again by dropping 10 days. The Gregorian Calendar, which is used today, brought the Vernal Equinox back to when it had occurred in the time of Julius Caesar. Gregory eliminated the leap year in years beginning a century unless they are divisible by 400. (For instance, 2000 will be a leap year, but 1900 was not.)

The system of numbering years before or after the birth of Christ was designed by an abbot, Dionysius Exiguus, who lived in the late 5th century A.D. The abbreviation A.D. stands for *anno domini* (in the year of the Lord in Latin), and B.C. represents the period before Christ. Unfortunately, the abbot made a mistake in calculating the date of Jesus' birth. Comparing the Gospels with other historical events in Roman and Jewish history, historians now know that he was actually born between A.D. 4 and A.D. 6 rather than the year A.D. 1, as popularly believed.

men in her Christian group were torn apart by wild beasts, including bears, leopards, and boars.

But Perpetua and Felicity, another woman who had just given birth, were gored by an enraged cow: "Perpetua was first thrown, and fell upon her loins. And when she had sat upright, her robe being rent at the side, she drew it over to cover her thigh, mindful rather of modesty than of pain. Next, looking for a pin, she likewise pinned up her disheveled hair; for it was not meet [acceptable] that a martyr should suffer with hair disheveled, lest she should seem to grieve in her

glory. So she stood up; and when she saw Felicity smitten down, she went up and gave her her hand and raised her up. And both of them stood up together and (the hardness of the people being now subdued) were called back to the Gate of Life." Felicity and Perpetua survived the first onslaught of the animals, but were later executed by swords.

On the whole, the persecutions probably strengthened adherence to Christianity, because the crowds were impressed by the strength of the martyrs' beliefs. But the real boost to Christianity's popularity came when Emperor Constantine converted in 313. Constantine's father, Constantinius Chlorus, was the caesar, or junior emperor, in charge of the westernmost provinces of the empire. His mother, Helena, was a Christian, who eventually went to Jerusalem and purportedly discovered the site of the Holy Sepulcher (the tomb of Jesus). To ensure that Constantine's father remained loyal, Diocletian, the senior emperor, insisted that Constantine be raised in his own court as both a pupil and a hostage. After his father's death, Constantine broke free of the court, escaping on horses that were stationed at convenient intervals to carry mail to the west. Fearing pursuit, Constantine hamstrung the horses at each post stop by cutting their leg tendons. Once in the west, he raised an army to fight the other contenders for his father's position. On the eve of a decisive battle that would make him emperor of the whole empire, he had a dream in which he saw a cloud pass before the sun and heard the words, "In this sign you will conquer" *(in hoc vinci)*. The next day he saw the sign, a

circle with a cross in it, during the battle and converted to Christianity.

Constantine's grasp of Christianity was limited. He continued to worship Mythras and the Roman pantheon of gods, but he won over Christians by revoking the edicts of persecution. Only toward the end of his life was he baptized. Despite his poor understanding of the Christian faith, he had a profound influence on the development of the religion. Following his lead, many people of all classes converted, including patricians. This large number of new converts presented certain problems, however. Some, like the emperor, did not understand the religion, and others believed that only their interpretations of the doctrines were correct. One of the early disputes arose from the question of whether Jesus was divine or human. Arguing for the humanity of Jesus was a monk named Arius; the movement that arose from his teachings was called Arianism. The Arians argued that if both Jesus and the Holy Ghost (who appears in

the New Testament as the manifestation of God in people and the Church) were considered divine, then the religion would no longer be monotheistic. They further maintained that if Jesus, the Holy Ghost, and God were all divine, then Christianity began to resemble the polytheism of the old Greco-Roman system. Tempers ran high over the question of Jesus' divinity; street fights even broke out over the controversy. In a similar debate a century later, St. John Crysostom wrote that when he asked the price of bread in the market he was given an argument about the nature of Christ in return.

In 325 Constantine called a council of bishops at Nicaea to decide the question of Jesus' divinity once and for all. He disliked the civil unrest the dispute had created, but he may also have been discomforted by his own doubts about the power of a religion that harbored so much controversy. At the council, Constantine oversaw the adoption of the Nicene Creed, in which the concept of the Trinity was formulated. According

Gladiators fight a variety of wild beasts in this fourth-century mosaic. Fighters risked their lives in these animal fights to the delight of amphitheater crowds.

The night before Constantine's decisive battle for control of the Roman Empire, he had a dream about a cross in a circle and the words in hoc vinci ("in this sign conquer"). The next day the same symbol appeared to him in the clouds. The sign influenced his decision to become a Christian.

Pilgrims to the Holy Land brought back various souvenirs from their pilgrimage. The sixth-century metal flask has a representation of the Ascension of Christ and contained oil from lamps that burned at holy shrines.

to the creed, God was the only divinity, but he had three persons: God the Father, God the Son, and the Holy Ghost. The council and its decision would have lasting implications. Following Constantine's example, emperors and lay rulers would assume a leading role in mediating disputes in the Church throughout the rest of the Middle Ages. Although the council dealt a great blow to Arianism, the movement did not die out immediately. While it continued, missionaries converted many of the barbarian tribes to the Arian version of Christianity. Thus when the tribes came into the empire, they were separated from the native population not only by language and culture but also by their type of Christianity.

Early Christians who longed for what they perceived as the "good old days," before these hordes of Christians-in-name-only joined the Church to please the emperor, began to retreat to the desert to practice their religion. St. Anthony was the most famous of the desert fathers, but he soon discovered, to his consternation, that others were eager to join him in his retreat. He had to organize his followers into a community of hermits. Gradually, monas-

teries—communities of men dedicated to celibacy and worship—became the common refuge from worldly concerns.

Women also wanted to seek salvation through retreat, but Christian leaders generally did not consider the desert an acceptable place for them. In particular, St. Jerome (c. 340–420), who had strong opinions on most matters relating to the practice of Christianity, felt that the excesses of hermits were not truly godly. He cited as evidence their poor hygiene and their beards. (He commented that if beards contributed to salvation, then all goats would be saved.) But St. Jerome was sympathetic to the women in his own family who did not want to marry for religious reasons, and organized a community in which women could live apart from society as nuns.

The writings of one early nun, Egeria, provide a sense of the cohesion of the Christian world and the peace in the empire during the fourth century. Historians speculate that Egeria came from a nunnery somewhere along the Atlantic, because in the records of her travels she compares the Red Sea to an ocean. Between 381 and 384, she made an extended pilgrimage to the sites of the Old and New Testaments and wrote of her journeys for the benefit of her sisters back home. She was an inexhaustible traveler, willing to climb mountains and go out of her way to visit shrines and holy monks. Among the hermits living in numerous cells surrounding one shrine at Golgotha she was reunited with a holy deaconess named Marthana, whom she had befriended in Jerusalem, where they had both been on pilgrimage. Marthana had become the leader of a group of virgins.

While at Golgotha Egeria wrote of the rituals of Holy Week—including fasting and night-long services—and finally of glimpsing a piece of the cross on which Jesus had been crucified: "As long as the holy Wood is on the table, the bishop sits with his hands resting on either end of it and holds it down, and the deacons round him keep watch over it. They guard it like this because what happens now is that all the people come up one by one . . . stoop over it and kiss the Wood. . . . But on one occasion one of them bit off a piece of the holy Wood and stole it away." Egeria's account gives a flavor of the devotion that early Christians felt for the religion, and records their desire to visit the shrines of its origin.

Among those who found Christianity attractive were Roman patricians, such as Augustine of Hippo, who had received a traditional education in Greek and Latin. Drawing from their intellectual back-ground, the patricians tried to fit Christian teachings into the context of Greek phi-losophy and rhetoric. The greatest of these thinkers were known as the Doctors of the Church. Among them was St. Jerome, who translated the Bible from Hebrew and Greek into Latin. (His translation, called the Latin Vulgate Bible, is still used in the Catholic Church.) Jerome's pagan heritage caused him considerable anxiety. He had a dream in which Jesus admonished him by saying, "You are a Ciceronian [an admirer of the essays of the Roman orator Cicero] rather than a Christian," because Jerome valued his rhetorical training so highly. Ambrose (c. 340–397), the bishop of Milan, used his great skill as an orator to convert his listeners

to Christianity. Indeed, he was such a persuasive preacher that patrician fathers supposedly did not want their daughters to hear his sermons out of fear that they would take vows of perpetual virginity and refuse marriages that were advantageous to the family. Among Ambrose's converts was Augustine of Hippo. Augustine became deeply interested in reconciling Greek phi-losophy with Christianity. The problem was not a new one. In the early first century A.D., Jewish scholars, including Philo Judaes, had tried to combine Biblical study with philosophy.

Even though Augustine died just be-fore one of the so-called barbarian tribes took over his home city in North Africa, his writings only indirectly reflected the major changes such peoples would bring to the Roman Empire. Their contribution to the unique culture of the Middle Ages can best be understood by looking at their way of life before they entered the empire. Historians have categorized the invaders as

St. Jerome, a doctor of the Church, translated the New Testament from Greek into Latin. His translation is still used in the Catholic Church and is known as the Vulgate. This 15th century illustration of Jerome in his study is obviously updated because the scene behind him is Florence.

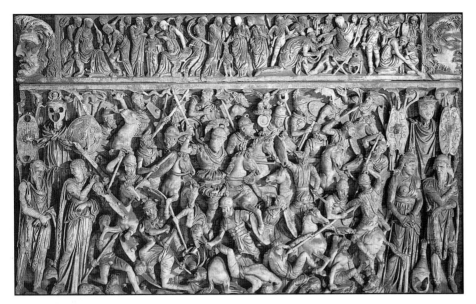

Oral tradition preserved the Old English poem Beowulf *for centuries. The first written version dates from the late 10th century. The edges of the page were charred by fire in 1731. The letters are easy to decipher, but the words are in Old English, which is close to German.*

Germanic (also called Gothic) because their language fell into a German linguistic group as opposed to the Greco-Roman or Celtic linguistic groups that had predominated in western Europe. They came into the empire from regions to the north and east, including Scandinavia. The Germanic tribes' values differed greatly from those of the Romans. Mediterranean civilization was based on cities and agriculture; the invaders preferred rural areas and hunting. Roman government was centralized; the tribes were organized loosely around kings, fighting bands, and family groups. Roman society had a high degree of literacy; the tribespeople were illiterate. Romans valued their public and private baths; the Germans were, to Roman nostrils, a dirty and smelly group.

Despite their differences, the Romans had frequent contact with the Germanic tribes on their borders through conquest, trade, and employment as slaves and mercenaries. In the 1st century A.D., a Roman historian, Tacitus, wrote a book about the tribes called *Germania*. Tacitus never visited the regions he described, however, so his information is not entirely reliable. Nevertheless, his book shows that this inquiring man was able to learn a great deal about the tribes' very different culture from soldiers, merchants, and even slaves. Other information about the barbarians comes from their laws, which they had transcribed in Latin in imitation of Roman law; scraps of their literature; and the evidence yielded by modern archaeology.

The economy of the Germanic tribes was based on simple agriculture, hunting, and plunder. For the most part, women and slaves cultivated grains and cared for domesticated animals, while the men hunted and fought in raiding parties. Gambling, storytelling, and drunken feasts served as pastimes for the men. In contrast to the Mediterranean taste for wine, they drank fermented brews of grain (beer) and honey (mead). According to Tacitus, the men would gamble until they had no stakes left but their own freedom. Some even gambled that away and became slaves.

In the mead halls men told stories of heroic adventures. Most of these were part of an oral tradition that was not preserved, but a few were written down later. The most famous is *Beowulf,* a story, written in Old English (Anglo-Saxon), which was set in Denmark. For 12 years a monster, Grendel, had ravaged the king's mead hall and devoured warriors. The poem describes his entry into the hall:

> Then came from the moors under the
>   misty hills
> Grendel creeping—he bore God's ire
> The evil-doer intended to entrap some
> of the kin of men in the high hall....
> The creature came then journeying to
>   the hall
> deprived of joy. The doors soon gave
>   way,
>   bound fast with forged bands,
>   after he touched them with his hands.

Beowulf, a young prince of the Geats, arrived from southern Sweden and offered to rid the kingdom of Grendel. When the

Sutton Hoo: Ship Burial for a Chieftain

In the summer of 1939, the richest find of Anglo-Saxon treasure ever discovered was unearthed on an estate in East Anglia. The owner of the estate was curious about a group of barrows, or burial mounds, on her property. She arranged for a local archeologist to investigate. The early results were disappointing: three small mounds showed signs of having been robbed. The largest mound, however, proved to be the magnificent, undisturbed burial chamber of a powerful chieftain. An entire ship, 86 feet long, had been buried in the large barrow, and inside it was a chamber that contained armor,

weapons, bowls, drinking vessels, and a large quantity of gold and garnet jewelry. This mound, too, would have been robbed, had it not been for plowing in the later Middle Ages that removed much of one end. When treasure-hunters dug into the mound in the 16th century, they dug into the center as it then existed thinking that it would contain treasure, but were misled by the missing part. Although no doubt disappointed, the would-be looters apparently stopped to eat a meal before leaving, as evidenced by pottery and part of a cook-fire found during the 1939 excavation.

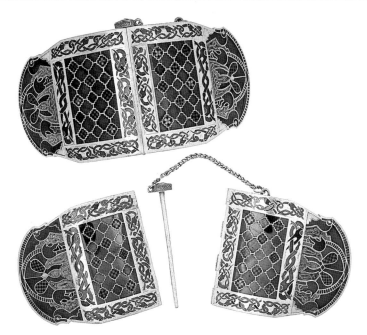

Among the treasures in the Sutton Hoo burial is a finely worked shoulder clasp for a leather tunic. The fine workmanship in gold, glass, and garnets indicates the level of skill that Germanic artisans possessed.

monster came to the mead hall that night and ate a Geat, Beowulf tore off his arm, and Grendel retreated to his lair to die. The Geats rejoiced in the prince's victory until the next night, when Grendel's mother came seeking revenge and killed one of the king's men. Beowulf then pursued her into a cave at the bottom of a sea, where he killed her.

Beowulf's return to Sweden with rich rewards was brief. The king of the Geats died, and Beowulf returned and served as their king for 50 years. But his story ended as it began, fighting a monster. The aged Beowulf again killed the enemy, but this time was mortally wounded. The story of Beowulf provides a sense of the tribes' wandering and mingling even before they moved into Roman territory. It also shows that they viewed nature as containing threatening, hostile elements, compared with the Roman's view of nature as providing an abundance of food for their benefit.

Germanic society was organized according to both family ties and a social hierarchy of kings and war chiefs under whom the warriors served. Below these groups were

slaves. War chiefs attracted a warrior band, or *commitatus* (literally, a group of fighters who have gathered together), by their prowess in fighting and by their success in taking plunder, which they distributed to their followers. Family groups and the commitatus formed loose units, but they coalesced into a tribe under the leadership of a king, particularly when they faced an external threat.

The tribes near the Roman Empire's borders were partially romanized. They knew something of the Roman economy, which was based on money rather than barter. They also had some knowledge of the Latin language and Roman military organization and law. Despite this exposure, however, the Germanic tribes preserved their own language and laws. Their laws dealt mainly with violence in interpersonal relationships. Because family honor was an important value, when a family member was killed, his or her relatives were bound to kill the murderer or one of his relatives in revenge. Such vendettas between families were obviously disruptive to the peace of the whole group,

so laws evolved calling for murderers to pay *wergeld* (human payment), or money compensation, to their victims' families. The amount depended on the value of the person killed. For instance, the murder of a king or a woman of childbearing age demanded very high wergeld. Other losses—such as the loss of limbs, teeth, and virginity—also required monetary compensation. The compensation for knocking out a front tooth was greater than for a molar because of its ill effect on a person's looks. Likewise, a thumb was worth a great deal more than a little finger.

Other laws governed theft, rape, adultery, and treason. Even relations with the Roman population were incorporated into the laws as the tribes moved across the empire's borders. A Frankish (the Franks invaded northern Gaul) law read: "If anyone has assaulted and plundered a free person, and it be proved on him, he shall be sentenced to 2500 denars, which make 63 shillings. If a Roman has plundered a Frank, the above law shall be observed. But if a Frank has plundered a Roman, he shall be

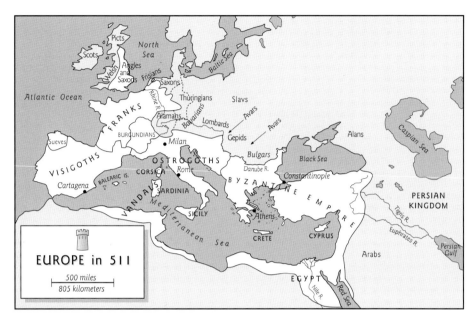

EUROPE in 511

500 miles
805 kilometers

sentenced to 35 shillings."

The Germanic tribes had already begun to move into the western empire by the early fifth century. By that time, the Anglo-Saxons had settled permanently in Britain, and the Franks had crossed the Rhine into Gaul. But this migration occurred with greater speed and urgency when a completely unromanized tribe, the Huns, forced the Germanic tribes to seek protection within the empire. The Huns were a nomadic people who traveled swiftly on horseback. Like other tribes, they tended to splinter into smaller groups, but they moved as a "horde" when poor pastures in central Asia drove them to migrate. Jordanes, a thoroughly romanized Goth, described the Huns as "small, foul and skinny; their faces were seamed with gashes, their noses broad and flat. They dressed in coarse linen tunics, which they never changed until they rotted; on their heads they wore a sort of helmet made with skins of wild rats patched together." He also said that they carried raw meat under their saddles all day and then ate it raw for supper as a sort of early version of steak tartare. Their drink was fermented mare's milk.

Jordanes had good reason to dislike the Huns. In time, the Huns so completely dominated the Gothic tribes of central Europe that they became indistinguishable from them. One small, remaining group of Goths, known as the Visigoths or west Goths, begged to be allowed into the Balkans. Thinking that they would be a useful buffer between the empire and the Huns, the Byzantine emperor settled them south of the Danube in 376. The emperor also agreed to pay the Visigoths for fighting, but when he reneged, they moved on into Italy under the leadership of their king, Alaric.

The emperor in the west, a young man named Honorius, panicked at the Visigoths' arrival, and retreated to the marshes of Ravenna, thereby allowing them to sack Rome in 410. Alaric gave his army three days to plunder the city; they then moved on with their booty and hostages. The image of a defeated, overrun Rome had a profound influence at the time and long after. St. Jerome wrote of his despair: "My tongue sticks to the roof of my mouth and sobs choke my speech." The animosity the Romans felt toward Alaric was so great that,

when he died, his followers feared his grave would be defiled. Legend holds that they diverted a stream and had captives bury him under its bed. They then killed the captives and redirected the stream, Alaric's body lying beneath it. To this day, no one knows where Alaric is buried.

The Visigoths chose Athaulf as Alaric's successor. The new king decided to move the tribe west through Gaul and into Spain, where they eventually established the Visigothic kingdom. Among the hostages they took with them was Galla Placidia, sister of Emperor Honorius. In fulfilment of an old prophesy, "the queen of the south married the king of the north" in January 414. At their Roman wedding Athaulf deferred to his bride, letting her lead the procession. Her lavish wedding gifts probably came from the sack of Rome.

Tradition has it that Galla Palacidia consented to the marriage and had a strong influence on her husband. She supposedly led him to accept Christianity and to become a defender of the Roman Empire rather than its invader. Certainly, his policy changed as he tried to form an alliance and friendship with his brother-in-law, Honorius. When Athaulf was murdered in Barcelona, Galla Placidia returned to Rome and married a Roman. She concluded her eventful life by ruling in the name of her infant son, who was made emperor.

The Huns continued to harass the Germanic tribes and threatened to invade the empire. Their leader from 433 to 453 was Attila, whose reputation for brutality is firmly planted in western European culture. At the time he was called the "Scourge of

God." Attila had his sights set on Rome. He claimed that he was coming to liberate Honoria, a Roman princess who had been disciplined for having an affair. She sent a ring to Attila proposing marriage. A Roman-Visigothic army forced him to retreat, but within a year he was plundering his way toward Rome, where only the city's bishop stood in his way. Again, probably because of plague in his army, Attila retreated. Taking yet another wife to join the many he had already, he died on his wedding night, perhaps of a surfeit of food and drink.

The Hunnish incursions again moved Germanic peoples to regroup into invading tribes. The Vandals moved through Gaul and Spain to set up a kingdom centered in Carthage, in North Africa. Augustine died only months before Hippo fell to them. The Vandals took to the sea as pirates, and in 455 they too sacked Rome. Their raiding left a permanent legacy in the English language—the word *vandalism*. Their name also remains as Andalusia, a province in southern Spain.

Once again Italy lay open to attack. The group that moved in this time was the Ostrogoths (or east Goths). The parts of Gaul that were not controlled by the Visigoths were invaded by the Burgundians and Franks, whose story will be told in the next chapter.

By the end of the fifth century, Rome, the founding city of the empire, had been sacked and its earlier prominence superseded by Constantinople. The Roman Empire had fragmented into a number of smaller kingdoms dominated by tribal lead-

ers. However, the eastern part of the empire, including Constantinople, remained wealthy and powerful, and its emperors came to resemble eastern potentates. Also during this period, the Christian church gained considerable stature and power among the Roman population. It had preserved Latin, the language of Roman culture, and in the west bishops increasingly took on the roles of Roman officials. They effectively governed cities and the surrounding countryside (called dioceses) for their Germanic overlords. With so much change taking place in the space of a century, the lives of people caught up in the new religious enthusiasms and in the myriad invasions and settlements also changed dramatically.

The Vandals quickly assumed the comfortable life of the upper class Romans, adopting their dress and living habits in northern Africa. They even learned to use Roman ships, and with a fleet they attacked and destroyed Rome in 455.

Chapter 2

Settling Down in the Old Empire

Major historical events usually create traumas and drastic changes in individual lives. The Visigoths' sack of Rome in 410 had an enormous impact on the invaders and the invaded. One Roman of patrician rank, for example, wrote to a friend complaining that the Visigoths had stolen his land, which ruined him and reduced him to beggary. Strangely, some years later one of the plunderers located him and offered to pay for the land he had taken. Although the Roman claimed that he did not receive the fair market value, he confessed that the return of a part of his wealth helped him to again hold his head up in the Roman society of Gaul.

With the invasion of Rome, people lost not only land. Many lost their lives, and many others faced the possibility of marriage to people whose appearance and customs were strange.

For people living in Europe from the fifth through the seventh centuries, waves of change altered or removed many of their familiar institutions. As a result, their children had to be reared differently from the way they themselves had been. For tribes accustomed to moving to greener pastures

and new forests when they had exhausted the old, becoming part of the empire meant encountering people who lived in one place and cultivated the same land year after year. Loose tribal confederations became kingships (*rex* was the Roman term for their leaders); Germanic laws had to be reconciled with Roman laws; and for the Germanic tribes individual ownership of land created an entirely new concept of making a living, that is, from cultivation rather than plunder. Adding to the confusion were Roman prejudices against the Germanic tribes. The Roman population, now Christian, regarded their new neighbors as land grabbers and heretics (religious dissenters who held incorrect views of Christianity), because many of the tribes had converted to Arianism (the interpretation of Christianity that had been banned in 325 at the Council of Nicaea).

The letters and some poetry of a patrician Roman named Apollinaris Sidonius (431–489) provide an insight into the experiences of at least one man and his correspondents during this turbulent period. Sidonius had followed the traditional career pattern for his class. He had entered public service,

Clovis was baptized after he promised his wife that he would convert to Christianity if he won an important battle. When he was successful, he also had all his troops baptized with him. This 14th-century manuscript shows a bishop pouring the baptismal water over the king's head.

Converted tribesmen often used both pagan and Christian symbols on their tombstones. This stone has the typical double-headed serpent from pagan art; the flask at the man's feet and the sword and comb in his hands suggest that these are pagan grave goods. The other side of the stone, however, has a representation of Christ carrying a spear.

becoming an official in Rome. He was of such high status that he married the emperor's daughter. After retiring to his country estates, he spent the final 17 years of his life serving as bishop of Clermont in what is now central France. As the Church became the last vestige of the old imperial system, many members of the patrician class became bishops and continued to administer both spiritual comfort and civic services to the urban population. Like many other bishops, Sidonius was charged with the task of organizing the defense of his city against the Visigoths and other tribes who besieged the countryside in the 470s. He wrote in 473: "Our own town lives in terror of a sea of tribes which find in it an obstacle to their expansion and surge in arms all around it." When the town fell, he spent three years as a prisoner of the Goths.

Despite the sack of Rome, Sidonius continued to consider the city "the abode of law, the training-school of letters, the font of honors, the head of the world, the motherland of freedom, the city unique upon earth where none but the barbarian and slave is foreign." But he was fully aware that the "Roman state has sunk to . . . extreme misery." Writing to his friends, Sidonius praised his correspondents' dedication to keeping the study of Latin and Greek alive: "The Roman tongue is long banished from Belgium and the Rhine; but if its splendor has anywhere survived, it is surely with you; our jurisdiction is fallen into decay along the frontier, but while you live and preserve your eloquence, the Latin language stands unshaken."

Sidonius also wrote of the transformation taking place among the tribespeople. He described Sigismer, a Germanic prince, who walked at the center of a victory procession:

> With charming modesty he went afoot amid his body guards and footmen, in flame-red mantle, with much glint of ruddy gold, and gleam of snowy silken tunic, his fair hair, red cheeks and white skin according with the three hues of his equipment. But the chiefs and allies who bore him company were dread of aspect. . . . Their feet were laced in boots of bristly hide reaching to the heels; ankles and legs were exposed. They wore tight tunics of varied color hardly descending to their bare knees, the sleeves covering only the upper arms.

Cloaks of skins secured with brooches completed their garb.

Bishop Gregory of Tours (538–594), writing about a hundred years later, presented a very different picture of Gaul. By this time, the Visigoths had moved on into Spain, and a new tribe, the Franks, had crossed the Rhine and settled in what was once Roman territory. The area eventually took the name France from this tribe. The Franks had had little contact with Romans and had not converted to any version of Christianity. Bishop Gregory's own world was far removed from Rome and the impe-rial traditions, but Christianity was strong. He wrote of his embarrassingly poor Latin, which indicates that he was not schooled by the old standards. His interests also show a shift of perspective from that of Sidonius. He recounted stories of brutal Frankish rulers and relished miraculous events rather than classical literary works. For example, Gregory wrote of an army of Franks who plundered the church of the holy St. Vincent, a martyr who died for his Christian beliefs. The troops found it filled with treasure that had been deposited by Christians who trusted in the saint's power to save their goods. Unable to open the church, the Franks set it afire. When they tried to retrieve the goods inside, however, divine vengeance was visited on them. According to Gregory, their hands were "supernaturally burned, and sent forth a great smoke, like that which rises above a fire."

Gregory also recounted the vicious politics of the Franks, who gradually seized all of Gaul. Clovis (481/2–511) emerged as the victorious ruler after many battles in which his family members were often killed. Gregory reported an emotional speech Clovis delivered before a large gathering of Franks: "Oh woe is me, for I travel among strangers and have none of my kinsfolk to help me!" Gregory went on to suggest that "he did not refer to their deaths out of grief, but craftily, to see if he could bring to light some new relatives to kill."

Clovis and the Franks, however, were set apart from other tribes by their conversion to Roman Christianity, that is, the Christian beliefs of the bishop of Rome (also known as the pope) as opposed to those of the Arian heretics. Clovis married a Christian woman, Clotilda. Her uncle had killed her father and drowned her mother by tying a stone around her neck. Clotilda's sister had retreated to a nunnery, and Clotilda might have followed suit if Clovis had not been taken by her beauty and married her. Gregory of Tours wrote that Clotilda immediately tried to convert Clovis to Christianity. She persuaded him to allow the first two sons she bore to be baptized, but because they died soon after birth her husband remained unconvinced about the new religion's worth. Finally, in a battle with another tribe, Clovis looked to heaven and promised to convert if he won. After his victory, he fulfilled his promise by being baptized along with 3,000 of his followers. Clovis knew even less than Constantine about Christianity, but because he and the Franks were baptized as Roman Christians, they were loyal to the pope. Later, when the Church needed help, its leaders looked to the Franks for aid.

Clovis unified the Franks under a long-lasting dynasty, the Merovingians—a name derived from a mythical ancestor, Merowech. The Franks practiced partible inheritance—that is, a father's lands were divided equally among his sons. Upon their father's death, brothers would fight each other until one dominated. Each change of king, therefore, resulted in the same sorts of brutal fights between brothers in which Clovis had engaged. The queens were no less capable of bloodthirsty tactics. Despite such fighting, the Franks became a strong power in Europe. They successfully assimilated their kin from across the Rhine and encouraged missionaries to convert their brethren.

Italy enjoyed a generation of peace and order under another tribal invasion, the Ostrogoths (or east Goths). Their leader was Theodoric (reigned 471–526), who had been a hostage at the court in Constantinople and therefore was very familiar with imperial government. Although the Ostrogoths were Arians, Theodoric did not try to persuade the non-Arian population to convert. Rather than destroying what remained of the Roman Empire and Roman ways, he worked with the conquered people to restore their aqueducts, repair their buildings, and improve the general order and economy of the Italian peninsula. In return for aiding the local population and defending them against other tribes, the Ostrogoths taxed a third of the proceeds from the estates of the wealthy. This policy was kinder to the local population than the outright plunder and confiscation of goods and land that other tribes had committed.

With the establishment of a general peace between mainstream Christians and heretical Arians, between Romans and Ostrogoths, learning once again flourished in Italy. Boethius (c. 480–524), a Roman who became an official for the Ostrogoths, realized that Greek might die out as a language of learning. Thus he translated portions of Greek philosophy, including the entire works of Plato and parts of Aristotle's writings. His translations were used throughout the Middle Ages. Cassiodorus (c. 490–585), another scholar who was close to Theodoric, retired from government service and became the abbot of a monastery. He set his monks the task of copying and preserving the works of Christianity and of pagan Greece and Rome.

Amalsuntha, daughter of a sixth-century Byzantine emperor, became regent for her young son on her father's death. This ivory shows her holding an orb, the symbol of ruling, wearing a typical Byzantine crown and sitting on a throne surrounded by pillars to suggest a palace.

Symmachus and his son-in-law Boethius were Romans who served as officials under the Ostrogothic king Theodoric. But when the Pope began to attack the Ostrogoths for their Arian heresy, Theodoric turned against his Roman officials and they were executed.

Mysterious Plague Kills Hundreds in Marseilles

The bubonic plague, like many other epidemics, comes in cycles. The first plague of the medieval period occurred during the reign of Justinian (527–565); the second, called "The Black Death," struck in 1348. Plague is a bacterial infection normally spread to humans through the bite of a household flea that has picked up the bacteria from an infected household rat. Gregory of Tours, who saw the plague's effects firsthand, wrote a very accurate description of the clinical symptoms of the disease:

> At this time it was reported that Marseilles was suffering from a severe epidemic of swelling in the groin. . . . I want to tell you exactly how this came about. . . . a ship from Spain put into port with the usual kind of cargo, unfortunately also bringing with it the source of infection. Quite a few of the townsfolk purchased objects from the cargo and in less than no time a house in which eight people lived was left completely deserted, all the inhabitants having caught the disease. The infection did not spread through the residential quarter immediately. Some time passed and then, like a cornfield set alight, the entire town was suddenly ablaze with the pestilence. . . . At the end of two months the plague burned itself out. The population returned to Marseilles, thinking themselves safe. Then the disease started again and all who had come back died. On several occasions later on Marseilles suffered from an epidemic of this sort.

The plague killed three-fourths of the people that it infected, so burial of the dead became a problem. In some places mass burials replaced the usual ritual of washing the body, putting it in a shroud (pictured in the center), and putting it in a coffin.

By the early sixth century, the world of learning was much changed from the time of Jerome and Augustine. Preservation of the past became the overwhelming preoccupation for the surviving Romans, as it had for Sidonius. Even Boethius's great work, *The Consolation of Philosophy,* had more to say about the comforts of contemplating Greek philosophy than it did about his Christian present.

The comfortable compromise between Theodoric and the Pope did not long survive. The Roman emperor of the east, Justinian (527–565), began an ambitious program to reconquer Italy, North Africa, and Spain—the wealthiest parts of the former western empire. The expeditions were very expensive, however, and Justinian's victories were few. The Byzantine armies defeated the Vandals but could retain only a small portion of North Africa. They did gain Sicily and southern Italy; however, the protracted campaigns weakened the Ostrogoths and destroyed more towns, villas, and Roman roads and viaducts than all the previous Gothic invasions. The senate finally ceased to meet, and the last public entertainment in the Coliseum was held in 549. Only Ravenna remained as a glorious outpost of Byzantine civilization in Italy.

The mid-sixth century was a grim time for Italy. Bubonic plague—the disease that would be called the Black Death in the 14th century—decimated the population. As a result of the Ostrogoths' campaigns and the plague, Italy lay open to invasion by a savage new tribe, the Lombards. As earlier in the face of the Huns, the bishop of Rome was left alone to ward off invasion. He

During the Middle Ages, sick people made pilgrimages to the shrines of saints, hoping to be cured by praying at the tomb or consuming dust from it. A superstructure with niches protected the tomb from being entirely scraped away by the pious; it allowed them to get only part of their bodies close to the tomb.

managed to preserve Rome and the land around it, but the Lombards took over most of the northern part of the peninsula around Milan, which became known as Lombardy. The Lombards represented yet another challenge for conversion and assimilation into something resembling the Roman way of life.

The brutality of the times is depicted in a story about a Lombard king and his wife. The queen's father had been a rival chieftain, whom her husband had killed. Proud of his deed, he carried the father-in-law's skull about as a trophy. During a banquet, he filled the skull with wine and forced his wife to drink his health. She complied but vowed to murder her husband—a promise she kept. Despite the gruesome infighting of the Lombard royal family, eventually the Lombards, too, were Christianized.

Although the original written legal codes of the Germanic tribes were intended to keep the Roman and Germanic populations separate, the distinctions between the two could not be maintained. Intermarriage frequently occurred, and the languages blended to create the Romance (or Latin-root) languages: Italian, French, Spanish, and Romanian. The two groups slowly assimilated into a common culture, but it is not known how people felt about this transition as it was taking place. Did Roman fathers think that their Germanic sons-in-law had crude table manners? Did Germanic boys think that their dark-haired Roman brides, whatever land and wealth that they brought to the marriage, were less beautiful (or more beautiful) than the blonde girls they were used to? Did Roman women

resent becoming wives to husbands who wore hides rather than tunics or had blond hair and blue eyes rather than dark hair and dark eyes? (Some women preferred a life in a nunnery to marriage, but not necessarily because they objected to the physical and cultural characteristics of a prospective husband.) In any case, the invaders settled, married into the local population, adopted hybrid languages of Latin and Germanic words, and produced children of mixed ancestry. Indeed, the entire Ostrogothic population was assimilated into the population of Italy. The western Mediterranean culture as well as the appearance of its people changed through genetic mixing that introduced fairer skin and blond and red hair into their population.

For some time the Romans managed to keep for themselves the distinction of serving as bishops in the old Roman towns. Gregory of Tours, for example, boasted that all but five of the bishops of Tours had been connected with his family. But his power and that of the other bishops depended on the tribal rulers. The bishops governed the towns and their surrounding countryside in a unit of land and government called the diocese. The church in which the bishop officiated was called a cathedral. Gregory of Tours described one built in Clermont-Ferrand: "It is one hundred and fifty feet long, sixty feet wide inside the nave and fifty feet high as far as the vaulting. It has a rounded apse at the end, and two wings of elegant design on either side. The whole building is constructed in the shape of a cross. It has fifty-two windows, seventy columns and eight doorways.

In it one is conscious of the fear of God and of a great brightness."

The cathedrals often contained the bones of early Christian saints. Pious Christians traveled to the shrines to cure their illnesses, for the religious experience of being near the body of a martyr, for the adventure of travel, or for the opportunity to buy and sell goods at their destination. They also left gifts, including extensive land holdings, to the cathedrals and churches that housed the bones of notable saints. Gregory had particular success as a bishop by making the shrine of St. Martin of Tours one of the most venerated stops for pilgrims. Another famous shrine was that of St. Denis the martyred, first bishop of Paris. His remains rested in a large and wealthy monastery. That monastery became even wealthier when it established an annual fair that attracted merchants from all over Europe as well as the eastern Mediterranean.

Despite the popularity of St. Denis and St. Martin among pilgrims, the status of these saints was far lower than that of St. Peter, one of Jesus' original apostles. The bishop of Rome held a special place in the hierarchy of bishops because Rome had been the center of the empire and because Christian tradition was woven around Jesus' words to Peter: "Thou art Peter and on this rock I shall build my church." According to Christian tradition, Peter had founded the first church in Rome and was martyred there. The bishop of Rome, as the successor of Peter, was considered the head of the Church and came to be called pope or *papa* (Latin for father). But the superior position of the bishop of Rome also owed much to

When monks took their final vows to join a monastery, they received a tonsure—the hair on the top of their heads was cut off. Here, St. Guthlac (c. 674-714), an Anglo-Saxon, receives a tonsure from a bishop while his abbess and other nuns observe.

Peter, as the favored apostle of Jesus, held a place of special reverence in the early Church. Tradition maintained that he had founded the first Christian church in Rome and had suffered a martyr's death in that city. In medieval illustrations he is depicted carrying two keys—the keys to heaven. The symbolism of the keys derives from words Jesus said to Peter: "I will give you the keys to the kingdom of heaven: Whatever you bind on earth will be considered bound in heaven; whatever you loose on earth shall be considered loosed in heaven." The name Peter, from the Greek word for rock (petra), becomes a pun when Jesus says "Thou art Peter and on this rock I shall build my church." The term "apostolic succession" —which was used often by medieval papacy—meant that the popes were directly descended by ordination from Peter and that they also held the power of the two keys.

the able men who held the office and their heroic leadership in both church and state matters. For example, Leo the Great (pope from 440–461) had defended Rome against the Huns, and Gregory the Great (c. 540–604) did much to increase the power of the papacy through missionary activity, reform of the church, and administration of the papal estates around Rome.

While the peoples within the old empire were gradually being Christianized, those on the fringes were either pagans or Arian heretics. Monks served as missionaries to these peoples. St. Patrick (c. 389–c. 461), for example, was a missionary in Ireland. According to his early biographer, he came from a Christianized family in Britain, but at the age of 16 Irish raiders captured him. He spent six miserable years as a slave in Ireland before he escaped and returned to Britain. He received further education in Christianity among the Roman population of southern Gaul. Summoned in a dream to go back to Ireland and Christianize the people there, he accepted the mission and began preaching and baptizing new converts. Although many of his followers were killed and he was nearly martyred, Ireland became Christian. The Irish then sent their own missionaries to the north of England, where a remarkable monastic culture was established at such places as Iona. The monasteries housed both men and women and were often supervised by an abbess rather than an abbot.

The monasteries in Ireland and the north of England (in the Anglo-Saxon kingdom of Northumbria) produced remarkable artists, scholars, saints, and missionaries. The designs in their books and of their statuary and altar ornaments combined motifs derived from indigenous animals with Christian symbolism. Their saints were remarkable for their perseverance and their relationship with animals. For example, the Irish saint Brendan set out in a small boat in the Atlantic with few provisions, but birds ensured that he was fed. St. Cuthbert once stood up to his neck in the cold waters of the North Sea to meditate. When he got out, otters came to dry his feet.

While the Irish and Anglo-Saxons in the far north were practicing their own type of monasticism, a young Roman noble, Benedict (c. 480–c. 550), decided that he did not want to follow the usual career path for his class. Instead of entering politics, he became a hermit. His reputation for piety grew, and he soon had more followers than he could easily settle near him. Furthermore, his disciples were overwhelmed by worldly temptations, and fought with one another. To provide them with a more peaceful refuge, Benedict moved his followers from outside Rome to Monte Cassino in southern Italy. His sister, Scholastica, set up a hermitage nearby, and became the patron saint of Benedictine nuns. Eventually, Benedict wrote a set of rules for his followers—the Benedictine Rule—that monastic orders in the west still follow. Indeed, the Benedictines are among the most numerous of the monastic orders in the world today.

The Benedictine Rule was based on three simple precepts: a vow of poverty, a vow of chastity, and an acceptance of complete obedience to the abbot. When a person entered a monastery or nunnery, he or she gave all personal possessions to the community and adopted the simple robes and sandals of the order. An initiate, or new member, commonly went through a period of trial, called a novitiate, before taking the final vows. The novitiate helped people make sure that the rigors of monastic life were what they really wanted. Once initiates had passed through the novitiate and taken their final vows, they wore the symbols of their order. Men shaved their heads, leaving only a ring of hair on the top called a tonsure. Women donned a distinctive veil.

Within the religious community, responsibilities were assigned according to the skills of its members. Some administered the monastery, while others copied and illuminated (decorated) manuscripts, educated children, worked in the kitchens and barns, or became priests. Everyone said prayers seven times a day. Recognizing the difficulty of waking up before sunrise to pray, the Rule asked that brothers gently encourage one another to do so. Their simple diet consisted of cheese, fish, bread, beans, and a good measure of wine every day. The young, sick, and elderly were also encouraged to eat some meat for strength. The residents of the monastery lived in dormitories supervised by the older monks. Other monastic buildings included a large kitchen, storage areas, barns, a chapter house for meetings, a chapel, a scriptorium for writing and keeping books, and a cloister for meditation and growing medicinal herbs. The monk's life was simple, orderly, and dedicated to prayer, learning, and service to the poor.

The Benedictine Rule was very popular, and soon many new monasteries were

The Illuminated Manuscripts

The word "illuminate" comes from the Latin *illuminare,* which means "to light up." In the Middle Ages, illuminated manuscripts were texts decorated with letters and images formed from colored inks. Usually red ink was used for the capital letter of the first word on a page or the first word in a paragraph. Such red letters were called rubrics (from the Latin *rubricare,* "to make red"). Decorations of important manuscripts were much more complex. They featured illustrations of scenes from the text or small pictures within the first letter of a word. Many of the most beautiful existing manuscripts are Bibles and Books of Hours (books of daily prayers). The paintings were usually small because they appeared within the text; for this reason, they are often called miniatures.

Illuminating manuscripts was exacting work, particularly in elaborate books in which various colors of inks were used. Design motifs varied from century to century. The *Book of Kells,* a richly

In this illumination from the Lindisfarne Gospels, snakes curl to form the initial letters (L, I, and B) of St. Matthew's gospel. The Celtic patterns within the snake's bodies transform into the heads of dragons and other creatures. In illuminated Bibles the first page of a Gospel was generally the most ornate, containing large decorative images with few words.

decorated manuscript of the four Gospels made in the eighth century, contains some of the most interesting early motifs, combining Celtic and Christian artistic traditions. In its complex borders, images of snakes and dragons surround religious scenes. The book was made in northern England or possibly Scotland or Ireland, but its name comes from the monastery of Kells in Ireland, where it was housed from about 1006 to 1653.

founded. Among the early adherents was a young man who would become Pope Gregory the Great. Gregory, like Benedict, came from a noble Roman family but preferred the monastic life. When he was selected as pope, he tried to hide from those who sought him out. Nevertheless, he was able to preserve and increase the power of the pope. He made peace with the Lombards and carefully administered the Churches' estates around Rome, which gave him the resources to defend the papacy against the Lombards. He also wrote a life of Benedict and a number of works on relics and the

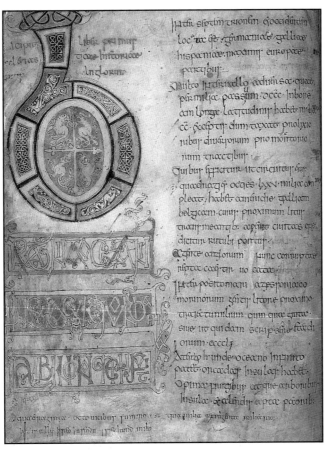

One of the oldest surviving copies of *The Venerable Bede's* History of the English Church and People *was printed in southern England in the early eighth century. Bede's history included the fanciful and miraculous lives of Anglo-Saxon saints, such as St. Cuthbert, but when he wrote about historical events, he carefully named the sources he used or the people he talked to in order to write an accurate account.*

Justinian was the last of the emperors to try to unite the eastern and western parts of the Roman Empire. In addition to many military campaigns, he sponsored the codification of Roman law, the Corpus Juris Civilis, *and many building projects. The diadem he wears indicates the shift from Roman to more eastern traditions.*

demonic temptations that plagued even saintly people. But his lasting achievement was the use of Benedictine missionaries to extend Christianity to the peoples who had settled on the fringes of the old empire.

One story told about Gregory held that he saw some beautiful, fair-skinned children for sale as slaves in the Roman market. He asked where they had come from and was told that they were Angles, people who had settled in the old Roman province of Britain. Gregory commented that they were not Angles but Angels. He then set about converting them to Christianity.

The conversion of England was in part the result of Gregory's missionary efforts, but was also facilitated by a line of remarkable women. Clotilda, who had helped Christianize Clovis and had earned the title of saint, had a granddaughter named Clodoswinde. She became queen of the Lombards and tried to convert her husband, Alboin. Clotilda's great-granddaughter, Bertha, married King Aethelbert of Kent. After their wedding, he agreed that she could bring along a Christian priest, even though Aethelbert intended to continue to practice

the religion of his ancestors. Gregory sent her a bishop who became known as St. Augustine of Canterbury because he succeeded in converting Aethelbert and his followers. Bertha's daughter, Ethelberga, married the king of Northumbria and converted him as well.

The north of England posed a particular problem for the Church. While the area was already Christian, the religious practices of the people there differed markedly from Roman traditions. For instance, they calculated the date of Easter differently, and their monks tonsured their heads from ear to ear instead of in a circle. The Synod (council) of Whitby in 664, presided over by the abbess of that great monastery that included both men and women, was called on to reconcile local practices with Roman traditions. The Northumbrian king declared that he found all the theological arguments for Roman practice confusing. He finally asked if both sides accepted that Peter founded the church of Rome. Because they both agreed, he decided in favor of Roman practice.

The combination of Benedictine monasticism and the strong traditions the English had inherited from Irish Christianity created a vibrant culture that would influence learning and missionary activities for several centuries. The most famous author of the period was the Venerable Bede (672–735), a Benedictine monk who spent his life at the monasteries of Wearmouth and Jarrow. The most learned man of his day, he digested all of the manuscripts available in their remarkable libraries. His writings present a summary of the learning of his time. Among his books

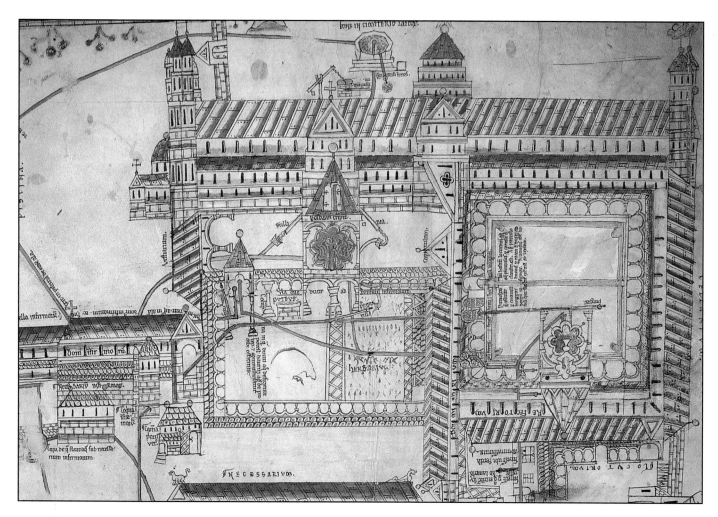

The plan for the Benedictine monastery at Canterbury shows Canterbury Cathedral at the top. The two squares are the cloisters with their open, arched corridors shown as a scalloped border. The center cloister has an herb garden. At the bottom is the necessarium or latrines for the monks. To the left is a chapel and infirmary; the dormitory abuts the cloister.

is the *History of the English Church and People,* which recounts the Synod of Whitby, various political events, and the lives of kings, queens, abbots, abbesses, and saints.

By the middle of the seventh century, separate kingdoms had begun to emerge in the western part of the former Roman Empire. The Anglo-Saxons, divided into several kingdoms, occupied England; the Franks had settled much of France; the Visigoths controlled Spain; the Lombards had taken over Italy; and the papacy, with its estates, was established in Rome and the surrounding countryside. Only the vast region of modern Germany had yet to be Christianized.

In the eastern half of the Roman Empire, however, the fifth and sixth centuries brought both great victories and major defeats. The eastern empire was able to preserve its territory partly through a policy of encouraging the Germanic tribes to move into the west and partly through diplomacy and bribes to the new tribes that appeared on its borders. Through these efforts, the wealthy crescent of territory around the eastern Mediterranean retained its rich, urban-centered culture.

Justinian (reigned 527–565) was the last of the Roman emperors to attempt to control the whole of the empire once again. Justinian was a colorful figure who surrounded himself with equally dramatic people. Because he had a keen sense of history, he hired a historian, Procopius, to write an official account of his reign. Although Procopius enjoyed this patronage and dutifully wrote two books about Justinian's wars and buildings, he also wrote a secret history containing all of the court gossip. Procopius particularly wanted to discredit the Empress Theodora, Justinian's wife, whom he maintained had an earlier career as a pornographic entertainer and courtesan in Constantinople. Rather than seeing the rise of this intelligent, beautiful woman to the position of empress as a heartwarming rags-to-riches story, he con-

Procopius's *Secret History* Reveals Court Scandal

A historian during the reign of emperor Justinian, Procopius lived between 500 and 554. While writing his official histories for Justinian, he composed another book, in which he reviled the emperor and his wife, Theodora. Of Theodora, he wrote: "To her body she gave greater care than was necessary, if less than she thought desirable. For early she entered the bath and late she left it; having bathed, went to breakfast. After breakfast she rested. At dinner and supper she partook of every kind of food and drink; and many hours she devoted to sleep, by day till nightfall, by night till the rising of the sun. Though she wasted her hours thus intemperately, what time of day remained she deemed ample for managing the Roman Empire."

Procopius was equally scathing in his descriptions of Justinian: "Now in physique he was neither tall nor short, but of average height; not thin, but moderately plump; his face was round and not bad looking, for he had good color, even when he fasted for two days.... Now such was Justinian in appearance; but his character was something I could not fully describe. For he was at once villainous and amenable; as people say colloquially, a moron. He was never truthful with anyone, but always guileful in what he said and did, yet easily hoodwinked by any who wanted to deceive him. His nature was an unnatural mixture of folly and wickedness."

This mosaic of Theodora, wife of Justinian, appears opposite his in Ravenna. The magnificence of court clothing and jewels indicate the wealth of the Byzantine Empire.

sidered Theodora a sorceress. In fact, she was very much her husband's partner in running the empire and showed considerable courage early in their reign when rioters burned much of Constantinople and threatened to depose them. Theodora refused to leave the city, declaring that she would rather die wearing the imperial purple (a color reserved for the clothing of the emperor and his family) than live in exile. Theodora and Justinian were able to quell the riots, and continued to rule.

Justinian decided to rebuild Constantinople on a grand scale. The most memorable monument was the Hagia Sophia, a great domed church that still stands today. It was once lined with mosaics of semi-precious stones and gold that shimmered in candlelight or filtered sunlight. The dome had a series of windows around its base so that in bright sunlight it appeared to be floating. One of the favorite ways to impress visiting barbarians was to take them to a religious service in the church. On one occasion a child was suspended from the dome to play the part of an angel and fill the dome with heavenly singing. Justinian and Theodora also built churches in Ravenna (St. Vitale) and Venice (St. Mark's).

Another of Justinian's cultural achievements was the codification of Roman law in the *Corpus Juris Civilis*. The Roman laws were a jumble of old practices and decrees of Roman emperors that had governed commercial transactions, criminal offenses, and the relationship of the emperor to the people. Justinian's jurists worked on eliminating duplications and inconsistencies to produce a unified code of laws, the *Codex Justinianus*. He also had them compile a summary of the main legal principles in the *Institutes*.

In the 12th century, the emperor's compilation of laws found its way back to the west, where it had considerable influence on western legal thinking. It also played a large role in the establishment of universities and legal practices. Much of modern commercial law and legal thought about the relationship of rulers to the ruled originated in the Roman law preserved in the *Codex*. It suggested that emperors were subject to the law just as the people were and that the power of emperors derived from the people. These ideas reflected the older Roman tradition, but Justinian himself was more of an eastern despot, inclined to take law and governance into his own hands.

The reign of Justinian marked a transition for the Roman Empire. His government was oriental in style, that is, power was concentrated in the office of the emperor and his subjects had little access to him. Those Justinian did see had to prostrate before him while he sat wearing a multilayered diadem instead of the traditional crown of laurel leaves. But Justinian was also the last of the Latin-speaking emperors. Greek language and culture had become so predominant that even though the people continued to refer to themselves as Romans, to westerners they were "the Greeks."

Justinian and Theodora envisioned the reconquest of the west, but their wars proved more devastating than successful. The expense of these campaigns, along with the couple's elaborate building projects, drained the treasury. Further religious conflicts over whether Christ was divine or human also left many people disaffected. Some argued that Christ was entirely divine (these adherents were called monophy-sites, meaning one purely spiritual body), while others held that he was entirely human. The compromise position maintained that he was both perfectly divine and perfectly human.

Because of threats from the east, the reconquest of the west proved impossible.

The Persians had managed to capture a Byzantine emperor, forcing him to serve the Persian emperor on bended knee. When he died in this humiliating service, he was stuffed and hung from the roof of the palace. After defeating the Persians in 641, the Byzantines finally were able to give the unfortunate emperor a Christian burial.

The interior of Hagia Sophia, commissioned by Justinian and Theodora, was originally covered with mosaics that shimmered with gold in the sunlight. The massive windowed dome seemed to float in golden light. When the Turks conquered Constantinople, they painted over the Christian mosaics in accordance with Islamic beliefs.

Muhammad (right) leads a group of his predecessors including Abraham, Moses, and Jesus in prayer. The Islamic religion considers Muhammad to be the last of God's prophets. This Persian manuscript shows that there were exceptions to the rule of not representing humans in pictures.

The long and draining wars left both empires vulnerable to yet another set of invaders, the Arabs.

The Arabian peninsula lay outside the domination of the Roman Empire, but through trade and caravan routes its merchants had contact with the Byzantine and Persian empires. The peoples of the area were polytheists (worshipers of many gods) and had no political unity. However, the peninsular Arabs all recognized the city of Mecca as a religious center. It was in Mecca that Muhammad was born about 571. He worked as a caravan trader for a wealthy woman who became his wife. In his travels, he had contact with Jews and Christians in the towns that bordered the Byzantine Empire. In his late 30s he underwent a mystical experience and had a series of revelations, which he attributed to God. Muhammad began preaching a new faith based on strict monotheism (worship of one God). Initially, only his wife and a few relatives converted, but his radical views worried the merchants of Mecca. They believed he was discrediting the Kaaba—a special shrine in Mecca that contained many statues and symbols of their gods, including a black stone that was said to have been given to Adam on his expulsion from Para-

dise. To escape the merchants' wrath, Muhammad fled to Medina; his flight is known among Muslims as the "Hegira." In Medina he preached and gathered a number of followers. His followers wrote down his sermons, and these notes formed the basis of the Koran. By 630 Muhammad's following was large enough to defeat Mecca, and he made a triumphant return to the city. He removed idols from the Kaaba, but kept the black stone. In the final two years of his life, he unified the Arabs under the new religion, Islam, and created a state in which he acted as both the religious and political leader.

Muhammad regarded himself as the last of the prophets and included Moses and Jesus among his predecessors. Islam tolerated Jews and Christians as "peoples of book," meaning the Old and New Testaments. A strict monotheist, Muhammad preached that his followers must submit to the will of Allah, the single, almighty God of the universe. The Koran provided instructions for living properly as well as religious guidance. The basic tenant of the faith was, "There is no god but Allah, and Muhammad is his prophet." Those who followed Islam were assured of salvation. Practice of the religion included praying

five times a day, refusing to eat pork or drink wine, offering charity to the poor, making a pilgrimage to Mecca once in one's lifetime, and perhaps fighting for the faith in a battle known as a *jihad*.

The unified Arabs spread quickly after Muhammad's death. During the first wave of conquest, from 632 to 655, they conquered Syria, Egypt, and the Persian Empire. They continued their expansion into North Africa, where they destroyed the remnants of Vandal and Byzantine rule. The Arabs then moved into Spain and defeated the Visigothic kingdom. Finally, in 732, their drive into Europe was stopped by the Franks.

The Arabs proved remarkably able to adapt to new circumstances and to the cultures that they conquered. After their arrival at the Mediterranean Sea, they became excellent sailors. They captured Byzantine islands in the Mediterranean and threatened Constantinople from the Bosporus. The emperor's armies fought back with Greek fire, a chemical compound similar to napalm that burned on water and set the Arab boats on fire. Only through great effort were the emperor's soldiers able to keep Constantinople, the Balkans, and a portion of Asia Minor in Byzantine hands.

The Arabs also borrowed from the art, architecture, and intellectual achievements of the people they conquered. On capturing Baghdad, the capital of the Persian Empire, they became acquainted with the astronomical learning of the Persians, which included accurate observations of the stars,

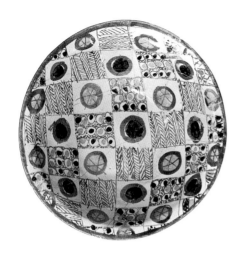

Islamic artists perfected elaborate geometric designs for daily objects such as this bowl, the walls of mosques, rugs, and clothing. The Koran forbade representations of God's creation, including humans and animals.

the phases of the moon, and eclipses. They also found the writings of the Greek philosophers and medical experts. These manuscripts had come to Persia by a curious path. When Christianity became the dominant religion in the Roman Empire, the intellectuals who remained true to the pantheon of the gods in Athens and elsewhere left the Christian area with their books and settled in Persia. There their works were translated into Persian. Arab scholars then translated them into Arabic and added their own commentaries. These texts made their way through Spain to western Europe centuries later.

The Arabs also drew on the decorative traditions of other peoples to create their remarkable and beautiful mosques (Islamic houses of worship). Islam prohibited representations of God or his creation, humans, so Muslim artisans developed their own intricate geometrical designs for pottery, mosaics, and fabrics.

Although Muhammad created his new religion for Arabs, Islam and its culture proved very attractive to their subject populations. Large numbers of Christians, Jews, and Persians converted, and mosques replaced some Christian churches.

By 700 the Mediterranean and northern Europe were very much changed. Rather than consisting of provinces in one large empire, northern Europe was splintered into a number of smaller, semi-tribal units ruled by kings. Although nominally Christian, the people who made up these units retained many pagan practices. For instance, the names used for the days Tuesday, Wednesday, and Thursday were derived from the names of the Germanic gods Tiu, Woden, and Thor. Sacred groves that honored these gods were referred to by Christianized names such as "Holy Wood" or "Hollywood."

Although its land mass was much reduced, the Byzantine Empire remained powerful in the eastern Mediterranean. Constantinople was a huge city with a population of a million people. Other large cities in the empire produced rich silks, glass objects, tapestries, carved ivories, and fine jewelry that were much in demand in the west. The Roman traditions were lost, and the emperors became more like eastern autocrats, with the ceremonies surrounding their persons becoming increasingly elaborate. Although they now ruled much of the former territory of Byzantium, the Arabs were unable to bring such a large territory under one ruler. Instead, parts were overseen by powerful leaders called "caliphs," who acted as both the supreme religious and political leaders of their lands.

By the beginning of the eighth century, the period of expansion of different peoples—from the Anglo-Saxons in northwestern Europe to the Arabs in western Asia—was coming to an end, leaving populations coping with new cultural experiences and new neighbors. This chapter has told the story of how the wealthy and powerful experienced these vast changes. The next will examine their influence on the population as a whole, both members of the invading tribes and those they conquered.

The Koran is the religious book of Islam. "Koran" comes from the Arabic word for "recitation." Muhammad recited his revelations with his followers every day first in Mecca and later in Medina. In Medina, he assembled a group of scribes to take down his words. After Muhammad's death, several different collections of his revelations circulated among his followers. Under the third caliph, Uthman, an official version of the Koran was assembled. It is written in a learned Arabic, which remains the standard for all scholarly Arabic writing.

EXCELSA VO...

Three Empires: Carolingian, Byzantine, and Arab

Charles the Bald receives his crown from the hand of God, which reaches down from the heavens. He is flanked by, but superior to, the two bishops standing on either side of him. To indicate that their power came from God and that they were heirs to the Roman emperors, the Carolingians took care to represent themselves below God and in Roman dress.

In 510, on the night that Clovis, king of the Franks, converted to Christianity, legend says that his wife Clotilda dreamed first of a lion, then a wolf, and finally a jackal. When she awoke, she told Clovis about her dream and prophesied that his royal line would follow the same sequence. The first rulers, including Clovis, would be lions among kings, but after a few generations they would become wolves, and in time his line would turn into jackals, or mere dogs. The prophesy was probably made much later and with hindsight, because the Merovingian dynasty Clovis established did follow that pattern. The last of the Merovingians were so inactive that their subjects saw them only when they appeared, riding in ox carts, on their estates.

As the Merovingians increasingly became figureheads, the real power passed to another family, who became known as Carolingians after their famous leader, Charlemagne (742–814), also known as Charles the Great or Carolus Magnus. The Carolingians descended from a line of bishops from the northeastern frontier of the Frankish kingdom. They rose to prominence through their military and administrative abilities and eventually conquered and ruled much of the Frankish territory in the east. Their early leaders held the position of mayor of the palace under the Merovingians, the equivalent of a prime minister. However, they never forgot their religious origins and were great supporters of monasteries and missionaries.

The era of colorful medieval nicknames began with the Carolingians. Charles Martel (meaning Charles the Hammer, born 688) embarked on a policy of fighting those who would not recognize Merovingian rule. By the beginning of the eighth century, he had brought most of the territory that Clovis had ruled into the Frankish kingdom. But Charles Martel was still not king, only mayor of the palace.

While Charles was unifying the Frankish territory, a new threat crossed the Pyrenees in the south—the Arabs. The Arabs swept into southwestern France just as they had earlier entered the Byzantine Empire, North Africa, and Spain. Charles marched to the region between Poitiers and Tours with an army partly composed of a heavily armed cavalry—the forerunner of the medieval knights—and defeated the Arabs in 732. He

Pépin the Short issued a silver coin for his realm with his name PIPI on one side. The new coinage marked his deposition of the ruling Merovingians and the assumption of the Frankish throne for himself and his heirs.

was then declared the "Hammer of Christendom." The pope perceived him as the savior of all Christians from the threat of Islam and invited him to come to Rome to deliver Italy from the threat of the resurgent Lombards. Charles refused to take on this fight.

Pépin the Short (reigned 751–768), his son, was not content to govern for the Merovingians. He wanted to be king in his own right. His accession to mayor of the palace coincided with the Lombards' success in taking Ravenna, the last Byzantine stronghold in Italy. Pope Stephen, worried about the survival of Rome, called on the powerful Christian leader of the north to save the city rather than turning to the Byzantine emperor. Pépin sent an embassy to the pope asking if it would be proper for him to assume the kingship. The pope quickly replied that "the man who had the actual power was more deserving of the crown than the one who was only a figure-head," by whom he meant the current weak Merovingian king. Pépin then called an assembly of Frankish nobles, warriors, and clergy and had himself elected their king. The last of the Merovingian kings was sent to a monastery where his hair, worn long as befitting a king, was cut in the fashion of a monk.

To legitimize Pépin's coup, the pope crowned him in a coronation ceremony modeled on the anointing of David as described in the Bible. This ceremony became the standard for all coronations in western Europe. Pépin made good on his side of the bargain: He twice invaded Italy and defeated the Lombards. After securing the land around Rome from Lombard

attack, he gave it to the pope in what became known as the "Donation of Pépin." This territory, which extended across the Italian peninsula from Rome to Ravenna, was referred to as the Papal States by the late Middle Ages.

Following the Frankish custom of dividing an inheritance equally among all a deceased's heirs, Pépin was succeeded by two sons. The early death of one left an able king, Charlemagne, in power. Much is known about Charlemagne because he had two contemporary biographers. Several statues of him have also survived.

Einhard, the more colorful biographer, wrote that Charlemagne had been his friend since childhood and that later he had lived close to the king at his court. He described Charlemagne as "large and strong, and of lofty stature, although not disproportionately tall (his height is well known to have been seven times the length of his foot); the upper part of his head was round, his eyes very large and animated, nose a little long, hair fair, and face laughing and merry. Thus his appearance was always stately and dignified, whether he was standing or sitting; although his neck was thick and somewhat short, and his belly rather prominent; but the symmetry of the rest of his body concealed these defects." (In the late 19th century Charlemagne's skeleton was measured; he was 6 feet 3 inches.) Einhard also explained that the king had a firm walk and a clear voice, although softer than one would have expected in such a large man. For recreation Charlemagne enjoyed horseback riding, hunting, and swimming. He swam in the hot springs at Aachen (Aix-la-Chapelle), often joined by his sons

This silver reliquary holds the bones of Charlemagne, who was regarded as the ideal Christian emperor. The crown and the scepter in his hand indicate his role as ruler, the small replica of a church in the other hand represents his role as protector of the Church, and the halo behind his head shows him to be a religious figure.

and nobles. He sometimes invited a troop of his bodyguards to swim with him as well.

According to Einhard, Charlemagne drank and ate moderately, preferring roast meats to the boiled ones that his physicians recommended when his health was failing in old age. In dress, he favored Frankish clothing over Roman garb. (Only on two visits to Rome did he dress like a Roman.) Next to his skin he wore a "linen shirt and linen breeches, and above these a tunic fringed with oriental silk, while hose fastened by bands covered his lower limbs, and shoes his feet." He always carried a sword with a gold or silver hilt. Over everything he wore a blue cloak.

Both Christianity and learning were dear to Charlemagne. While he ate, he liked to have Augustine of Hippo's books read to him, particularly *The City of God*. But he also enjoyed recitations of the old Frankish stories similar to Beowulf. He could, Einhard tells us, speak Latin as well as Frankish, but he could not write: "He used to keep tablets and blanks in bed under his pillow, that at leisure hours he might accustom his hand to form the letters; however, as he did not begin his efforts in due season, but late in life, they met with ill success."

Charlemagne saw that both his sons and daughters were educated. He also encouraged the education of the clergy by starting schools in the cathedrals. To keep himself informed of intellectual matters, he surrounded himself with scholars from the monasteries of northern England and other parts of Europe. Notable among them was Alcuin, a scholar from England who brought to the continent the learning preserved by English and Irish monks. He and other

scholars studied astronomy, grammar, and rhetoric. Perhaps their most lasting contribution was the development of Carolingian minuscule, a form of handwriting with capitals and small letters that influenced modern writing and typography.

It is remarkable that Charlemagne ever had time to sit and listen to books being read or to pause for a swim. He spent most of his reign in military campaigns or supervising his vast kingdom. He pushed the boundaries of the Frankish lands north into the modern Netherlands, east of the Rhine into Saxony, and into other areas that even the Romans had not conquered. Using monks as missionaries, Charlemagne encouraged the peoples of these newly conquered territories to convert to Christianity. The monks used extreme measures, such as cutting down the oak trees that the local people worshipped and using the timber to build

Charlemagne's exploits as a warrior are commemorated on a panel of the reliquary above. The emperor sits in his tent dressing for battle. His fully armed knights, clad in chain mail, are either sleeping or already on horseback. Charlemagne spent almost every year of his life in warfare.

Carolingian Minuscule

The Romans used a script composed of all capital letters (majuscule). In formal documents these capitals looked much like our capital alphabet. The Romans also developed a cursive (informal) script that was written so quickly that the words ran together, making reading very difficult.

Merovingian scribes were even more careless.

In some parts of Europe, notably Ireland and Northumbria, a combination of the majuscule and the cursive were used. The beginnings of sentences were in capitals, but the rest was in a cursive. Because many of Charlemagne's scholars (including Alcuin) came from northern England, the writing that Charlemagne mandated for preserving laws, liturgical documents, bibles, and government records resembled these scripts.

Capital letters were clearly distinguished from small letters. Space was left between words, and the letters themselves were well rounded and distinct. Carolingian minuscule outlasted the Carolingian kings and influences our printing today.

A page from the book of Exodus from a bible written in Tours about 834–43 shows the capital letter and the small letter combination typical of Carolingian minuscule.

churches where the oaks had stood. When peaceful conversion did not work, Charlemagne backed up such efforts with threats. He told the Saxons that if they did not convert, he would put them all to death. They converted.

The most famous of Charlemagne's battles was recorded in a distorted form in *The Song of Roland,* a poem that was written down several centuries after the event. Charlemagne thought that he could take advantage of internal dissension among the Arab rulers to take over Spain. He was unsuccessful, and on his return from Spain in 778, his troops were attacked by Christian Basques at a pass in the Pyrenees Mountains called Roncevaux. In the epic poem, Count Roland, the leader of the rearguard, is attacked by Arabs (rather than Basques) at the pass because of the treachery of Ganelon, another of Charlemagne's nobles, who was jealous of Roland. The poem first appeared in written form in the 12th century as the story of a warrior's loyalties to his fellow warriors and of a man to his lord.

Charlemagne's relations with the pope in Rome were as intense as those of his father. He finished the task of subduing the Lombards and took their territory in northern Italy. But squabbles in Rome brought him back there as a peacemaker during the Christmas season of 800. The pope, Leo III, had been deposed, and his enemies had cut out his tongue. When he appealed, in writing, for help, Charlemagne came to Italy with an army. He reinstated Leo as pope on December 23, and on December 25 Leo crowned him emperor.

Einhard claims that Charlemagne did

not want this title and that if he had known what Leo was planning, he would not have gone to church that day even though it was Christmas. Despite Einhard's protestations, Charles most likely orchestrated the coronation himself. Leo could hardly have been hiding a crown behind his back, only to plop it on Charles's head as he lingered at the altar to pray. Neither the pope nor Charlemagne, of course, had any legal right to claim the imperial title in the west. Indeed, Charlemagne had earlier tried to secure the title in a more legal fashion by proposing marriage to Irene, the empress of Byzantium. She turned him down.

The Carolingian Empire, as Charlemagne's realm came to be known, had little in common with the Byzantine Empire. The government relied on the presence of the emperor to keep everything running smoothly. If Charlemagne was not fighting, he was visiting various places in his empire to ensure his subjects' loyalty. Fortunately, he enjoyed horseback riding, because he spent much of his time in the saddle. His household administration, including a chamberlain who was in charge of the royal treasure, traveled with him. For the most part, the emperor's income came not from taxes as was the case in Byzantium, but from estates that Charlemagne owned. Indeed, he was the biggest landowner in the country. Likewise his cellarer, who oversaw the vineyards and wines, drew his stores from the emperor's private estates. A constable was in charge of the stables and the army. A private chaplain and his assistants carried on both private and official correspondence, because only the clergy knew Latin well

enough to do so. And because it was impossible to cart or ship all the goods grown on his estates to a central capital such as Aachen, his favorite residence, Charlemagne literally had to travel from place to place with his army, friends, family, and household officials to eat and drink the wealth of his harvests.

Realizing that governing such a vast territory was too much for one person, Charlemagne tried to delegate some of his power. The border provinces were a particular problem, because the native populations were only recently conquered, thus still rebellious. These areas he put in charge of marquises or dukes—titles derived from Roman military leaders. They were to look after the defenses of their assigned territory. In the more established

areas, Charlemagne relied on counts, who had mostly civil, or administrative duties. The counts, marquises, and dukes were drawn from the upper class of Franks and came to regard their positions as hereditary. Charlemagne could count on them to look after their own interests in the countryside and perhaps try to preserve some of his interests if he visited them with an army often enough.

He could also ask them to raise an army from their territory if it was threatened with attack. Only those with adequate land to support themselves and their attendants for a three-month campaign could serve. But asking a man to turn up with a horse, weapons, and armor was demanding more than most could afford. Charles Martel had rewarded those who withstood the Arabs

CHARLEMAGNE'S EMPIRE, 811

Marches were certain frontier provinces that were organized for the military defense of the empire.

500 miles
805 kilometers

with grants of land for their life use. Pepin and Charlemagne did the same when they required warriors for their many wars. Warriors, therefore, came to assume that they would receive a reward of land and its income in return for military service. In order to keep his counts loyal, Charles had to grant them even larger tracts of land and the rights to administer them. This policy was bound to weaken the emperor's control of his territory unless he frequently appeared in person to remind his noble counts, marquises, and dukes that he had ultimate authority over the land and its income.

After the Franks had arrived in the former Roman territories and the Carolingians had conquered the tribes on their borders, the way of life for most men and women proceeded as it had for centuries. The men did the hunting, fighting, gambling, metal work, and governing while the women did the farming, herding, brewing, clothing, and childrearing, and kept the religious practices. But a revolutionary change in these roles occurred when the tribes settled down in one place, became Christian, and had to cultivate the land for a living. From the earliest traditions of Mediterranean civilization, men's lives had been closely tied to the plow, so much so that the plow became a metaphor for men. Similarly, women were so closely associated with spinning wool and weaving cloth that the

spindle was often used to represent women. The men and women who came under the influence of Mediterranean culture gradually adopted these tasks and their respective symbols. Because metal was a scarce commodity in those times, men must literally have beaten their swords into plowshares. Women retreated from the fields to concentrate their labor about the house. These people must have had strong feelings about this radical change in patterns of behavior, but their emotions and thoughts are not recorded.

The records from the reign of Charlemagne provide a picture of the lives of those who became peasants rather than paid warriors in the new regime of settled agriculture. The agricultural workers who cultivated the old Roman estates blended with the tribespeople who arrived and settled with their families. The estate books of the Carolingian period, in which details of the land, people, and produce from the estates were recorded, point to the diverse backgrounds and conditions of those who worked the lands. Their names are of Roman, Germanic, and Old Testament origin, suggesting a considerable amount of intermarriage. For example, Electeus and his wife Landina had Roman names. Abrahil had a wife named Berthildis, and they had three children Abram, Avremarus, and Bertrada. This family, therefore, used both Biblical and Frankish names. The family of Ceslinus—which included his wife Leutberga and their two children, Leutgardis and Ingohildis—combined Roman and Frankish names.

The estate records also noted the degree of freedom enjoyed by each person listed.

Electeus and Abrahil were slaves, but their wives were *colona,* or free peasants. Berthildis, Ceslinus, and Leutberga were described as *lidi,* or half-free peasants, because they owed labor on the estate. They may have been Germanic settlers. Those with free status were free only in terms of their bodies, labor, marriages, and families. They were not free to leave the land or estate on which they lived.

The invasions of the fifth century destroyed much of the long-distance trade in Europe and around the Mediterranean. Although luxury items were still traded and an active trade continued in local markets, most of the population of Europe lived by farming the land, and most of the land was organized into large estates. In Roman times these estates were called *latifundia,* and they provided people such as Sidonius, the bishop and Roman patrician, and his friends with a comfortable, pastoral life. The estates changed hands in the Middle Ages. The large estates then became known as manors, and were owned by abbots, bishops, popes, counts, dukes, marquises, kings, and emperors. Part of the land, the best part, was put aside for the exclusive use of the owner. The rest was divided among the agricultural laborers or peasants, who produced crops and raised animals to feed themselves and their children. They paid their lord for the use of this land by performing services on his portion of the property, by giving him goods such as cheeses, or by paying rent in money. Electeus, for instance, held half a farm that included both arable land and meadow. In return for the use of the land, he carted manure and plowed a portion of the lord's fields for winter and spring plant-

ing. Abrahil, Ceslinus, and another *lidus,* Godalbertus, held a farm together. During the month of May, they had to cart goods to local city markets for their lord. They also had to transport two loads of wood to the estate in the winter, mend the fences to keep the lord's cattle from wandering off, and harvest his crops. They, too, plowed for winter and spring planting and hauled manure. In addition, they paid four pennies a head as a tax.

The records from Carolingian estates are complete enough to allow us to imagine a day in the life of Abrahil and his family. It is early spring, the day that the lord's plowing must be done. Berthildis has risen early to start a fire in an open hearth in the center of the family's hut. The smoke rises through a hole in the roof. She heats water for the family to use for washing. The morning meal—a gruel of cooked grain—needs only to be heated. Abrahil sends his son, Abram, to the shed that serves as a barn to fetch the ox and make sure that it has water and some

Peasant women provided services for both their family and the owner of the manor. Transporting water and milk and caring for livestock were daily activities.

Carolingian artists, imitating Byzantine styles, lavishly illustrated their bibles. Here, Luke writes his gospel with his symbol of the winged ox behind him on one page, and the gospel begins on the facing page.

fodder before the long day's work. Abram will accompany his father into the fields to goad the ox. Abrahil will do the plowing, because his partners in the farm are busy with other tasks. Ceslinus is carting grain to Paris with the help of his son, and Godalbertus has gone to fetch wood. Abrahil and Abram meet up with the other villagers, and the steward organizes them into work teams for plowing. Berthildis, meanwhile, has washed and swaddled baby Bertrada and placed her in a cradle by the fire. Avremarus, who is eight years old, goes to get water from the well for brewing beer. He then takes the cow to pasture and watches it and the cows of the others who share the farm. Berthildis heats the water and begins the process of brewing. She will have only a light lunch. Her husband and sons will eat the bread and cheese that they have taken

with them to their work. Those doing the plowing will have beer supplied by the estate's steward. Returning tired in the evening, the family consumes bread, a porridge of peas boiled with ham, and beer. They are too weary to sit around the fire, so Berthildis extinguishes it with a clay cover, and they turn in early. Their beds are straw pallets on the floor, their bedding rough linen sheets and wool blankets woven by Berthildis. A peasant's day is hard work from sunup to sundown.

Management of these estates required continual oversight. Among Charlemagne's many administrative duties, he took time to send directives to the stewards who ran his estates. One such directive survives. In it, Charlemagne's first concern was that the profits go directly to himself, not to anyone else. His second concern was for his peasants: "That the people on our estates be well

taken care of, and that they be reduced to poverty by no one." He did not want the stewards forcing the peasants to labor for them rather than their lord, nor did he want them extracting bribes from the peasants in the form of wine, fruits, chickens, and eggs. On the other hand, if the peasants stole or did not fulfill the written rules, they were to be whipped if they were slaves and fined if they were *coloni*. Charlemagne's directive then discussed the care of livestock, vines for wine, fields, fish ponds, mills, woodlands, and the weaving houses where women wove cloth. Stewards were to render accounts on Palm Sunday every year and have all produce—such as cloth, wax, wine, mustard, cheese, salted meats, butter, beer, mead, honey, and flour—ready for the emperor's arrival.

Charlemagne's arrival at one of his estates undoubtedly caused a great stir among its inhabitants. Cooking for the emperor and his retinue took days. The preparations included butchering, tapping and tasting barrels of wine, cleaning stables, scrubbing out the stone house where he would stay, and repairing the road on which he would enter the estate. Even though Charlemagne dressed like a Frank and rode a horse like any other Frankish warrior, his clothes were of much better quality than the peasants would ever have seen, and his horse would be a spirited stallion. He might even be accompanied by one of his daughters, who would be traveling in an ox-drawn cart and well bundled up in fine furs. Such a visit would be a time of feasting even for the peasants.

Feast days occurred at other times of the year as well. When the missionaries and clergy were occupied with converting the pagans, they made a number of compromises about the dates of Christian feasts. Even the date of Christmas, Christ's birth, was assigned to December 25 to coincide with pagan winter solstice celebrations. The Gospels did not give a date for Jesus' birth. The revelries lasted 12 days as they had during the Roman holidays that were traditionally held at the same time. Other feast days, such as Michaelmas, marked the end of harvest in September. St. Martin's Day, celebrated on November 11, was the traditional butchering day.

Ordinary people's understanding of Christianity was very slight and somewhat tentative. Many people combined old and new beliefs by worshipping both the old gods and the new one. To discourage this practice, the clergy sought to turn the old gods, such as Venus, Mars, and Jupiter, into demons who tempted Christians' souls. Christians who still worshipped these representatives of the devil would go to Hell, the clergy promised. Artists represented Hell on church walls as a terrifying place where demons tormented sinners with forks and threw them into burning pits. Even with such powerful weapons for dissuading people a tone of exasperation often crept into the clergy's sermons: "For to light candles before rocks and trees and streams and at crossroads—is this anything else but the worship of the devil? To observe divinations and auguries and days of the idols—is this anything else but the worship of the devil?" asked Bishop Martin of Braga. The population, however, went on saying spells over their land, giving herbs to their sick, and consulting men and women thought to

Omens of Charlemagne's Death

In the Middle Ages, as in the ancient world, natural phenomena and calamities were seen as omens of a major event. Of course, most of these signs were recollected after the event they supposedly foretold had occurred. Following the death of Charlemagne on 28 January 814, Einhard wrote:

Very many omens had portended his approaching end, a fact that he had recognized as well as others. Eclipses both of the sun and moon were very frequent during the last three years of his life, and a black spot was visible on the sun for the space of seven days. The gallery between the basilica and the palace, which he had built at great pains and labor, fell in sudden ruin to the ground on the day of the ascension of our Lord. The wooden bridge over the Rhine at Mayence ... was so completely consumed in three hours by an accidental fire that not a single splinter of it was left, except what was under water. Moreover, one day in his last campaign into Saxony against Godfred, King of the Danes, Charles himself saw a ball of fire fall suddenly from the heavens with great light, just as he was leaving camp before sunrise to set out on the march. It rushed across the clear sky from right to left, and everybody was wondering what was the meaning of the sign, when the horse which he was riding gave a sudden plunge, head foremost, and fell, and threw him to the ground so heavily that his cloak buckle was broken and his sword belt shattered.

Charlemagne's crown is preserved in Aachen, where his reliquary is also kept. The crown resembles the one he is wearing on the reliquary.

have the power to find lost animals or make love potions.

Charlemagne spent the last years of his life at his favorite residence of Aachen. There he had built a beautiful chapel decorated with gold and silver in the Byzantine style that still stands today. Einhard wrote that as he neared death, Charlemagne called his son, Louis, to him and before all the chief men of the kingdom, placed the imperial crown on Louis's head, proclaiming him emperor. Charlemagne then spent the fall hunting, but in January became very ill. After a reign of 47 years, he died at the age of 72.

While Louis took the title of emperor, he was not able to fill the shoes of his

Strasbourg Oaths: First Written Example of French and German

As Latin ceased to be the language of everyday speech, vernacular languages took its place. French is a Romance language, meaning that it derives from the Roman language of Latin. German belongs to the Germanic language group, which also includes the Scandinavian languages. English is a combination of French and German elements. All these languages belong to a greater, Indo-European language group.

The earliest texts written in French and German are the Strasbourg Oaths. By reciting these oaths, Charles the Bald and Louis the German publicly pledged their loyalty to one another.

English translation: "For the love of God and the common salvation of the Christian people and ourselves, from this day forth, as far as God gives me wisdom and power, I will treat this my brother as one should rightfully treat a brother, on condition that he does the same by me. And with Lothair I will not willingly enter into any agreement which might injure this, my brother."

French: "Pro Deo amur et pro Christian poblo et nostro commun salvament, dist di in avant, in quant Deus savir et podir me dunat, si salvarai eo cist meon fradre Karlo et in adiudha et in adiudha, et in cadhuna cosa si cum om per dreit son fradra salvar dist, in o quid il mi altresi fazet; et ab Ludher nul plaid numquam prindrai, qui meon vol cist meon fradre Karlo in damno sit."

German: "In Goddes minna ind in thes Christianes folches ind unser bedhero gealtnissi, fon thesemo dage frammordes, so fram so mir Got gewizci indi madh furgibit, so haldih thesan minan bruodher, soso man mit rehtu sinan bruodher shal, in thiu, thaz er mig sosama duo; indi mit Ludheren in noheinin thing ne geganga, the minan willon eino ce scadhen werben."

Charles the Bald, shown here in an illustration from his own bible, became the king of the original Frankish part of the Empire.

energetic father. He was well educated and very devout—deserving of his nickname "the Pious"—but he was neither a good statesman nor a skilled military leader. Reverencing the language of the Old Testament and of Jesus, he learned Hebrew, and encouraged Jews from the Mediterranean to settle in the empire, particularly in the newly conquered German areas. Perhaps the Carolingian Empire was too large and made up of too many different groups for one person to govern. Louis soon divided his land among his sons, giving them some of the responsibility for ruling, but this move simply created further divisions. His sons had no sooner claimed their titles and property than they began to fight among themselves.

When Louis the Pious died in 840, civil war broke out among his sons. Lothair, the eldest, had been made emperor of the whole territory, with his power base of land in Italy. Charles the Bald was made king of the west Franks (in the original part of the empire), and Louis the German was made king of the east Franks (in the newly conquered territories east of the Rhine in modern-day Germany).

Charles and Louis quickly made an alliance against Lothair to curtail his power. To cement this alliance, they swore the Strasbourg Oaths. Louis swore loyalty to Charles in French and Charles made the same oath to Louis in German. They used these vernacular languages so that the retainers and troops of each would understand what their king had said. The oaths are of great interest today because they are the first written examples of French and German and indicate that Latin was no longer understood by ordinary people.

Charles and Louis defeated Lothair and imposed on him the Treaty of Verdun in 843. The treaty confined Lothair's power to a central section of land running north from Italy into the Netherlands. This "middle kingdom" included no natural or linguistic boundaries. On the west side of Lothair's kingdom was that of Charles the Bald, which included much of modern France. On the east side was the kingdom of Louis the German, which included the German provinces of Saxony, Franconia, Swabia, and Bavaria. Some historians have suggested that the rationale behind the territorial divisions was to distribute the estates that still belonged to the monarchy among the three brothers. Whatever the reason, the middle kingdom continued to present a problem into the 20th century, because both France and Germany would claim parts of it as their own. Some historians even claim that World War I and World War II were the direct result of the Treaty of Verdun.

While Charlemagne was expanding his empire and his grandsons were fighting over its division, the Byzantine emperor was trying to preserve as much of his empire as possible. Political intrigues in Byzantium initially hindered an effective fight against northern encroachers, including Slavs, Bulgarians, and Russians. Irene (reigned 797–802), the empress whom Charlemagne proposed to marry, had risen to the throne by having her own son blinded and deposed. Further intrigue brought the Macedonian dynasty to power. Michael III (reigned 842–67)—"the Drunkard"—was a great devotee of

chariot-racing and raised to power his favorite horse trainer, a Macedonian named Basil. Basil repaid the favor by having Michael murdered and taking the crown for himself.

One way the Byzantines tried to dissuade the tribes on the northern border of the empire from attacking was to convert them to Christianity. Michael III sent two brothers, Cyril and Methodius, as missionaries to the Slavs. Before they left, the brothers devised a Slavonic alphabet based on Greek letters and translated the Gospels into Slavic. Their missionary efforts and those of their disciples were successful. By 867 they had also devised a liturgy (mass) in Slavonic, which is still used. (The early version of the Slavic language is called Old Church Slavonic.)

Meanwhile the Bulgars, a tribal group from central Asia, had moved into an area south of the Danube River in modern Bulgaria and mingled with the local Slavic population there. They too agreed to accept Christianity. But by now the pope and the patriarch of Constantinople, the head of the Greek-speaking Byzantine church, were engaged in both political and theological struggles. Among the issues was whether the clergy and the population of the Balkan peninsula would accept the pope's or the patriarch's version of Christianity. In the end, Croatia accepted Rome, while Serbia and Bulgaria adhered to Constantinople. These two types of Christianity are now called Roman Catholicism and Greek Orthodox.

The final triumph of Byzantine missionary work was the conversion of Russia a century after the conversion of the Slavs and Bulgars. The Rus were Swedish Vikings who had come from the area around

The Radziwill Chronicle, *written in Russian, chronicled the conversion of Vladimir, prince of Kiev (top), in 988. Envoys from Vladimir witnessed a Christian mass in Constantinople and returned to explain the mass to Vladimir (bottom).*

In 987 Basil II of the Macedonian dynasty was faced with rebellions in his capital. He called on the king of Kiev, Vladimir, for assistance. Vladimir agreed, but asked to be rewarded with a Byzantine princess, even though he already had several wives and more than 800 concubines. In desperation, Basil promised his own sister, Anna. Anna was strong-willed and refused to marry a pagan polygamist, so Vladimir agreed to accept Christianity and accept only Anna as his wife. Soon Kiev and later all of Russia was converted to the Byzantine model of Christianity. Once again, a Christian princess had been instrumental in bringing about the conversion of her husband and his people. Eventually, the Russian king was called a tsar, a corruption of the Roman title of caesar.

While the Byzantine Empire was engaged in preserving itself from further attacks by tribes migrating west and south, the Arab Empire had split into a number of smaller caliphates. (A caliphate was the territory over which a caliph, an Arab religious and secular leader, presided.) Spain became a separate caliphate, with its capital in Córdoba. Morocco, Egypt, Syria, and other states split off as well. The divisions also represented religious disagreements. A group of Muslims held that Ali, the cousin and son-in-law of Muhammad, should have been the first caliph and that he was unjustly passed over. When Ali and his sons were assassinated, a conflict broke out between his followers and those of the first four caliphs. Most of the adherents of Ali were

the Baltic Sea down the Dnieper River to trade in Constantinople. They had established two powerful cities—a northern one, Novgorod, and a more southern one, Kiev. They too had blended with the native Slavic population. By the mid-10th century, the Rus were speaking Slavic and using Slavic names.

Persian so that part of the split was along national lines. But deeper religious divisions created more serious differences. The followers of Ali, or the Shiites, rejected many of the oral traditions of Muhammad in which the majority group, the Sunni, believed. The split among Muslims continues to this day.

The Abbasids, who replaced the original Arab caliphs, were far more worldly. They resembled the former Persian emperors more than the original followers of Muhammad. The Abbasids established their capital in Baghdad and built fine palaces there. The grandson of the dynasty's founder, Harun al-Rashid (reigned 786–809), became a great patron of writers and scientists. He knew of Charlemagne and sent him an elephant along with other gifts. Charlemagne used to take the elephant with him as he traveled throughout his realm.

In spite of the religious and political splits, Arab culture remained unified by the Arabic language and a common acceptance of Islam and the Koran. All scholarship was in the language of the Koran, even though the population was now a mix of Greeks, Jews, Egyptians, and Persians, among others. With Arabic as the common language, the Abbasid dynasty became a time of remarkable learning. It was at the court of Harun al-Rashid that the *Thousand and One Nights,* or *Arabian Nights,* was composed. *Thousand and One Nights* is a series of anonymous oriental stories, including those of Ali Baba, Sinbad the Sailor, and Aladdin. The tales are loosely woven together through

Mosques

The Arabs did not have a building tradition before they had conquered the Byzantine and Persian empires. Initially, they used the structures they found in their new territories as mosques. But in time the caliphs wanted to construct their own religious buildings to rival the Christian churches. The first of the grand new mosques, the Dome of the Rock, was built in Jerusalem in the seventh century. The dome was set on an octagon of masonry, and the entire building was decorated in fine mosaic. The mosque in Damascus, built in the eighth century, was the first to serve as a place of worship, political center, and school. The building was surrounded by minarets, slender towers from which a muezzin (cryer) called the faithful to worship. Mosaics were also used to decorate the Damascus mosque. In addition, mosque architecture incorporated several types of arches, which showed more variation in design than those found in western cathedrals.

The Dome of the Rock mosque is built over the stone on which, according to the bible, Abraham was going to sacrifice Isaac. Islamic tradition calls it Ascension Rock, from which Muhammad was taken to heaven.

The great flourishing of learning during the Abbasid dynasty in Persia led to advances in mathematics, astronomy, medicine, and literature. Scholars met to discuss their work in mosques and palaces.

Here with a Loaf of Bread beneath
   the Bough,
A Flask of Wine, a Book of Verse—
   and Thou
Beside me singing in the
   Wilderness—
And Wilderness is Paradise now.

Western Europe did not learn about Khayám's poems until they were translated in the 19th century.

Like the Christians before them, Arabic and Persian scholars tried to reconcile the writings of the Greek philosophers Plato and Aristotle with their own religious texts. But their most important and lasting contributions were in mathematics and science. By translating the works of Greek mathematicians such as Euclid and Ptolemy, Arab scholars were introduced to arithmetic, geometry, and trigonometry. They then added their own scholarship to these fields. But their major contribution to modern mathematics and astronomy came from studying Hindu (Indian) works on these subjects. Drawing on Hindu thought, they created Arabic numerals—that is, the numbers 0 through 9. Greeks and Romans had used letters—I, V, X, C, M—for numbers but had not developed the concept of zero. Lacking numerals, the Greeks and Romans had performed their computations on an abacus—an instrument with beads or counters set on wires. Addition and subtraction were easy with these simple tools, but multiplication and division were very difficult. The introduction of numerals and zero as a placeholder made these calculations much easier.

Other branches of science also flourished in the Arabic world. Avicenna

a framing sequence in which Scheherezade, the wife of King Scariar, tells her husband a new story for each of 1,001 nights to keep him from killing her. She succeeds.

Poetry also flourished during this period. Among the most notable works was the *Rubaiyat* of Omar Khayám. Omar Khayám was born in the first half of the 11th century in the city of Nishapur in Persia. Almost no information about his life survives, but he was well known for his mathematical and astronomical scholarship during his lifetime. He wrote poems for his own amusement, and it was only after his death that they were discovered. His most famous verse is:

(980–1037) wrote medical books that expounded on those of Galen (200–130 B.C.), the Greek physician. Arabic thinkers also studied Greek, Persian, and Hindu astronomy and improved on the astrolabe, a Greek invention. The astrolabe helped to determine the position of a heavenly body so that mariners could establish the latitude of their boats. The first known division of musical melodies into equal intervals of time, or measures, was also the work of an Arab mathematician.

Of the three empires that grew out of the old Roman Empire, the Muslim one had perhaps the greatest influence on learning. While the Carolingians studied fragments of Greek scholarship preserved by the Irish monks and Boethius, the Muslims had access to the full body of work by both Greek and Hindu philosophers and scientists. The learning of Baghdad spread west into Spain, Sicily, and southern Italy. From these centers, Latin scholars of the west eventually came to learn more about their own Greek tradition and the Arabic additions to it. In contrast, the Byzantine Empire did not add significantly to the learning that the Greeks originated.

All three empires, however, experienced problems intrinsic to large political units put together by conquest and governed largely by single individuals and their advisers. Even the empire of Charlemagne had been shattered by fighting among his grandsons. The Arab Empire splintered into various smaller caliphates and other political units. The Byzantines managed to recapture some of their territory in the north through war and the spread of Christianity, but a succession of weak rulers could not hold on to this advantage. Weakened internally, the empires fell prey to outside attack. The west was attacked by Muslim pirates to the south, Magyars or Hungarians in central Europe, and Vikings from the north and west. The Byzantine and Arab empires were threatened by the Turks. In a sense, Clotilda's prophecy held true for all these empires: they started with lions and ended with jackals.

Astrolabe

The astrolabe was the most widely used astronomical instrument of the Middle Ages. It could determine the elevation of the sun or another star above the horizon. In addition, the charts incised on its moveable plates helped solve the complex geometrical problems that arose in astronomy and navigation. The instrument had a round brass plate with a sighting bar attached at the center. The outermost plate was a star chart—the apparent movement of the constellations around the earth could be simulated by rotating this plate. A horizon plate helped locate the angle of a star overhead. Different horizontal plates had to be used in different latitudes.

Sailors' astrolabes were simpler than those of astronomers because they had to withstand the winds on the oceans. Treatises on the construction of astrolabes survive from as early as the sixth century B.C. Most surviving astrolabes have Arabic, Latin, and Hebrew writing on them. Texts on how to use the instrument were widely available. Even Geoffrey Chaucer, the great English writer of the late 14th century, wrote a treatise on the astrolabe.

Astrolabes were usually made of brass so that the plates could move smoothly and they could stand up to frequent use either for astronomy or for navigation.

Chapter 4
The Turning Point

New invaders swept into Europe in the late ninth century. Most devastating were the Vikings, the men from the fjords of Scandinavia. The anguish of the local population was well expressed in a contemporary Irish account: "In a word, although there were a hundred hard steeled iron heads on one neck, and a hundred sharp, ready, cool, never-rusting, brazen tongues in each head, and a hundred garrulous, loud, unceasing voices from each tongue, they could not recount, or narrate, or enumerate, or tell, what all the Gaedhil [Irish] suffered in common, both men and women, laity and clergy, old and young, noble and ignoble, of hardship, of injury, and of oppression, in every house, from these valiant, wrathful, foreign, purely-pagan people."

The weak governments of ninth-century Europe were no match for the vigorous new invaders. England was split into small kingdoms. Ireland had never had a strong government. The Carolingian Empire had first divided into three parts, and then, as wars continued over the Middle Kingdom, the provinces became more and more independent in both the French and

German parts of the empire. Who then could withstand the determined groups of raiders and pirates who came from Scandinavia?

Scandinavia had little agricultural land—mostly concentrated in southern Sweden and Denmark—but a growing population in the ninth and 10th centuries. As in the fourth century, when the Goths left Scandinavia, the population outstripped the ability of the land to support it. Fishing, trading, and plunder supplemented the people's farming, but were still not enough to sustain their growing numbers.

To facilitate their trade and plunder, the Swedes had developed remarkable boats that could navigate both the rough seas of the Atlantic and the shallow rivers of Europe. The boats used oars and sails and varied in size, from those built for crews of 40 to those capable of carrying 100 warriors. They traveled at speeds of up to 10 knots. The boats permitted the Swedes to travel throughout the Baltic Sea and down the rivers to Constantinople. They established the cities of Novgorod and Kiev, where they were known as the Rus and gave their name to Russia.

The Vikings buried their dead with goods that they thought would be useful to them in the afterlife. These included boats, carts, sleds, and horses. Decorations on these objects, such as this wagon stave, were often fierce dragons or warriors.

Viking Ships

Before the Vikings were Christianized, they buried the bodies of their dead with objects that they had used during life and might need for the afterlife. The wealthy and noble were buried in their boats, so some excellent examples of these vessels have survived. In Gokstad, Norway, near Oslo, a large ship burial was excavated in 1880. The Viking buried in the ship was 6 feet tall and about 50 years of age. At least 12 horses, six dogs, and an imported peacock were buried with him. Beds, tent posts, sleds, three small rowboats, and many other items were also found there.

The main ship was built of oak, the decking and masts of pine. The keel consisted of one 58-foot-long timber. The boat itself was 76.5 feet in length and 17.5 feet wide at midship. The boat was very shallow draft, as are all the Viking boats that have been discovered, and drew only 3 feet of water even with a full load. The hull was clinker-built (the planks overlapped and were riveted together) and lashed to the ribs of the boat with spruce roots. The result-ing boat was flexible and capable of traveling equally well on the high seas and up the rivers of Europe. A replica of the boat was built in 1893 and sailed across the Atlantic for the Columbian Exposition in Chicago. The Gokstad boat and others may be seen in Oslo, and the replica is displayed in Chicago.

Near Gokstad, in Oseberg, a boat burial for a noble woman was excavated. She was buried with horses as well as two oxen, carts, and three sleds. She must have traveled a great deal during her lifetime.

This excavation photograph of one of the ship burials at Oseberg, Norway, shows the condition of the ship when archaeologists first uncovered it.

The Danes and Norwegians had first come to Europe as traders but, with the population pressure, they turned to plundering. England was close and wealthy. The first Viking attack occurred in 787 when they destroyed the monasteries of northern England, including Lindisfarne and Jarrow, which had been the home of the Venerable Bede. In their attack on London they used typical tactics. They plundered the city, but could not get their boats further up the Thames River because of London's bridge, which was built on pilings driven into the riverbed. By attaching ropes to the pilings and rowing their boats rapidly downstream, the Norse managed to destroy the bridge.

They moved down the coast of Europe, plundering Paris by 845 and reaching Aachen in 881. They had taken Ireland by the mid-ninth century and all of the rivers leading to the interior of France. The Vikings' greed also led them to Spain and into the Mediterranean, where they plundered the southern coast of France as well. Going beyond the lands known to earlier travelers, they settled in Iceland and Greenland in the late 800s.

The Vikings found that plundering was more efficient if they established permanent bases at river mouths. On the coast of France, the Danes settled on the mouth of the Seine and Loire rivers. They also settled in the north of England and Ireland.

At first, nothing seemed capable of stopping their raiding. One monastery in France, that of St. Philbert, changed its location three times in 35 years to avoid repeated raids. But finally some rulers did succeed in halting the Vikings' advances. Alfred, the Anglo-Saxon king of Wessex in southwest England, stopped the Norse advance in the 870s and began to take back other English territory from them. He finally established a diagonal boundary across England. The area north of the boundary was named the Danelaw. In its place names, this territory preserves the Danish influence to this day.

Ships were so important to the Vikings that they appeared on their coins. One side shows the high-bowed ship with its sail up. The other side shows the boat loaded with shields of the fighters.

In the eastern Frankish kingdom, the Carolingian monarch, Arnulf, defeated the Danes in battle and thus spared Germany from further Viking attacks. In fact Arnulf's victory was doubly fortunate for the Germans, because they were also facing an attack from the east by the Hungarians, or Magyars. Traveling on horseback, the Hungarian raiders took plunder and murdered the population. They eventually settled in what is today called Hungary.

The western Carolingians were less effective. The Vikings wanted to plunder eastern France by taking their boats up the Seine. The bridges of Paris, however, were not as easily destroyed as the one in London. Furthermore, the count of Paris had strung a chain across the Seine. The Vikings offered to spare Paris if the Parisians would let them pass the city. The Parisians refused, and the city withstood two years of siege. In the end, however, their heroic stance was a wasted effort. Emperor Charles the Fat eventually allowed the Vikings to go beyond Paris to plunder the interior of France.

As the Vikings became Christianized and settled down, their threat to Europe diminished. Still, this process took one and a half centuries. In the meantime, the population sought protection against the invaders. With the exception of Alfred in England and Arnulf in Germany, the kings had proven useless in defending their subjects against outside attack. The Carolingians had agreed to give away a whole province, now called Normandy after the Norse who settled it. The most able of the Carolingians, Charles the Simple, had died chasing a peasant girl. She ran into the enclosed courtyard of her father's house, and Charles,

following on a horse, hit his head on the beam on top of the gate and broke his neck. After his death, the Carolingians offered their subjects little leadership or protection.

King Alfred of England (849–899) was renowned in his own time and after. Like Charlemagne, he had a biographer, Asser, who modeled his life of Alfred on Einhard's life of Charlemagne. Asser describes the idyllic life of the young Alfred. He was loved by his parents, brought up in the royal court, and learned to write and hunt. He had a wonderful memory, and Asser wrote that "his mother one day was showing him and his brothers a certain book of Saxon poetry which she held in her hand." She promised the book to the first boy who learned it by heart. Alfred was attracted by the beauty of the illuminated initials in the book and took it off to ask his tutor to read to him. He then returned to his mother and repeated it word for word, thereby winning the book.

Alfred's interest in learning and books was evident throughout his reign and was shared by other Anglo-Saxons. He encouraged the translation of Boethius and other authors from Latin to Anglo-Saxon and contributed to the translations himself. In a preface to Gregory the Great's *Pastoral Care,* he noted that it was written "before everything was ravaged and burned, when England's churches overflowed with treasures and books." But more significant for our appreciation of the rich culture that flourished under Alfred's encouragement was the recording of Anglo-Saxon hymns and poems, including a written version of *Beowulf.*

Under Alfred's successors, the kingdom of Wessex gradually spread even farther. In

The Vikings used long, double-edged swords that took two hands to swing. The cross bar was designed to keep the hands from sliding down the blade. The pommel (handle) was of wood, bound with leather to soften the effects of blows to the user's hands. Since this sword comes from a tomb, the pommel has long since rotted away.

Alfred (right) successfully defended his kingdom from Viking invasion. In making the peace with one of their leaders, Guthrum (left), he was able to settle them in a region of northeastern England called the Danelaw. But the victory was hardly complete, and the Anglo-Saxons had to pay tribute, or Danegeld, to the Vikings to keep them from invading again.

time the whole of England as far as the Welsh and Scottish borders was united under one king. The Danes, however, did not give up their ambitions to conquer England, and, with new invasions in 1016, King Canute managed to take Norway and England and incorporate them into his kingdom of Denmark. He died in 1035, and his successors were unable to hold on to England, which reverted to a pious descendent of Alfred's Wessex dynasty, Edward the Confessor.

In France and elsewhere royal authority had failed to provide the protection that Alfred had given his people, and the population sought help from local strongmen. In Paris, the local count, Hugh Capet, proved capable of defending his city, so the inhabitants were more loyal to him than to the Carolingians who had sold them out to the Vikings. In 987 Hugh Capet took the title of king and thus founded the Capetian dynasty that ruled France until the early 14th century. Initially, however, Hugh controlled only the area around Paris. Other counts and dukes assumed control over their own territories and fought off the Viking raiders in these areas. Sometimes a local strongman or a bishop had the greatest success in defending the people against raids. Whether or not the strongmen had a title, they were generally referred to as "nobles."

The nobles maintained households of armed retainers to help them defend their territory. In many ways, the idea of a war chief surrounding himself with a band of fighting men resembled that of the Germanic *comitatus* (literally, a group of fighters gathered together). But this system was more formal: the nobles were assured of a

gift of land and membership in the upper class. All men in the nobility trained to become knights—that is, they were instructed in the use of arms in preparation for becoming professional warriors. Some of them were warriors all their lives. Others were given land by the lords and became vassals, men who swore to defend and serve their lord in return for the land. In the hierarchy of the nobles, kings had the highest title, followed by dukes, counts, marquises, and barons. What set these nobles apart from knights was their possession of land and enough wealth to secure other lords or at least knights as their clients.

Boys began the training in arms for knighthood when they were seven or eight. Often they were taken into another noble's household where they would be trained with other boys of their age. They learned to ride horses, wear helmets and chain-link mail (armor), use swords and spears, and carry a shield.

Warfare had changed under the Carolingians. Romans had used legions of foot soldiers, while the Germanic tribes had a light and highly mobile cavalry. Battles were often fought on foot. But the Carolingians had acquired, perhaps from the Byzantines, a larger type of horse that could support a rider wearing a shirt of mail, leggings, and helmet and carrying a shield, lance, and sword. Romans stayed on their horses by clasping their knees around them. The Carolingian mounted warriors, however, had stirrups that permitted them to remain in their saddles on the large horses even when they were hit by a lance held by another warrior riding toward them at full speed. The stirrups may have first been used by the nomadic tribes that invaded Europe. Not only was the training exacting for knights, the horse and equipment were very expensive. A war horse was equivalent in price to four oxen. Adding the armor and weapons, the cost of equipping a knight was 22 oxen. The biggest plow teams used by the peasants had only eight oxen, therefore becoming a knight was far beyond the means of any of them.

Another military development during the period of invasions was the castle. Because the Vikings did not want to waste time on protracted sieges, they tended to leave fortresses and protected cities alone and raid the surrounding countryside instead. The castles at this time—called motte-and-bailey castles—did not resemble the elaborate stone structures of the later Middle Ages. The motte was a natural hill or one that had been built up from nearby stone and earth. It was topped with a fort or stockade made from tree trunks sunk into the ground and sharpened at the top. The bailey had a larger, lower palisade constructed in the same way that enclosed a larger space and was attached to or surrounded the motte. The bailey was large enough to hold and protect animals and other valuables of the lord and his peasants. If the raiders took the bailey, the people could retreat into the motte fort and, they hoped, at least save their lives.

Building up the motte often left a circular trench around the mound that was called the moat. Filled with water, it was so muddy that attackers sank in it. The mounds themselves were quickly covered with grass that was slippery to climb. At the top was the stockade of tree trunks that shielded the

castle's defenders, who shot arrows and threw stones at the besiegers. As castles became more permanent, the wooden walls were replaced with stone ones, which had the added advantage of resisting fire.

Castles represented an investment of labor and money. Those who had them built became the protectors of their neighbors, who in turn became the castle owners' clients, beholden to them for protection. A whole system of personal ties and mutual obligations, which modern historians have termed feudalism, characterized the social and governmental arrangements of France at the time. Powerful lords, such as the counts and dukes, needed a group of fighters

Anglo-Saxon society valued literacy. In addition to histories, poetry, instructional literature, and religious texts, they preserved their legal documents in written form in Old English or Latin. This charter, by which King Canute granted land to a monk, Aefic, is written on parchment in Latin in the careful lettering typical of the Anglo-Saxons. The land is described above and the names of the witnesses are written below.

Chain Mail and Knight's Weapons

Mail, an iron mesh tunic, was made from iron rings that were interconnected. The rings were pieces of wire with the ends riveted together. On some mail, these rings were alternated with solid disks. The rings were fashioned together to form a tunic, called a hauberk, that was heavy, but flexible. It was suspended from the shoulders and hung down to the knees so that a knight's thighs would be protected. Knights also wore padded tunics stuffed with wool called gambesons. A gambeson stopped the metal from chafing the skin and provided further protection. Warriors might also have worn mail on their legs.

Mail could be penetrated by spears and arrows, so some knights wore hardened leather or whalebone as well as armor. Their helmets were conical and had a nasal bar in the front to give the face some protection. In addition, the knights carried large, kite-shaped shields to ward off blows and arrows. Their weapons included axes, swords, lances, and maces.

Although chain mail continued to be used throughout the Middle Ages, as bows became more powerful knights favored steel plates for armor. These were harder to penetrate and had convex surfaces to deflect arrows. Knights also favored a helmet with a visor that could be lowered so that the entire face was covered. Gauntlets protected the hands from arrows. A fully clad knight in mail and plate armor riding a horse that might also be clad in armor was the equivalent of a medieval tank.

The sword was the single most important implement of war. A sword needed to be both strong and sharp. Viking smiths made the blades from several strips of iron, which they twisted and hammered out many times to ensure their durability and strength. The blades were double-edged, with a groove running down the center. The groove made the blade lighter and more flexible. The guard was a simple crosspiece intended to keep the

By the 15th century knights preferred a full suit of plate armor. Where the plates joined—at the neck, over the upper legs, and at the elbows—they used chain mail for protection.

hand from running down on the blade. A pommel surrounded by wood and bound with wire or leather made the handle. The blades were used for cutting rather than thrusting.

weak, however, the counts and dukes had considerable control over the land granted to them. They took their names from their provinces. For example, there was a Duke of Aquitaine and a Count of Flanders. Lesser nobles, such as Geoffrey de Mandeville and Roger de Beaumont, took the names of their principal castles.

A warrior who received a fief from an overlord swore that he would be his *homme* ("man" in French) and serve him in times of need. This oath was called homage. Here is an early 12th-century example: Count William of Flanders asked a warrior if he was willing to become his man, and the warrior replied that he was. The warrior then clasped his hands together, and the count put his own hands around them. The two men exchanged a kiss of peace. Next the man did fealty—that is, he swore on his faith to keep the terms of his vassalage: "I promise on my faith that I will in future be faithful to Count William and will observe my homage to him completely against all persons in good faith and without deceit." The man then took this oath on the relics (bones) of a saint. Finally, Count William gave him a little rod that he held in his hand to indicate that he was now invested with the fief.

Giving over land as a fief was risky. A lord needed to ensure that the vassal would meet the obligations that the gift implied. By the 13th century the arrangements had become more formal. Written charters spelled out the services the lord and his vassal owed each other. Because the institution began as a military one, fighting, not surprisingly, was the vassal's first obligation.

To avoid abuse, specific terms were set.

to protect and administer their territory, so they offered lesser nobles land to support themselves if they would look after their interests in a particular district. The grant of land was called a fief (rhymes with "leaf") and is derived from the old German word *fihu* for property.

In theory the king held all the land, and the counts and dukes simply used it at his pleasure. They, in turn, granted it to the barons and knights. Because the kings were

The vassal was to serve his lord in war at his own expense. He was required to provide the armor, horses, and men needed to support the war effort. If the period of service was more than 40 days, however, the lord had to help pay the costs. The vassal also had to accompany his lord in times of peace and be present at his castle for two or three months each year.

The lord also had certain rights that he could exercise to protect his land. He always reserved the right to take the land back from an insubordinate vassal. In practice, however, retrieving land could be difficult, because an angry vassal might besiege the lord's castle or cause a revolt among his fellow vassals. A more convenient way of addressing the problem was to impose controls over inheritance. When the vassal died, the lord retained the right to relief, that is, to impose a tax for passing the estate onto the heir. If the vassal died leaving minor children, the lord claimed the right to wardship of the children until they reached the age of 21, the usual age of majority and of knighthood.

The lord could take the proceeds of the estate during this period. He also reserved the right to marry the widow and daughters to anyone of his choice. The lord could demand that the vassal contribute to the marriage gifts (dowries) of his daughters and the knighting of his first son. Finally, the lord could go to his vassal's estate with his retinue, which might include a hundred men, and sit and eat for a period of his choice. This right was called "purveyance." In the 16th century Queen Elizabeth I took advantage of this right as a way of keeping her potentially rebellious nobles sufficiently

A noble father presents his reluctant young son to the care of monks. Since the first-born son was the only one who could inherit property, fathers often dedicated younger sons to monasteries, whether or not they wanted to become monks. Since fathers had to make marriage alliances for daughters, they often found it convenient to put extra daughters in nunneries. If the noble family had endowed the monastery, the son or daughter might rise to be the abbot or abbess.

poor that they could not afford to form armies against her. In return for what seemed like burdensome rights, the lord gave the fief and offered his vassals protection in times of war or raiding.

The solemn oaths of loyalty and the contracts of service would seem a peaceful solution for local government, yet warfare was endemic in feudal Europe. Vassals accepted fiefs from different lords, so they often had conflicting loyalties. When a weakling or a daughter inherited a fief and could not defend it, lords and competing kin fought on the battlefield and in the courts to win control of the land.

Furthermore, the Frankish custom of equal inheritances for all sons had given way to primogeniture, or inheritance by the firstborn son and, when there were no sons, by the daughters in equal portions. Thus younger sons were disinherited, and had to look for other ways to make a living. Some became priests or monks, sometimes against their will. Because younger sons were often raised to be knights like their eldest brother, many found the peaceful ways advocated by the Church difficult to adhere to. Clergy were not supposed to spill blood, so they could not carry swords. (However, they were permitted to use spiked clubs known as maces.)

Other younger sons became knights in the service of various lords, and still others tried to conquer land for themselves. Fighting was so disruptive that influential abbots and bishops in France acted as peacekeepers. They persuaded the local lords to agree to the Truce of God, which protected the vineyards and the peasants' animals and limited fighting to about four days a week, excluding holy days. They also established a treasure chest that could be drawn upon by local lords to ensure the Peace of God by supporting armed intervention in local fights.

The social values that feudalism produced are best expressed in the poem *The Song of Roland,* which was first written down in the early 12th century. A nephew and vassal of Charlemagne, Roland was a member of the rear guard for Charlemagne's troops. The army managed to fight off the Arabs, but in the end was reduced to himself, his friend and fellow nobleman Oliver, and Archbishop Turpin, who was armed with a mace as befitted his clerical status.

A somewhat foolhardy young man, Roland could have summoned help long before this desperate situation occurred because he had a famous horn, Oliphant (a horn made from an elephant tusk). When, at last, he decided to blow it, Oliver chastised him by saying, "Wise courage is not madness, and measure is better than rashness. Through thy folly these Franks have come to their death; nevermore shall Charles the king [Charlemagne] have service at our hands. Hadst thou taken my counsel, my liege lord would be here, and this battle ended." Charlemagne heard Oliphant but arrived too late to save the three. Archbishop Turpin died on the ground: "His

bowels had fallen out of his body, and his brains are oozing out of his forehead." Count Roland lay down to die under a pine tree and called to mind "all the lands he had won by his valor, and sweet France, and the men of his lineage, and Charles, his liege lord, who had brought him up in his household." He then wept and died.

Absent from *The Song of Roland* and other such poems of valor and warfare from this period is a strong role for women. Roland has a fiancée in France, but as he dies he thinks of his liege lord, not of the girl he would have married. Noble women in this period of constant warfare had to be resourceful and capable of taking control of a castle. They did not learn to fight, as their brothers did, but they did learn to administer estates, run a household full of rough warriors, and defend a castle if it was besieged. If they were heiresses to a fief, they took the vows of homage and fealty to their lord but had to supply a knight to fight in their place. Likewise, many abbots and even bishops held their lands from the king or another lord and had to swear homage and fealty for their fiefs.

As membership in the nobility and the transfer of fiefs became increasingly hereditary, women became more and more important as pawns in marriage alliances. A woman who had no brothers was a valuable heiress because the man she married would get the use of her fief. Women in such circumstances were married off by their fathers or liege lords when they were quite young. They had no say in the matter, but would be married to the man who offered their father or their lord the best potential for political alliance, land acquisition, or

military aid. Thus, the Duke of Aquitaine's only heir, a young daughter, Eleanor of Aquitaine, was married to Loius VII, king of France. Through this union, Eleanor's entire estate, which included a large portion of southwestern France, came under the control of Louis VII. The couple was so mismatched, however, that the marriage was eventually annulled.

When the nobility were not at war they spent their time in and around the castle. Hunting was very popular, and even women took part. Banquets and feasting, accompanied by recitations of *chansons de geste* (literally, "songs of great deeds"), were also favorite pastimes. Off the battlefield, men wore a loose-fitting tunic that was belted at the waist and dropped to the knees or slightly above. The legs were covered with a sort of tights. A mantle, fastened at the throat or the right shoulder with a brooch, completed the costume. They wore their hair short and are frequently represented as clean-shaven.

Women wore long tunics that covered them from the chin to the feet. They too wore belts and mantles attached by brooches. When they were young, their hair hung free, but later it was bound up with ties. Older women and married women wore headdresses or veils over their hair. Hoods provided both sexes with protection from rain and other inclement weather. Most clothing was made of linen and wool. Furs might be used as decoration or as lining for mantles to provide additional warmth. Silk was reserved for special occasions and for use by the clergy. Women in all ranks of life used a spindle to turn wool and linen into thread for weaving. In addition, upper-class women embroidered tapestries and ceremonial clothing.

Several elements contributed to the nobility's exclusivity, including the expense of horses and armor, the importance of castles for defense, and the long training required to use arms. Certain behavior and values, as reflected in *The Song of Roland,* also set members of the class apart from those of lower rank. Most importantly, to be noble meant being born into the class, because its privileges of membership could be gained only by heredity. The members of the noble class, along with the clergy, who were often the younger sons of nobles, comprised about 5 to 10 percent of the total population. The other 90 to 95 percent were peasants. Very few people fell outside the categories of noble and peasant during the early Middle Ages. Artisans and merchants were few. Long-distance trade was much less important than it had been in Roman times. The populations of towns had dropped to the level of villages, and the inhabitants engaged as much in agriculture as in crafts.

The Roman *latifundia* system of farming on large estates was readily adaptable to the needs of both the peasantry and the nobility in the early Middle Ages. The Carolingians had adapted the system on estates that included both the remnants of the Roman agricultural population and the more newly arrived Franks. It was further modified during and after the period of Viking invasions.

These agricultural estates were called manors. Manors were an effective system for organizing agriculture and were found all over Europe in areas where grain was

Poems Recount the Lives and Battles of Heroes

Seeing his knights being massacred by the Arabs, Roland, the hero of The Song of Roland, *finally blows his horn, Oliphant, to summon Charlemagne.*

The warrior societies of both the Vikings and the early feudal period enjoyed the recitation of poems, which recounted histories, battles, tales of deceit and valor, and deeds of gods, kings, and adventurers. The poems were recited to the accompaniment of a harp.

The Icelandic sagas were written down in the 12th and 13th centuries. Some of them, such as the *Volsungasaga,* tell the same story as the German *Nibelungenlied*— that of a dragon protecting a magic treasure. Others narrate the adventures of actual people and events, such as Leif Ericsson and the discovery of Vineland.

The *chansons de geste,* or, literally, songs of great deeds, were more deliberate compositions in French. Although harkening back to the Carolingian era, they reflect the society of 11th- and 12th-century France. The *Chanson de Roland* (Song of Roland) is the best known of the *chansons de geste.* The poem includes stirring battle scenes and descriptions of an aged and venerable Charlemagne, who is presented as a prototype of the ideal feudal king. Also memorable is the trial by battle of the traitor, Ganelon, and his final execution, during which he is bound to four war horses and pulled in four directions:

And so they order four
   war-horses brought out
To which they tie
   Ganelon's feet and
   hands.
These are proud chargers,
   spirited, bred for speed:
Four servants urge them
   the way they ought
   to go.
There where a river across
   a meadow flows,
Count Ganelon is utterly
   destroyed:
His ligaments are twisted
   and stretched out,
His every limb is cracked
   and split apart;
On the green grass the
   bright blood runs in
   streams.

cultivated. Usually, but not always, they coincided with villages. Fiefs ranged in size from a portion of a manor to many manors. The peasants had houses in the village with some garden and yard space around them for fruit trees, outbuildings, and straw stacks. The village also had a church and residence for the local priest. It might also have a manor house for the lord to stay in when he visited and a residence for his estate manager, the steward. The fields, which

surrounded the village, might be divided into two or three large areas, depending on the type of agriculture undertaken. Each field consisted of several hundred acres.

These large fields were not cultivated as units but were divided into a series of strips to be farmed by village families. The strips were scattered through all three fields. The best strips were reserved for the lord of the manor and were called demesne (literally, belonging to a lord) lands. The parish priest also had strips reserved for his use, and these were called glebe (literally, soil or earth) lands. The rest of the strips in the common fields were divided among the peasants for their use. This land was apportioned so that all received a mix of good and bad holdings, but the number of acres that each family held varied considerably. The better-off peasants had 30 acres or more, the moderately well-off peasants had about 15 acres, and the poorer ones had 5 or 6 acres.

The division of the manor into two or three large fields and the distribution of strips were also done for conservation reasons. The division of the fields depended on the fertility of the soil. The thinner soils, such as those found around the Mediterranean or in hilltop areas, could be cultivated only every other year. Consequently, a two-field system predominated in those regions. One of the large open fields was

allowed to remain fallow, or uncultivated, for a year to regain its fertility while the other field was cultivated. In river valleys and other regions with deeper, richer soil, a three-field system was employed. Under this system one third of the land lay fallow each year, and the other two fields were cultivated. The strips in the fields were laid out in such a way that they would capture moisture, avoid erosion, and get plenty of sunshine. On hillsides, for instance, the strips ran horizontally around the slope rather than vertically. Where necessary, drainage ditches were constructed to draw water off wet ground. Likewise, terraces were built to trap water in arid areas.

Crop rotation also increased fertility. Under the three-field crop rotation system, the first field would be planted in the fall with winter wheat. Wheat was a heavy feeder, taking many nutriments from the soil, so the next year the field was planted with peas or oats. Peas had many advantages. Legumes (peas and beans) fixed nitrogen in the soil, renewing its fertility. Peas were also a source of protein, and thus provided the peasants with a more balanced diet than one containing only wheat and other grains. The third year the field lay fallow and was used to graze the village herds so that their manure fertilized the soil. Animal protein, however, did not

make up a large part of the peasants' diet because they did not have enough grass and grain to feed all of their animals throughout the winter.

The second field was planted with peas or oats the first year, lay fallow the second, and was sown with wheat the third. The third field lay fallow the first year, sown with wheat the second, and planted with peas or oats the third. By rotating the crops in this way farmers had a field of wheat and one of peas or oats every year.

The exploitation of the fields was similar to that practiced on the Carolingian estates. The duties of each peasant on the manor were spelled out in the *custumal,* the register of customary services and rents that each family owed. Slavery, prevalent on Carolingian estates, disappeared, but peasants were still categorized as free or unfree. The unfree peasants were called serfs or villeins. ("Villein" derives from *villa,* meaning "farm.") On the surface, the differences between the two groups did not seem too great. Both free peasants and serfs had to work for the lord. They did the same sorts of work as the Carolingian peasants: They had to plow the lord's land, plant it, reap and harvest it, carry the crops to market, and mend his fences, roads, and home.

But the serfs had to provide other types of services and dues that free peasants did not. Free peasants had title to their lands, whereas custom dictated that serfs had only the right to take over their father's holding and had to pay a death due to do so. Usually the due included a serf's best plow oxen as well as an entry fee. Serfs also paid an annual rent for their land. Furthermore, whereas free peasants could leave the manor as they wished, serfs were bound to the land and had to pay the lord if they wished to leave.

Certain other dues were also part of a serf's lot in life. When his daughter married, he had to pay a special tax to the lord, known as the merchet, and if his son wished to leave the manor, he had to pay for that as well. He also owed special rents and gifts, including the traditional gifts of fowl on feast days such as Christmas, and eggs at Easter. Our customs of having fowl for Christmas dinner and eating eggs at Easter derive from these practices.

As in the Carolingian period, marriages between the free and unfree peasants were common, so it was hard to keep the two groups distinct. In practice, there was little difference between them in the 10th and 11th centuries. A free peasant could move his family about if he wished, but there were few places to move. If he had a lord who offered him protection from the Vikings or Hungarians (Magyars), he was happy enough to stay where he was. If the manor was sacked, both the free and unfree peasants might leave and seek their fortunes elsewhere. Basically, livelihoods were so tenuous that people were grateful for the security of having land to work and protection during invasions. Only in the 12th century, when new lands opened up and towns began to grow, offering an opportunity for new ways of earning a living, did peasants begin to care about whether they were free or unfree.

Like the innovations in knights' fighting equipment, innovations in the tools of cultivation profoundly changed medieval society. The larger horse was not only a better cavalry animal, but also made a better cart horse and plow beast. Romans had not used horses as draft animals because they did not have the horse collar. Instead they used oxen, which could be yoked to a plow or a cart. Horses in harnesses could pull only light objects, such as a chariot, because they would choke if the harnesses were pulled too tightly around their throats. The medieval invention of the horse collar, however, distributed the weight around a horse's shoulders so it could pull a plow or heavily loaded cart.

In the early Middle Ages the horseshoe also came into use. It allowed horses hooves to withstand a heavier load, be it a fully armed man, a cart, or a plow. Oxen continued to be used for agriculture, but horses were faster as draught animals. They were, however, more expensive to feed because they needed grain rather than just pasture.

Improved plow technology revolutionized agriculture in the Middle Ages. The Romans had used a simple plow that was really a hardened, sharp stick drawn by oxen. It was very effective in the sandy,

The new plow used in the Middle Ages for the heavy soils of northern Europe had wheels to help move the plow along and a coulter, a sort of long knife, to cut through the sod. The actual plowshare is attached to the end of the shaft that the man holds. A mold board on the shaft turned the soil over and formed a furrow. The horses are equipped with collars that distributed the burden of pulling the plow to the horses' shoulders. The man in the background is planting seeds.

When William the Conqueror won the Battle of Hastings in 1066, he commemorated his victory by establishing a monastery on the site of the battle. The monks kept a chronicle of events and in this 12th century manuscript initial depicted a king on a throne to represent their benefactor. It is not a real likeness.

light soils of the Mediterranean area, but not adequate for the heavier clay and alluvial soils of the fertile river valleys of northern Europe. The plow invented for these areas employed a coulter, or knife, to cut the heavy grass sod before the plowshare turned it. Added to the plowshare was a moldboard that turned the soil over into furrows, thus burying the weeds and grass to rot. After plowing, a harrow (a tool used to pulverize lumps in the soil) went over the furrows to break up the soil and prepare it for planting. Such improvements in plowing meant that lands that had not previously been used for agriculture could now be brought into cultivation.

The overall result of these improvements was that yields from planting increased dramatically. In the Carolingian period, every bushel of wheat planted yielded only two or three bushels at harvest. One of those bushels, of course, had to be saved for seed wheat for the next year. With crop rotation and a better plow, yields went up to as much as seven bushels harvested for every bushel planted. The implications of this early agricultural revolution were immense for medieval Europe. Everyone's diet improved, so the population increased in all social classes. Lords and peasants alike began to trade their surplus grain for other items. This desire, in turn, encouraged a renewal of long-distance trade and the development of towns where goods were manufactured for expanded markets.

In 1066 the Norse made one more major foray into England—the Norman Conquest. The English king, Edward the Confessor, had married Edith, the sister of the Anglo-Saxon nobleman Harold Godwinson, but they had no children. As the king aged, three powerful men weighed the possibilities of taking over his kingdom. Harold Godwinson's family was not of royal blood. Still, for the Anglo-Saxons, his was the strongest claim because of his sister's marriage. King Harald Hardrada of Norway, who was the subject of a Norse saga, made his claim through Denmark's King Canute who had also been king of England. Duke William of Normandy, a Dane by descent, maintained that Edward the Confessor had promised the throne to him and that Harold Godwinson, on a visit to Normandy, had sworn an oath to uphold this claim. Edward the Confessor was half Norman and had grown up in Normandy.

In 1066, as Edward the Confessor neared death, a comet appeared in the sky. Modern astronomers have since identified it as Halley's Comet, but people in England interpreted it as a dire prediction of terrible events to come. The Anglo-Saxons met and elected Harold Godwinson as their king. Harald Hardrada immediately invaded the north of England and pressed toward York. Harold Godwinson managed to defeat him, but two weeks later, on October 14, Duke William's fleet arrived from Normandy. William was well prepared. He brought supplies, war horses, and even a prefabricated castle. His neighbors in France and many of the younger sons of the nobility joined his army in the hope of being rewarded with fiefs of their own. The two armies met at Hastings on the southern coast of England. Harold's troops had the better position on a rise, and made a shield wall to protect themselves. The Normans had to attack by going uphill. At some point, however, the shield wall broke down, and Harold was shot in the eye with an arrow. The Normans were victorious.

One battle did not amount to a conquest, however. William set off to the west with his army, building castles in every county and castles in every location where he met resistance. He proceeded north, where he met the greatest opposition. He killed many people there and destroyed much of their farmland. London was his final target. By the time he reached the city, the rest of England had been conquered, and London could no longer hold out. There William built the biggest of his castles, the Tower of London. Along the

route of his conquest, he killed or drove out the Anglo-Saxon noblemen, but married their women to his followers when he gave them the noblemen's land. His followers were thus richly rewarded with fiefs, and England came to experience the feudal system as it existed in France. Likewise, the English peasantry became serfs and were organized into the manorial system by their Norman and French overlords.

When the conquest was complete and the English population subdued, William returned to Normandy and ruled England from a distance. By 1086 he began to survey the real estate and wealth he had acquired in such a brutal way. He sent out his officials to inquire about and record the number of fields, farm animals, agricultural implements, and people he had under his control. This great survey was preserved and is called the *Domesday Book*, or the lord's *(dominus)* book.

In addition to the *Domesday Book*, two remarkable sources survive for the study of the Norman Conquest. One, which gives the English side, is the *Anglo-Saxon Chronicle*.

The Bayeux tapestry was commissioned by the Normans to tell their version of events leading up to the conquest and battle. The Normans brought food, horses, weapons, and even a prefabricated castle in boats that were still built in Viking style. They wore chain mail, carried sail-like shields, and were armed with swords and lances.

St. Maurice brings Otto I into the presence of Christ. Otto carries a replica of the church he has built in honor of St. Maurice. St. Peter stands to the right holding his symbol, two keys. The Ottonians were great patrons of the Church.

It had been started in the days of Alfred and continues through the death of William. In it William is described as:

> a very wise and great man, and more honored and more powerful than any of his predecessors; . . . he caused castles to be built and oppressed the poor; . . . he was of great sternness, and he took from his subjects many marks of gold and many hundred pounds of silver, and this either with or without right and with little need. . . . The rich complained and the poor murmured, but he was so sturdy that he recked naught of them; they must will all that the king willed, if they would live, or would keep their lands.

The author comments that for the Domesday survey "so narrowly he had them investigate that there was not a single hide nor a rood of land, nor—it is a shame to tell though he thought it no shame to do—was there an ox or a cow or a pig that was not set down in the accounts." But in the end, the author concedes that a man could travel from one end of the kingdom to the other with a bosom full of gold and not be robbed. William had, at least, brought peace.

The other source is the *Bayeux Tapestry,* named for the town in France in which it is housed. Commissioned by the Normans, it is really an elaborate embroidery rather than a woven tapestry and tells the story of the conquest from the Norman point of view, through pictures and a running commentary in Latin. The tapestry is 230 feet long and 20 inches wide (70 meters by 51 centimeters). The death of Edward, the comet, Harold's oath, the preparations for the expedition, the feast before the battle, the battle, and the portable castle are all represented. On the border are other illustrations, including plowing scenes.

Germany's response to the end of the Viking invasions was very different from that of France or England. Germany had not suffered as much, so its recovery was quicker. Otto I the Great (reigned 936–973) managed to bring some unity to the territory of Germany and even to the Middle Kingdom that had been given to Lothair by the Treaty of Verdun a century earlier. He defeated the Magyars, and the process of Christianizing northeastern Europe began. Moving down into Italy to rescue the pope, much as Charlemagne had done, Otto took the title of "Roman Emperor" in 962. The German Kingdon became known eventually as the Holy Roman Empire.

Feudalism was late in coming to Germany. Although the great lords became vassals of the emperor, they did not have vassals of their own. The emperors governed their territory with bishops and abbots rather than their vassals because they could appoint the churchmen, whereas the vassals held their positions by hereditary claims. Furthermore, the bishops and abbots were educated men and made very good administrators. They were also loyal to the emperor who appointed them.

Under the patronage of Otto and his dynasty, the Ottonians, learning flourished in Germany. Two scholars stand out from this period. One is the nun Roswitha of Gandersheim (c. 937–1004). She came from a noble family of Saxony but was put into a Benedictine nunnery at an early age. Gandersheim was founded by the Duke of Saxony in 852 and was governed by women who belonged to the Saxon dynasty. Otto the Great's younger brother, a bishop, encouraged learning at the nunnery, so Roswitha was educated by a series of learned nuns.

During her early education, she wrote religious poetry on the life and miracles of the Virgin Mary and lives of other saints. She then read the comedies of Roman playwrights. Roswitha was beguiled by their language but bothered by the worldliness of their subject matter. Nevertheless, seeing the potential of drama, she began to write religious plays—the first plays written since Roman times. Finally, she turned to writing histories, including the *Deeds of Otto* about Otto the Great.

The other great scholar of the age was a monk, Gerbert of Aurillac in France (d. 1003). Gerbert came from a peasant family, but his genius was recognized by the local monks who educated him. He was taken to Spain, where he came into contact with the great learning of the Arab and Hebrew populations in Barcelona. Although he studied with Christian scholars there because he did not know Arabic, he learned something of Arab mathematics. Back in Europe, he demonstrated the mathematical basis of music by using vibrating strings. He also taught astronomy. Although he had an abacus with Arabic numerals, he did not use the zero as the Arabs did. His fame in France brought him patronage from the Ottonians, who appointed him pope. He served as Sylvester II. So great was his knowledge that people thought he was a necromancer, or sorcerer. In reality, he was a man ahead of his time.

By 1050, Europe was beginning to develop a strong economy and a vibrant culture that brought Roman, Christian, and Germanic elements into a coherent whole. The feudal arrangements among the nobility, and the manorial system for organizing land and labor, spread all over Europe. Kings such as William the Conqueror of England and Otto the Great of Germany were reviving a sense of unified monarchies. Towns and trade were beginning to develop and Europeans began to travel, explore, and conquer new territories. Once again scholars had the leisure and intellectual curiosity to ask new questions. Even the weather cooperated as Europe experienced several centuries of warmer than usual weather. The 12th century was such an expansive period that a growth metaphor is often used to describe it: the flowering of the Middle Ages.

In dem pñj tag do kumpt
der planet venus vnd lan
zeit ob dem mone An dem
ist gut mit frawenn zu red
kinder werdenn mbenn

Chapter 5

The Flowering of Medieval Europe

Courtly love, the recommended standards of polite relationships between knights and ladies in medieval Europe, changed manners at the time and has had a long-lasting influence on our ideas of courtesy.

Eleanor of Aquitaine, heiress of the Duke of Aquitaine, married the king of France as a teenager. While in Paris she perhaps heard the leading philosopher of the day (Peter Abelard) lecture, was chastised by a saint (Bernard of Clairvaux), and advised by Abbot Suger, who commissioned the first Gothic building. Eleanor also went on the second Crusade to the Holy Land before, at the age of 30, she divorced her husband and married the 18-year-old king of England. As Duchess of Aquitaine and Queen of England she participated in the creation of the culture of courtly love and bore four sons, two of whom would become kings. While Eleanor's life was extraordinary, her personal experiences reflected the remarkable burst of creativity and energy of the period between 1050 and 1150. It was a time of new ideas, increasing prosperity, and fervent religiosity which to some degree touched all the people and institutions of Europe.

In the political arena, both the papacy and the monarchies began to bring stability to their respective domains. Political stability allowed trade to flourish once again and all classes to take advantage of increased agrar-

ian prosperity. It also led to a revival of piety among the ordinary people—inspiring them to build new churches and undertake pilgrimages and crusades. Philosophy and learning revived as scholars reinterpreted ancient texts. The peace of the era forced the rough manners of war to give way to the polite behavior of the court, creating a new impetus to write romances and love lyrics.

The founding of one new monastery had particularly far-reaching consequences for lay piety, architecture, learning, and the papacy. It had become customary for kings and lords to endow monasteries and nunneries with sufficient land for their inhabitants' livelihood and with laborers to support them so that they could spend their lives in prayer. Their motives were twofold. They wanted the monks and nuns to pray for their souls so that their afterlife would be spent in heaven rather than hell. But they also saw these establishments as offering an honorable career for the extra daughters and sons who would not marry or could not be endowed with lands.

Placing these superfluous noble children in monastic institutions sometimes had good results. Some became worthy abbots and

The Order of Cluny was responsible for great church reform, for an increase in piety, and for a new style of architecture known as the Romanesque. The rounded arches on the windows and the massive walls of the abbey church at Cluny are typical of the Romanesque style.

abbesses and occasionally even saints. But often the children had no taste for monastic life and lived very corruptly. They spent more time with their married brothers and sisters in their castles and, against monastic rules, took lovers and concubines themselves.

To counteract the strong lay influence on monasteries, the Duke of Aquitaine founded a monastery at Cluny in 910. The Cluniac monks used the Benedictine Rule and were permitted to select their own abbot rather than accepting the duke's choice. The abbot was answerable only to the pope, not to the duke. The monastery gradually gained respect and adherents. Other monasteries reformed and declared themselves Cluniacs. The movement inspired Emperor Henry III of Germany, who reformed the Church in Germany. He then crossed the Alps to Rome, where three men were claiming to be pope. He deposed all of them and put in their place a series of popes who also supported the reform of the Church.

The new wave of piety inspired the laity as well as the clergy. Because they no longer feared that their churches would be destroyed in warfare, the laity began to contribute some of their excess profits from agriculture to building parish churches, cathedrals, and new monastic houses. The architecture of the churches they built was derived from previous Roman models and is therefore called Romanesque. Romanesque architecture incorporated rounded arches and vaults, and ceilings or roofs of masonry (including barrel vaults and cross vaults). The buildings also tended to be low, and required a massive amount of masonry to hold up their stone ceilings. Some churches had wooden ceilings that allowed for height in the nave, which in turn allowed more windows in the clerestory (the wall extending above the aisles to the roof of the nave).

To counterbalance the massive appearance of the masonry and the absence of large windows, the interiors of churches were brightly painted with Biblical scenes, including the lives of the saints, pictures of heaven and hell, and other such paintings that would instruct the congregation as they attended services or visited the churches. In the apse (a semi-circular room on the east end of a church) was a very large picture, often a mosaic, of Jesus giving the law to Christians. The effects of the heavy masonry were further lightened both inside and out with carvings featuring biblical scenes, saints, and Christian symbols. A popular theme for the carvings over the main entrance to large churches was the symbols of the four gospel writers, Matthew, Mark, Luke, and John. This set of carvings was called the tympanum, from the Greek word for drum.

Romanesque architecture could be found throughout Europe, although it varied from area to area. William the Conqueror constructed several cathedrals in England. Durham, one of the best examples of the Norman style, is a massive structure capable of inspiring worship but also of withstanding siege. Normans favored geometric designs for their arches. French versions of Romanesque architecture tended to have more elaborate exterior and interior carvings, such as those that can be seen today at Vezelay and Autun. The French also added small chapels in the apse area for private worship. In Sicily, elements of Moslem architecture were added to the arches, making them appear less weighty.

As the laity contributed more to the building of their parish churches and cathedrals, they demanded more from their clergy. They wanted the clergy to know the liturgy (the rites used for public worship), to be able to instruct them, and to remain unmarried and lead exemplary lives. The quality of the clergy did improve. In the spirit of Cluny, the clergy wanted to remove themselves from the control of the ruling elite, so that they could regulate their own ranks. Most important, of course, was liberating the papacy from the control of the emperors. Ever since Charlemagne's rule, the emperors had claimed the right to reform the papacy when it became embroiled in local fights. Henry III of Germany was acting on the same tradition when he set up a reform pope in Rome.

To gain its freedom, the papacy needed to develop a way of electing its successors without outside influence. The man credited with working out the details of papal election was a Cluniac monk named Hildebrand, an Italian who had moved into the Church hierarchy in Rome. He developed

Romanesque Cathedrals Show New Building Techniques

Masonry ceilings for Romanesque churches were either barrel vaults or cross vaults (groin vaults). Barrel vaults looked like half of a barrel or half of a cylinder of masonry perched on the supporting masonry walls. Cross vaults were composed of two half barrel vaults intersecting at a right angle. A series of these vaults formed the ceiling. The weight was concentrated at the four corners of the vault and the two groins. Cross-vaults had the advantage of adding some height and allowing for an arch that could provide space for a clerestory window, which let light in at the ceiling. Cross vaults were well suited for the aisles of a church because the wall of the nave and the outside wall could hold them up. However, the bigger expanse of the nave needed heavier, oblong vaults, and the weight of their heavy masonry required large piers to hold up each corner. Clerestory windows were minimal in the nave area. Sometimes wedge-shaped buttresses (supports) were used on the exterior of churches to hold up the masonry. Romanesque churches tended to be rather low and dark because the walls, piers, pillars, and, sometimes, masonry buttresses had to be very thick in order to hold up the ceiling.

Durham Cathedral is one of the most powerful examples of the Romanesque style. It has a massive, austere quality that represented both the piety of the Cluniac reform movement and the substantial conquest of the Normans in England.

The struggle between Emperor Henry VI and Pope Gregory VII showed the tensions between the secular rulers of European monarchies and the power of the pope. In the famous fight between Henry and Gregory, each used his most powerful weapons. The pope used his spiritual power to excommunicate Henry in the first round, but Henry appeared as a penitent and had it removed. Later Henry used force of arms to set up an antipope, Guibertus, and expel Gregory from Rome. Gregory again excommunicated Henry, but the pope died soon afterwards in exile.

an electoral system called the College of Cardinals. In his plan the pope was to be elected by the most important clergy in Rome, that is, by the bishops, priests, and deacons of the churches in Rome and its surrounding countryside. The plan was an adaptation of the old custom of having the priests attached to a bishopric (or district) elect the new bishop. The College of Cardinals, which still exists, was later enlarged to represent all of the clergy by giving some of the archbishops and important ecclesiastical officials outside of Rome the title of Cardinal so that they could vote. Hildebrand's plan removed the emperor entirely from the process of electing a new pope. The first election went smoothly because Henry III had died, and his son, Henry IV (1056–1106), was only a boy and too young to interfere.

In 1073 Hildebrand himself became Pope Gregory VII (1073–1085), but not through an election by the College of Cardinals. He was so popular in Rome that the clergy and populace alike proclaimed him pope. Emperor Henry IV went along with Hildebrand's elevation to the papacy because he was trying to establish control over his rebellious German nobles.

Contemporaries described Gregory as a small man with a weak voice, but a strong vision of what the papacy should be. He claimed that the mission of the popes was to be the voice of St. Peter on earth and argued that, by the doctrine of the Petrine Succession, the pope was accountable to St. Peter and to God for the sins of humans. If an emperor sinned, the pope had a duty to call even him to account. In Gregory's eyes, Henry IV had become a sinner because he continued to appoint bishops and abbots in Germany and to invest them with the symbols of their spiritual office—the bishop's crook (staff) and ring. Investiture by a layman such as the emperor, as Gregory saw it, was unacceptable. From the early days of the church, monks customarily elected their abbots and the clergy elected their bishops—a principle that Gregory had invoked in creating his system for papal elections.

Henry IV had learned the hard realities of politics as a young boy. His mother had acted as regent, ruling in his stead while he was too young to do so, but during this time he became the virtual prisoner of the Bishop of Cologne. After freeing himself from these influences when he came of age, he began an active campaign to form his own power base. Realizing that he needed a wealthy region under his control, he selected Saxony, in part because it had silver mines. By 1075 he was successful in his campaign and feeling flush with impending victory.

By the same year, however, Pope Gregory VII was also feeling powerful enough to strike at the heart of lay investiture. Although Gregory was adamantly opposed to lay rulers selecting abbots and bishops, he recognized that ecclesiastical authorities might hold fiefs from a lay ruler, and he would permit them to receive those from a monarch, but he would not permit lay rulers to appoint ecclesiastical officers or invest them with the spiritual symbols of that office. In 1075 Gregory wrote several letters to Henry—calling him "beloved son"—in which he praised the emperor for not selling ecclesiastical offices and for upholding the principle of unmarried clergy. But he then attacked Henry for appointing bishops.

In one letter his address moved beyond a firm remonstrance: "Gregory, bishop, servant of God's servants, to King Henry, greeting and the apostolic benediction— but with the understanding that he obeys the Apostolic See as becomes a Christian King." He went on to stress his own spiritual power over Henry, "considering and weighing carefully to how strict a judge we must render an account of the stewardship committed to us by St. Peter, prince of the Apostles, we hesitated to send you the apostolic benediction." Gregory was angry that Henry was appointing and investing bishops in both Germany and Italy against the papal edict and threatened him with excommunication (expulsion from the Church) if he continued to do so.

In 1076 Henry responded in a letter to his bishops. He called Gregory "not pope but false monk" and referred to Gregory's own assumption of the papal throne as a usurpation because he was neither appointed by the king nor elected by the College of Cardinals. The salutation of one of his letters to Gregory reads, "Henry, King not by usurpation, but by the pious ordination of God." Henry argued that he too had a sacred trust from God because of his consecration during the coronation ceremony. In his estimation, a monarch had a duty to God to cleanse the Church of a false pope. He rallied the bishops of Germany and Italy, who were loyal to him, and with their support closed his letter with the statement: "I, Henry, King by the grace of God, together with all our bishops, say unto you: Descend! Descend!" He was asking that the pope abdicate because of his false election.

Gregory realized that he could make no headway with the bishops that Henry had appointed in northern Italy and Germany, so he appealed to the German lay lords. They had resented Henry IV's conquest of Saxony, and distrusted his plans to curtail their own independence. They were quite willing to listen to Pope Gregory's suggestion that they rebel against their feudal overlord if he were excommunicated. Excommunication meant that a Christian was not allowed to participate in Holy Communion, but its ramifications went far beyond this religious ceremony. It also dissolved all feudal bonds of loyalty and forbade anyone from serving the excommunicated former member of the Church. In other words, excommunication put the offender outside of the community of be-

lievers. If Henry were excommunicated, the German nobles were released from all feudal vows and could select anyone they wanted as their ruler.

Gregory excommunicated Henry in 1076. The German nobles immediately met and declared that, if Gregory did not revoke the excommunication order within one year, they would depose Henry. Gregory's triumph was short-lived, however. Because Henry could find no loyal supporters among his nobility, he made a trip to Italy in January 1077 to waylay the pope, who was on his way to a meeting with the German nobility.

At Canossa in the Alps, Henry appeared before the walls of the castle in which the pope stayed, standing barefoot and clad in the rough wool garments of a repentant sinner. After the penitent king had stood in the winter cold and snow for three days, the pope finally relented. As he wrote to the German nobility, Henry "ceased not with many tears to beseech the apostolic help and comfort until all who were present or who had heard the story were so moved by pity and compassion that they pleaded his cause with prayers and tears. All marveled at our unwonted severity, and some even cried out that we were showing, not the seriousness of apostolic authority, but rather the cruelty of a savage tyrant." As pope, Gregory could not refuse absolution to a sincere penitent, so the excommunication order was lifted.

Henry regrouped his power and in 1084 marched into Rome and selected a new pope. Gregory died in exile in 1085, reportedly exclaiming: "I have loved righteousness and hated iniquity; therefore

In Florence and other cities, the grain supply was crucial for the survival of the population, so the city regulated it. When grain was scarce, the poor and indigent who did not contribute to the economy of the city were evicted. When the city had abundant grain, officials distributed it liberally to the poor (right).

I die in exile." But Henry did not triumph, either. Papal reform was by now too strong a movement for the emperors to control, and future popes continued to pressure Henry. While Henry was engaged in Italy, the German nobles again rebelled and supported Henry's son against him. In 1122, at the Concordat of Worms, the Church was able to persuade his son, Henry V, to agree that only the clergy could invest the bishops with the symbols of their office and that the emperor could not appoint bishops and abbots. But the bestowing of fiefs remained the right of a king or an emperor.

The papacy was not the only institution that reestablished itself in the late 11th century. The surplus of grain and the restoration of peace also allowed trade to flourish once again. Both peasants and nobles had surplus grain to sell and, therefore, money to buy practical items such as plowshares as well as luxury goods such as silks and ribbons, and spices to make their bland foods taste more interesting.

With the revival of trade and crafts, towns became an important part of the European landscape, just as they had been during the Roman period. Lords were so interested in attracting people to their towns that they offered peasants freedom from serfdom if they migrated. Other serfs took advantage of town laws that promised freedom to those who managed to live for a year and a day in town without their former masters claiming them. "Town air breathed free" is how they put it at the time.

Towns flourished throughout Europe, but none as much as those in Italy, where Venice, Genoa, Pisa, Milan, and Florence became major trading and industrial cen-

ters. Milan was known for its fine armor and its control of the overland trade with Germany. Venice, Pisa, and Genoa rivaled each other for their overseas trade in the Mediterranean and even across the Atlantic to countries including France, England, and the Low Countries. As townspeople prospered, they also sought freedom from kings and bishops so they could govern themselves and set their own rules of trade, government, and citizenship. Towns came to be governed by the merchants who dealt in luxury items and bulk shipments. The merchant class, in contrast to the nobility, enjoyed wealth derived from trade as opposed to land. Furthermore, the merchants needed goods to trade overseas. This demand encouraged artisans to produce high-quality cloth, art, and other products that would be valuable in trade. Peasants, who were also enjoying new prosperity because crop yields were improving, wanted to purchase better shoes, plows, tools, and pottery. Town markets and trades flourished, and so did the artisans.

The growing population moved into previously unsettled parts of Europe. As village populations became too large for their old sites, lords who held forests and swamps urged their serfs to clear the trees and drain the fens. To encourage them to take on this extra work, the lords offered serfs better terms and freedom from the servile duties they performed in return for their land on established manors. The new settlements adopted place-names that are still in use. Some of them were named for nearby settlements; for example, Little Horewood was a new settlement whose population came from Great Horewood.

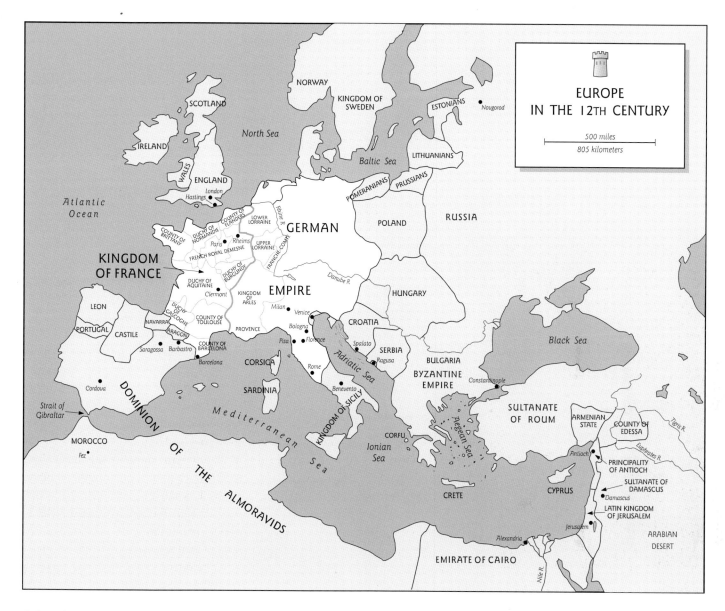

NORWAY

KINGDOM OF
SWEDEN

ESTONIANS

Nougorod

SCOTLAND

North Sea

IRELAND

Baltic Sea

LITHUANIANS

WALES

ENGLAND

Hastings

London

Atlantic
Ocean

COUNTY OF
FLANDERS

LOWER
LORRAINE

Rhine R.

POMERANIANS

PRUSSIANS

POLAND

RUSSIA

COUNTY OF
BRITTANY

DUCHY OF
NORMANDIE

GERMAN

Paris

Rheims

UPPER
LORRAINE

FRANCHE-COMTÉ

KINGDOM
OF FRANCE

FRENCH ROYAL DEMESNE

DUCHY OF
BURGUNDY

Danube R.

HUNGARY

DUCHY OF
AQUITAINE

Clermont

KINGDOM
OF
ARLES

EMPIRE

LEON

DUCHY
OF
GASCOGNE

COUNTY OF
TOULOUSE

PROVENCE

Milan

Venice

Bologna

CROATIA

Black Sea

PORTUGAL

CASTILE

NAVARRA

ARAGON

Saragossa

Barbastro

COUNTY OF
BARCELONA

Pisa

Florence

Spalato

SERBIA

Ragusa

BULGARIA

Barcelona

CORSICA

Rome

Adriatic Sea

BYZANTINE
EMPIRE

Constantinople

Cordova

SARDINIA

Mediterranean

KINGDOM OF SICILY

Benevento

Ionian
Sea

Aegean Sea

SULTANATE
OF ROUM

ARMENIAN
STATE

COUNTY OF
EDESSA

Tigris R.

Strait of
Gibraltar

DOMINION

Sea

CORFU

Antioch

Euphrates R.

MOROCCO

Fez

OF

THE

ALMORAVIDS

CRETE

CYPRUS

PRINCIPALITY
OF ANTIOCH

SULTANATE OF
DAMASCUS

Damascus

LATIN KINGDOM
OF JERUSALEM

Jerusalem

ARABIAN
DESERT

Alexandria

EMIRATE OF CAIRO

Nile R.

Others had names that indicated a new foundation, such as Newcastle or Villeneuve (literally, New City in French).

During this period, Netherlanders began to settle the marshes bordering the North Sea, establishing a system of dikes and windmills to drain these areas. The German emperors also conquered more land in the Slavic east in an expansion called the *drang nach Osten* (drive to the east). They encouraged people in the heavily populated areas of the Low Countries to move east and settle along the Baltic Sea and in Hungary and Bohemia. Just as in the United States during the 18th and 19th centuries the call to the adventurous was "Go West, Young Man," in the 11th and 12th centuries, agents of German lords recruited serfs to go east and settle the new lands, bringing

with them their technology of plowing and draining fens.

If the peasant population was expanding both within the old territories and in newly conquered lands, the nobility was growing at an even faster pace. Noble mothers had a better diet than peasant mothers and produced children who were more likely to survive the dangers of childhood. The sizable family of a minor noble, Tancred de Hauteville in Normandy, serves as a notable example of the circumstances of this large and aggressive group. He had 12 sons; five by his first wife and seven by his second. Because only one son could inherit the small ancestral lands, the others set out to seek their fortunes.

Three of the brothers—William Iron-Arm, Humphrey, and Drogo—

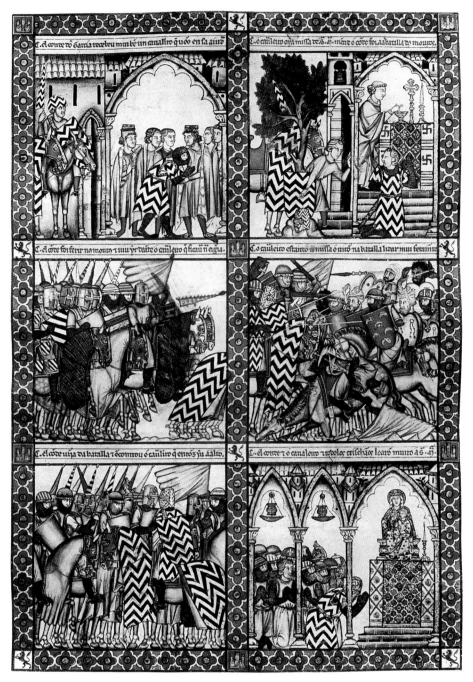

The Reconquista *in Spain was part of the armed expansion of Europe in the 11th and 12th centuries. The knights who sought their fortunes taking land from the Arabs and from each other viewed their warfare as a holy endeavor. A century after the events, a Spanish king who was also a crusader commissioned a book that showed the blessing of the troops before battle (top), the final victory of the Christians (center and bottom left), and a ceremony of thanksgiving for victory before the Virgin and Child (bottom right).*

recognition as ruler of the territory. His brother, Roger, captured Sicily and held it with papal approval by 1072. The brothers established a Norman kingdom in these two areas similar to the organized state that William the Conqueror had established in England.

Other younger sons of the nobility sought their fortunes in Spain by fighting against the Moslems there and carving out principalities. This fight became known as the *Reconquista* (reconquest) and was portrayed in the epic poem *El Cid.* The poem's hero is based on a historical figure, Rodrigo Díaz, a Castilian noble who is born in about 1043. (His nickname, "el Cid," means "lord" in Arabic.) In the poem, Díaz is a champion of the Christian faith. In reality he was an opportunist who fought both Christians and Moslems, plundering both churches and mosques. By the early 12th century, Moslem control in Spain started to crumble, and the kingdoms of Aragon, Castile, and even Portugal began to expand.

During this period, the Arab world began experiencing reverses that would lead to its decline. While the French and Norman nobility were creating separate kingdoms in Sicily and Spain where the Arabs had previously ruled, the Seljuk Turks (a nomadic tribe that had converted to Islam) were making major conquests in the east. The Turks conquered Baghdad and moved west, where they defeated the Byzantine army and acquired Anatolia (part of modern Turkey), which they called the sultanate of Roum (an adaptation of "Rome"). Jerusalem and other areas of the Christian and

became warriors, sometimes acting as mercenaries and sometimes as bandits. During their pilgrimage to Jerusalem, they discovered that Sicily and southern Italy were fine places to practice their skills of warfare. The Arabs and Greeks who were fighting in these places were both willing to hire mercenaries. Soon the remaining de Hauteville brothers had joined their kin and began carving out their own kingdoms rather than fighting for local factions. The half-brother of William, Robert Guiscard ("the Fox" or "the Sly"), managed to conquer southern Italy and receive papal

Jewish heritage came under the Turks' control. Thus, when western Christians began to make extended pilgrimages to the Holy Land, they were greeted at inns and shrines not by the tolerant Arabs, but by the Turks, a group newly converted to Islam. Pilgrimage thus became more difficult and much more dangerous, and the native Greek Christian population complained to the pilgrims of persecution.

Relations between the Greek-speaking church in Byzantium and the Latin-speaking church in Rome also were strained. Although both parties believed that they were part of the same Christian church, the Roman Church, flexing its muscles during the reform movement, sought to dominate the patriarch of Constantinople. The "Great Schism" of 1054 was the culmination of a number of clashes over the centuries. Controversies had arisen over such issues as the use of the Roman or Cyrillic alphabet among the Slavs, the wording of the Nicene Creed, the question of whether Christians should use two fingers or three to cross themselves, and the position of the pope in Rome as the titular leader of Christianity. These tensions led to a split between the two branches of the Church.

The increasing strength and belligerence of the European nobility and the papacy, together with the Turkish threat to Constantinople, led to an explosive clash of cultures called the Crusades. Literally, the word crusade meant "pilgrimage," but the pilgrims were armed men from Europe who sought to retake the area around Jerusalem and any other rich territory that they could conquer, including the Byzan-

tine Empire. While the ideal of crusading—to make Jerusalem a Christian city—lived on for centuries, many crusaders simply wanted to gain territory.

A volatile combination of interests, ambitions, and religious feeling gave rise to the first crusade. Pilgrims complained that they risked their lives going to Jerusalem, and that the Greek Christians, even though they were erring in their ways, were in grave danger of being killed. The merchants of Italian towns maintained that they were being ill-treated in Constantinople because of the schism and that trading in the former Byzantine and Arab territories had become increasingly dangerous. The economy of the Italian towns was suffering as a consequence. The Byzantine Emperor, Alexius Comnenus, wrote to the pope in consternation after a defeat suffered by the Byzantine army and asked that he send mercenaries, perhaps some of those fierce and footloose Normans. In return for such help, the emperor hinted that he would mend the schism by investing Rome with greater power than that of the patriarch of Constantinople.

The pope at the time, Urban II, held a council of French clergy and nobility at Clermont in 1095. There he preached a sermon that was a stirring call to arms to liberate the Holy Land. Addressing the French laity, he flattered them by praising their fame as warriors and called on them to avenge the Christians in the east. He noted that the Turks, followers of Muhammad,

The liberation of Jerusalem from the Turks became the goal of the Crusaders. A map of the city drawn at the time of the Crusades showed the city wall with its five gates. The three major religions, Judaism, Christianity, and Islam, all had their sacred structures in the city: the Temple of Solomon, the Church of the Holy Sepulcher, and the Dome of the Rock.

Pope Urban II met with the French nobility at Cleremont in 1095 and gave a stirring sermon calling upon his audience to recapture the Holy Sepulcher from the Turks, relieve the Byzantine Empire from the threat of annihilation, and enrich themselves by conquering fiefs for themselves in the Biblical land of milk and honey. He called upon them to undertake a glorious holy war—which became the First Crusade.

Holy Land, the traditional land of milk and honey, and carve out estates there. For those who went, he promised remission of their sins so that they would go to heaven, for this was to be a glorious pilgrimage.

The audience responded enthusiastically, crying out *"Dieu le veut!"* ("God wills it!"). But Urban quickly realized that too much enthusiasm would not raise an army but a rabble. He cautioned that "we neither command nor advise that the old or feeble, or those incapable of bearing arms, undertake this journey. Nor ought women to set out at all without their husbands, or brothers, or legal guardians. Let the rich aid the needy; and according to their wealth let them take with them experienced soldiers." Clergymen were not to go without the consent of their bishops.

Urban had, indeed, anticipated the problems that might arise. He and Emperor Alexius Comnenus needed an army of knights under the direction of a western king or at least a duke. But the pope's first appeal inspired a mob of second sons, peasants, poor knights, and members of the clergy. Persuading the nobility to join up took more time. Finally, the Duke of Normandy (Robert, son of William the Conqueror); Count Raymond of Toulouse; Bohemund, son of Robert Guiscard; and several other French nobles agreed to go on the crusade.

While the main army of nobles and knights took time to organize themselves, amass supplies, and negotiate with Italian merchants for ships, the popular crusade set off by foot across Europe. It was led by an impoverished knight, Walter the Penni-

had killed Christians, destroyed churches, and dismembered the Greek empire. The Franks could liberate the Holy Sepulcher (the tomb in which Jesus had been buried) and aid the Greeks. The pope also alluded to the overpopulation of France: "This land which you inhabit, shut in on all sides by the seas and surrounded by the mountain peaks, is too narrow for your large population." He pointed out that instead of fighting one another for land, they could go to the

less, and a preacher, Peter the Hermit. Their followers believed that the year 1100 would bring a second coming of Christ, and they wanted to be in Jerusalem when this happened. They also believed that the walls of Jerusalem would come tumbling down like those of Jericho, when they marched around them and blew their horns. Some people argued that they did not even need to go to the Holy Land to fight infidels; they could do just as well by attacking Jews in Europe. The first po-groms—in which Jews were rounded up, robbed, killed, and burned—occurred in Cologne. Most of the popular crusade, however, headed on through Hungary and the Balkans. The crusaders also believed that, as an army of God, the local inhabitants should feed them. When this charity was not forthcoming, they stole food. When they finally arrived at Constantinople, the emperor was so disgusted with them that he forced them to camp outside the city. Even so, they committed petty thefts and harassed the local population. Finally, the emperor agreed to ferry them over the Bosporus. There the Turks attacked them, and most were killed. Peter the Hermit, however, managed to return to Constantinople.

In the meantime, the main body of crusaders assembled in Constantinople. Relations between Emperor Alexius and the westerners were not cordial. A remarkable account of the Greek viewpoint was written by Alexius's daughter, Anna Comnena. Anna claimed that the crusaders could not be trusted: "There were among the Latins such men as Bohemund and his fellow counselors, who, eager to obtain the Roman Empire for themselves, had been looking with avarice upon it for a long time." Anna was right about Bohemund. She described an incident in which her father greeted Bohemund and invited him to a feast. Knowing that Bohemund would be suspicious of this, Anna's father had his cooks bring raw meat to his guest and told Bohemund to have his own cooks prepare it if he preferred. With a great gesture of liberality, Bohemund divided up the cooked food and gave it to his followers, but did not take any for himself. The next day he asked them if they were feeling well or if the meal had been poisoned. They were all well. Anna concluded: "Such a man was Bohemund. Never, indeed, have I seen a man so dishonest. In everything, in his words as well as his deeds, he never chose the right path."

After numerous squabbles between the crusaders and the Greeks, Alexius and the leaders of the crusade reached an agreement. Alexius would supply the crusaders with the provisions necessary for their warfare, and in return the crusaders would deliver to him the cities of Asia Minor, which the Byzantine Empire had lost to the Turks. The emperor would also continue to supply the crusaders with food and drink. The first town the crusaders captured was Nicaea. Anna wrote that they did not, however, turn over the city as promised, but forced Alexius to pay for the city once again.

The crusaders' real test came at the siege of Antioch in 1098. Alexius stopped their supplies just as they attacked the city. The situation became desperate as food ran short

Medieval bestiaries described animals, both real and fictional. Sometimes the animals were characters in fables written to teach the readers moral lessons about covetousness and other sins. Other times the descriptions are of animal behavior, habitats, and origins of names.

The assault on Antioch was long and brutal. The Turks held the city while the crusaders tried to attack it from the outside. The crusading army suffered from hunger and disease that decimated their ranks and led to fights among the leadership.

and continued on to Jerusalem. The Italian cities sent fleets to supply food and siege equipment. In the summer of 1099, the crusaders took Jerusalem. It was a terrible defeat. One eyewitness said there was so much blood in the streets that it came up to the knees of the horses.

The leaders of the crusade discussed what to do with the territory. The petty fighting and land-hunger that had characterized the conquests seemed inappropriate in the holy city itself. So they selected Godfrey of Lorraine, the only noble who had not participated in the internal dissensions, to be the first king of Jerusalem.

The Latin conquests in the Near East established the Latin Kingdom of Jerusalem, and several principalities were given as rewards to the nobles who fought. The whole experience of colonizing the region also had an enormous impact on Europe. Among the things that the crusaders returned home with were a better knowledge of building stone castles and machines to besiege them, a taste for more highly spiced foods, an appreciation of the luxury of silk and cotton garments, and a number of relics of saints from the early days of Christianity.

Life in Europe, particularly for the nobility and merchants, was becoming more refined even without the influence of the crusades. Contact with the Arab population of Spain had taught them to appreciate lyrical poetry as opposed to the heroic poetry of the *chansons de geste* and the sagas. Internal warfare decreased because younger sons went to Spain to fight Arabs or joined the crusades, and the resulting peace brought about a remarkable change in the nobles'

that winter. Finally, in the spring, an Italian fleet arrived with more supplies. According to the accounts of a person who was there, Bohemund suggested that whoever broke the siege and entered the city would be allowed to keep it. But the chronicler went on to say that Bohemund had already made contact with a Christian inside the city walls, who let him climb up at night and open the gates for the crusading army. The crusaders were victorious, but the victory was short-lived. The Turks soon recovered and sent a large force against Antioch. Now the crusaders were stuck between a castle in the city center still held by Turks, and the Turks outside the city walls. They were reduced to eating rats. In desperation, Bohemund suggested that they try to drive off the Turks encamped outside the city walls. The crusaders won this battle, and Bohemund claimed the city for himself in defiance of Alexius.

The other nobles accompanying Bohemund were so angry with him that the crusade nearly fell apart at that point. The leaders resolved their differences, however,

The refinements in court culture that courtly love brought to Europe included round dancing.

manners. The knights who went on the crusades had been warriors, trained to fight in battle. Those who remained in Europe, however, imbibed a new culture of military virtue called chivalry, from the French term for a mounted warrior, the *chevalier*. According to the code of chivalry, a knight was to be courageous (sometimes to the point of foolhardiness), loyal, trustworthy, generous to a conquered foe, and eager to defend the Christian faith. But chivalric behavior was to be practiced only by nobles and, for the most part, by males. The 12th-century refinements in living led to additional requirements for knights' behavior: Noble women became objects of respect and elaborate courtesy; religious ceremonies surrounded the initiation of knights; and tournaments, or ritualized combat and warfare, became an entertainment.

Eleanor, Duchess of Aquitaine, established a court in which the new noble values flourished. Her grandfather, Duke William of Aquitaine, was a romantic figure known both for his love affairs and for the lyrical poetry he sang to his mistresses. Eleanor became the Duchess of Aquitaine upon her father's death when she was a teenager. The adviser to the French king, Abbot Suger of the monastery of St. Denis outside of Paris, had arranged a marriage, with her father's blessings, between Eleanor and the young king of France, Louis VII (1137–1180).

The marriage was not a happy one because the two were so different. Eleanor had come from a sophisticated, worldly court in the south of France and disliked the damp chill of Paris. Louis had been raised to

Anna Comnena, Byzantine Princess and Historian

Anna Comnena, born in 1081, was the firstborn daughter of Emperor Alexius and the oldest of his 11 children. Because of the long gap between her birth and that of her oldest brother, John, she harbored the idea that she would become empress. In her book, the *Alexiad*, she wrote that her real troubles with John began when she was eight. She was to be married to the rightful heir to the throne, who was then a boy of about her age. She assumed that together they would take over from her father, who had usurped the throne. But the marriage never took place, and she was eventually married to another man. Thereafter, she blamed her brother, John, for her failure to become empress. With a male heir, Alexius did not need her for the succession.

Anna received a fine education that included the study of literature, medicine, astronomy, and the mechanics of siege equipment. She wrote in the introduction of her book: "I, Anna, daughter of the Emperor Alexius and the Empress Irene, born and bred in the Purple [born and raised as a princess], not without some acquaintance with literature—having devoted the most earnest study to the Greek language, in fact, and being not unpracticed in Rhetoric and having read thoroughly the treatises of Aristotle and the dialogues of Plato, and having fortified my mind with the Quadrivium of sciences (these things must be divulged, and it is not self-advertisement to recall what Nature and my own zeal for knowledge have given me, not what God has apportioned to me from above and what has been contributed by opportunity)." She not only observed firsthand the events of her father's reign, but also had access to men who had advised him and to other writings, including those of her husband who also wrote history.

become a member of the clergy, perhaps even abbot of St. Denis, and was more clerical than knightly in temperament. He was forced to take the throne on the death of his elder brother.

The real difficulties between the couple occurred during the Second Crusade. Eleanor had given birth to two daughters but no sons, so she accompanied her husband on the crusade in the hopes of conceiving an heir to the French throne along the way. Dressed as female warriors, she and several other noble French ladies set off in high spirits. As if this behavior did not

Battling dragons (left) and fearsome knights (right), the legendary knight Lancelot fulfills his chivalric duties. In the Middle Ages, romances about the feats of the nobility were popular in the courts, and the most popular subjects of all were the stories that related to King Arthur, Queen Guinevere, Lancelot, and the other knights of the Round Table.

cause enough scandal, when the couple arrived in Antioch Eleanor announced to Louis that she would remain there with her uncle, Raymond. Rumor abounded that she and Raymond, a handsome man and great warrior, were having an affair. She was said to have commented of Louis, "I thought to have married a king, but I married a monk." After their return to France, she still had not produced a male heir, and Louis agreed to solicit the pope for an annulment of their marriage. The marriage was dissolved and she returned to being Duchess of Aquitaine.

But as an heiress, Eleanor remained a very desirable marriage partner. She was pursued by Henry, Count of Anjou and Duke of Normandy, who had met her in Paris when he had come to pay homage to Louis VII. He was only 18 and she was nearly 30, but marrying her would make him the Duke of Aquitaine. Furthermore, he was in line to become the king of England. They were wed barely eight weeks after the annulment of Eleanor's first marriage. It is hard to imagine a bigger blow for Louis VII. Henry was his greatest rival, and now his rebellious vassal had combined his inheritance of

Normandy, Anjou, and England with that of Eleanor. Together these counties and duchies were larger than the land that Louis personally controlled in his kingdom. As a further wound to Louis's dignity, Eleanor produced four sons by Henry. A mighty feud arose between Henry and Louis.

Her marriage to Henry left Eleanor with responsibilities for maintaining his interests in the duchy of Aquitaine, but it also gave her a considerable amount of free time. Henry had political responsibilities in England, Normandy, and Anjou, so Eleanor was often alone in her own duchy. Her court was one of the most cosmopolitan in Europe. Her personal understanding of the world included the learned philosophy of Paris, the ways of Norman and English nobility, the exotic culture of the East, and the traditions of her grandfather, the poet. Poets and nobles were attracted to her brilliant court at Poitiers.

The combination of poets and young courtiers with the time to pursue refinement produced new standards of polite behavior around the court (*courtoisie*, or courtesy), a new emphasis on the importance of women as epitomized by courtly love, and new lyrical poetry and tales of romance that celebrated the changing relations between men and women of the noblility. Under the patronage of Eleanor and her daughter, Marie (daughter of Louis VII), rules of behavior in love were established. Men were instructed concerning in how to address ladies and were punished in a "court of love" if they offended a woman. Poets known as troubadours composed lyrical poetry in celebration of their love for women and wrote tales called romances, in which the love of the hero and heroine were tested by a number of separations and adventures. Many of the romances retold legends from the past about King Arthur, Lancelot, Guinevere, and the knights of the Round Table. Troubadours traveled widely seeking patronage from various nobles, and in this way the poetry, tales, and rules of behavior of courtly love became fashionable all over Europe.

Troubadours could be either professional musicians or nobles. Bernard de Ventadour, for example, was the son of a servant in a castle. Viscount Ventadour was his patron, but Bernard was very attracted to the viscountess and addressed a number of his love poems to her. When her husband became jealous, Bernard sought the patronage of Eleanor of Aquitaine. Other poets included a noble man, Bertran de Born, who wrote with tenderness about his love of war. He wrote of his enjoyment of the lusty spring with the songbirds singing and of the sight of the tented armies in the field. But what he liked most was to hear the cries of battle and the din of swords on armor and to see "horses mad, with rolling eye, who frenzied through the battle fly." The warrior, he wrote, thinks "but of blood and butchery and yearns for death or victory."

Authors of romances included Marie de France, an educated woman living in England. She told the story of one of Arthur's knights who had never known love. He was out hunting one day and shot an arrow at a white doe, but the arrow glanced back and struck him in the thigh. The doe told him that he would not be healed until he won the love of a lady. He then took to the sea, but his boat was shipwrecked on the shore of a beautiful garden. There a lady, who was imprisoned in a tower by her cruel husband, found him and nursed him back to health. But the husband discovered the knight and sent him off again. After a long separation, the husband was slain, the knight and his lady love were reunited, and they lived happily together. Having found love, the knight's leg healed.

The music for lyrical poetry differed from church music. The plainchant, in which all voices sang the same parts in unison without instrumental accompaniments, had been common in church services since the time of Gregory the Great. But the *chansons de geste* were sung to the accompaniment of a harp, and the troubadours played a stringed instrument with a bow—probably in imitation of Arabic musicians. Polyphonic compositions, which include parts for different voices such as tenor and bass, gradually became part of both religious and court functions.

St. Bernard of Clairvaux, one of the most influential figures of the day, contributed hymns to the Virgin Mary to the music and poetry of the period. Bernard was raised with the traditional values of a nobleman,

Stringed instruments, perhaps adopted from the Arabs, accompanied lyric songs and played carols for round dances. The fiddle was an oval instrument with three strings that was played with a bow. The guitar was also a popular instrument in court music.

Tournaments, or mock battles, became both a way of keeping up fighting skills and of entertaining the nobility. They were an opportunity for rich display of fashions, feasting, horses, and armor as well as feats of fighting prowess. Ladies attended, cheering on their favorite knight. The fighting was highly ritualized, with lists (wooden barriers) to confine the fighting space. Heralds made sure that the rules of fighting were followed.

The worship of the Virgin Mary became very popular in the 12th century as hymns and churches were dedicated to Mary. Mary was shown as a gentle mother with the infant Jesus on her lap. People found it easier to direct prayers to this motherly figure than to the more distant God or Jesus.

but had a conversion experience during an outing with some of his companions and joined a monastery at Cîteaux, where he entered the new Cistercian order. Although they followed the Benedictine Rule, Cistercians tended to be stricter in their observance than the Cluniacs, and emphasized manual labor. By the time of Bernard's death in 1153, the same year that Eleanor established her court in Aquitaine, the Cistercian order had spread throughout Europe. It was Bernard who had persuaded Louis VII to undertake the Second Crusade, and he had been an adviser to Louis and Eleanor. But he could not prevent their separation, and he grieved at the failure of the crusade.

Bernard was a great leader in theology as well as an inspiration for monks and monarchs. Among his major accomplishments were the hymns to the Virgin Mary, which greatly increased her popularity in the Church at the time. More and more, churches were dedicated to Mary, and ordinary worshipers found that addressing prayers to Mary was more comforting than addressing them to Christ the lawgiver, as he was depicted in the apses of cathedrals. Mary became the subject of popular veneration and was often addressed in the same terms of adoration as the noble ladies were in love lyrics.

Noble men organized tournaments, or war games, that were suitable to the new court culture. Knights who did not go on crusades or engage in combat for long periods saw tournaments as an opportunity to exercise their skill with arms with minimal potential for loss of life and limb. Tournaments were organized by nobles to celebrate the knighting of a son, the marriage of a daughter, the coronation of a king, the heroic entrance of a prince into a city, or as part of yearly urban celebrations. In fact, any excuse was a good one for these mock battles. If single combat was the order of the day, then lists were set up in such a way that the combatants could charge each other on horseback with lances. If a mock battle, or *melée,* was planned, then a field for two opposing sides was laid out. Elevated seating permitted spectators, including women, to view the fights. In elaborate contests, whole towns were turned into fighting quarters, and the streets were filled with sawdust or sand so that the horses would not slip on the cobblestones. The mock battles were fought from street to street.

The tournaments not only permitted the knights to display their fighting prowess, but also included a number of other rituals that emphasized courtly behavior. Observance of the rules of the game was crucial. First, weapons and horses were inspected. The participants then presented a coat of arms declaring the origin of the fighter to the assembled dignitaries and ladies. (Anonymous fighters could display false coats of arms. Sometimes kings used these, because no one would knowingly fight against his king in open combat for fear of being charged with treason.) A fighter might also wear some favor from his lady, such as a scarf or sleeve, and fight in her honor. Although the knight might have wanted to gain the love of a lady, he could win material rewards as well. Organizers offered winners a piece of armor, a horse, or the right to take the suit of armor and horse of the knights they defeated.

This remarkable period also saw a revival of learning in Europe. Boethius's translations of parts of Plato and Aristotle received new attention in the schools that grew up around the cathedrals. Students flocked from all over Europe to listen to famous teachers lecture. Lectures were given in Latin, the common scholarly language, so that students from all reaches could understand them. By far the most famous teacher was Peter Abelard (1079–1142). He wrote an autobiography, *Historia Calamitatum* or *The History of My Misfortunes,* thus much is known about his life. He was born into a knightly family in Brittany. He could have inherited his father's lands, but instead became fascinated by theological and philosophical arguments, and traveled

Every noble had his own distinctive coat of arms and registered it in a book of heralds. Heraldry terminology was an elaborate language of symbolism that included such terms as chevrons (peaked stripes), rampant lions (on their hind legs), fleur-de-lis (lily flowers), and various bars drawn left to right or right to left.

throughout France to listen to various teachers. Paris was the center for these debates, and Abelard soon developed a reputation as the most subtle of thinkers. He had a number of students who paid fees to hear him lecture. He became famous throughout Europe, but especially in Paris. His book *Sic et Non* (*Yes and No*) presented arguments for and against a whole range of difficult questions, such as whether faith can be supported by reason, whether good angels and saints who enjoy the sight of God know all things, and whether God is a substance.

In relating the history of his misfortunes in his autobiography, Abelard told of his romance with Héloïse. The uncle of this very bright and beautiful young woman was a high official at Notre Dame cathedral. Wanting to provide the best instruction for his niece, he engaged Abelard as her tutor. Abelard's description of their lessons recounted how they moved from reading books to kissing each other. The affair became more serious, and she became pregnant. The couple was faced with a dilemma. If they married, he would not be able to pursue a career in the Church, because the clergy had to remain unmarried. Héloïse, not wanting to ruin his career, refused to marry him. But when their son was born, they were secretly wed. Not knowing that they had married, her uncle was outraged when he learned of the birth, and arranged for a group of thugs to assault and castrate Abelard. Abelard retired to a monastery and urged Héloïse to do the same.

Although Abelard continued to write and lecture, some people, such as Bernard of Clairvaux, believed that his thinking was close to heretical. While living in the monastery, Abelard wrote his autobiography. It was circulated widely, and Héloïse read a copy. She, like Abelard, had by now become the head of a religious community. Reading the account of their love reopened the old wounds. She wrote a letter to Abelard in which she sympathized with his misfortunes but reminded him that she too had suffered. She did not think of their love affair as a sin and recalled that he was a singer of love songs in those days. Héloïse wrote: "But in the whole period of my life I have ever feared to offend thee rather than God; I seek to please thee rather than Him. Thy command brought me, not the love of God, to the habit of religion." She felt like a hypocrite for loving Abelard and becoming a nun only to please him. Abelard wrote back as a father confessor rather than as a former lover.

The remarkable flowering of the arts in Europe had lasting effects, even into our own time. Courtly love and chivalry became the basis for polite relations between men and women and in society in general. The crusades marked the first major expansion of Europe into Asia since the Roman period and brought Europeans into contact with new products and ideas. The spirit of expansion and conquest never left people's imagination and led to the age of discovery in the 16th century. The revitalized Church and the intellectual developments of the 12th century came to further fruition in the 13th century as lay governments—of both towns and monarchies—also began to prosper as peace prevailed.

William Marshall, the Ideal Knight

William Marshall was a younger son of a minor English nobleman. He grew up in a period of struggle for the English throne. During a siege, his father offered him as a hostage to King Stephen, as a pledge that he would give up his castle if he could not find reinforcements. When his father reneged on the deal, King Stephen determined to kill William, who was five or six at the time. The king marched him to a tree to hang him, but was so overcome with pity for the boy that he stayed the execution and kept him with him for two months during the siege.

When William was a teenager, his father sent him to Normandy to be a squire and learn the use of weapons. At the age of 21, William, according to his biographer, "seemed so well and straightly made that if one judged honestly, one would be forced to say that he had the best formed body in the world." He was knighted in a simple ceremony. His lord buckled on his sword and gave him a ceremonial blow on the shoulders. William participated in his first battle soon afterward, but during its course he was pulled from his horse and the animal was killed. In the celebrations that followed, the lords told him that fighting was for profit as well as for the cause of the fight. He should have tried to capture an enemy soldier, for whom the lords could have demanded a ransom.

Without a war horse, William could not participate in tournaments. Finally, his lord relented and equipped him with a horse. William became a famous fighter on the tournament circuit and never forgot to make a profit from his victories. But he had his share of defeats as well. During one battle his horse was killed under him, and he had to fight with his back to a hedge. An enemy knight came up from behind and wounded him in the leg. He was taken prisoner and thrown on a horse. He had nothing to bind his wound with until his captors made a stop at a castle. There a lady noticed his wound. She gave him a loaf of bread, the center of which she had cut out and stuffed with linen bandages. Queen Eleanor eventually agreed to pay to set him free.

Between the ages of 25 and 40 William pursued a career as a knight-errant, earning his living by fighting. It was said that fully armed he could scale a siege ladder on the underside, lifting himself up the rungs with his own strength. He became so famous for his chivalry that Henry II made him the instructor of his heir. By this time William's brothers had died, and he had inherited the family lands. He married the heiress of an English earl and thereby gained more land, and a title, the Earl of Pembroke. William continued to play a role in both Norman and English politics. When John I died in 1216, the English barons appointed him regent for John's son and successor, the young King Henry III.

Many younger sons of nobles, such as William Marshall, earned their livings as knights-errant. For these men the best hope was to find a patron to support them or an heiress to marry them.

Chapter 6

New Architecture, Ideas, and Monastic Orders

In Pope Innocent III's dream, St. Peter's church and papal palace are about to collapse and fall on his bed chamber, but the young St. Francis holds up the building and saves the pope, the church of St. Peter, and the Church in a more general sense. In many ways the picture is not an exaggeration. In 1200 the Church was in trouble. Heretics offered attractive, alternative teachings about Christianity. The laity was critical of the worldliness of the Church and its involvement in politics. While Innocent worked to reform the Church, it was St. Francis and his followers who reached out to the laity.

While Eleanor of Aquitaine represents the innovations and new spirit of the revival of Europe in the 12th century, no single figure can personify the late 12th and early 13th centuries. Henry II, Eleanor's young second husband, was an energetic man who established many of the laws and government systems in England that are still used today. Among Eleanor and Henry's children were two sons who also made a major impact on historical events—Richard I ("the Lion-Hearted"), who led the Third Crusade, and John I ("Lackland"), who signed the Magna Carta.

But perhaps the man who presided over the most far-reaching changes in Europe at the time was Innocent III, who was only 37 when he was made pope. He had the vision to see that the new ideas of Francis of Assisi, founder of the Franciscans, and Dominic, founder of the Dominicans, about mingling among the laity might prove better than the seclusion of the older monastic orders.

Enthusiasm for religious revival remained strong among lay Christians, but they began to voice their own concepts about religion, which they gleaned from the teachings of priests, stories of the lives of saints, and art in the churches. The contact between merchants, pilgrims, crusaders, and scholars and Byzantines, Turks, and Arabs also introduced new ideas about religion. The laity's religious views often were counter to those of the Church, and the Franciscan and Dominican orders offered to teach by example and by preaching where the true path to salvation lay. But those who strayed far from the Church's view were few in number and most lay people continued to support the building of parish churches, cathedrals, and monasteries.

An exciting new architectural style, called "gothic" by modern art historians, also revolutionized church building. Gothic architecture takes us back to the days of Eleanor of Aquitaine, Louis VII, Henry II, and that shaper of European politics—Suger, Abbot of St. Denis (d. 1151). He had been a mentor to Louis, had helped to arrange his marriage to Eleanor, and had governed France in their stead during the Second Crusade. He was an energetic man, who found time to patronize the development of a new architectural style in order to glorify his abbey church. His portrait, in which he is

Gothic Architecture

The term "Gothic" is a misnomer because the style had nothing to do with the Gothic tribes. It was first applied to late medieval architecture during the Renaissance, when all medieval artistic production was looked down on as barbaric. The identifying characteristics of Gothic style were "flying" buttresses, pointed arches, ribbed vaults, expanses of stained glass windows, and a soaring height. The Gothic buildings were towering frameworks of masonry piers or columns and arches that were supported on the outside by flying buttresses. Only if all these elements were perfectly balanced would the structure be stable. Unlike Romanesque churches, in which the walls supported the roof, Gothic churches were held up by the skeletal structure. Their stonework, therefore, could be thinner and used as a decorative element. Gothic churches were higher and lighter, and, because of their taller piers, had more space for windows in the clerestory as well as in other walls. A great rose window of stained glass dominated the front wall of the

The front of Reims Cathedral in France, with its two rose windows, shows the extensive use of glass in Gothic architecture. The exteriors of Gothic churches were ornately carved with Biblical figures to instruct the laity.

structures. All the windows had stone tracery that supported the glass; that of the rose window gave the appearance of a rose in its tracery. Filling in the stone were pieces of glass in bright colors set in a framework of lead. Figures of the saints, apostles, biblical characters, animals, and flowers were painted on window glass. Taken together, the images on a church's windows often told a story. The sculpture that appeared on both the external and internal portions of churches also frequently represented biblical stories, the four Gospels, or the Last Judgment.

shown in prayer, appears in a small corner of one of the stained glass windows of his church.

Romanesque churches were limited in height and number of windows because they required heavy masonry to support their barrel and cross vaults. As a result, the buildings were dark inside. Because candles were too expensive to illuminate an entire church, churches usually were quite dark even during services. Gothic architecture approached the building of large structures, such as cathedrals, very differently. Rather than placing all the weight of the structure on the walls, an external skeleton composed of buttresses supported the internal building skeleton of columns and vaults. The buttresses are described as "flying" because an external column of masonry supported arches that met the stress points of the building itself. Because the skeletal structure supported the building, the walls could be pierced, allowing for portions of the wall to be used for windows. The change was revolutionary. Within 50 years of the development of Abbot Suger's new style of architecture, cathedrals and large churches all over Europe had abandoned Romanesque architecture and adopted the new, Gothic innovations.

Of course, some calamities resulted. Sometimes the engineering was faulty and the whole roof of a church caved in, as happened to the church at Beauvais. Many European cathedrals successfully melded elements of the Romanesque and Gothic styles, however.

Building a cathedral was a complex undertaking that often took centuries. Some say that cathedrals are never really com-

pleted, but are continually added to. The bishop and his clergy financed the building of a cathedral and hired an architect to design it. Sometimes they could afford to construct only part of the building, then the project lapsed until more money could be raised. Architects moved from one job to another, often from England to France to Germany and back again. Some became famous throughout Europe. Architects trained on the job and often integrated ideas inspired by other cathedrals into their own designs. Even so, an architect had to be able to draw plans of his proposed buildings and have a good knowledge of the principles of mechanical engineering.

The sketchbook of Villard de Honnecourt, a French architect of the 13th century, shows the way in which an architect developed his ideas. De Honnecourt designed the cathedral at Cambrai, but seems to have observed the construction of the cathedrals at Laon, Chartres, and Reims. In about 1250 the queen of Hungary commissioned him to build churches in that country. His notebook contained sketches of animals—such as a parakeet, crawfish, and dragonfly—but also drawings of the features of the cathedrals he most admired. Inventions depicted in the notebook included siege equipment and a sawmill powered by water. Much of the book was dedicated to engineering questions, such as estimating the height of a tower from the ground, constructing a vaulted roof in wood, and finding the center of a given area. He observed in the introduction that "in this book may be found great help in learning about the principles of masonry and of construction by carpentry. You will also

find in it methods of portraiture and drawing, according to the requirements and teachings of geometry."

A cathedral architect was also the foreman of the project and hired master masons, carpenters, stonecutters, sculptors, and carvers. Preparation included acquiring timber for a scaffolding, stone for building the walls and the tracery of the windows and ornamental designs, lime and sand for mortar, metal for bells, and fine quality sand and pigments for window glass. Master craftsmen designed and supervised each stage, but the apprentices and less skilled craftsmen under their direction did most of the work. The marks of the masons, stonecutters, and sculptors can be seen on the building blocks of cathedrals. In addition, the building of such a large structure required a number of unskilled laborers to dig the foundations, carry the stones, set up the scaffolding, lift the timbers, and perform other heavy labor.

The 12th and 13th centuries must have been golden years for architects, masons, carpenters, and even laborers. The developing towns were building walls around their perimeters, partly to protect themselves, but also to indicate that they had charters from the king that licensed them as independent cities. Nobles and even members of the clergy were building city

dwellings in the major urban centers to be their residences when they were in town on official business. In the countryside, monarchs and nobles alike were building bigger and better castles. Many of the ideas for constructing better fortresses came from those that the crusaders had found in the Near East, such as Antioch.

Castles became far more complex than the simple motte-and-bailey structures of the 11th and early 12th centuries, although many of the basic features remained the same. The motte became a defensible tower made of stone. The parts below the ground served to stabilize a construction of masonry with walls as thick as 15 feet. The basement rooms were used as dungeons or prisons. The first level above the ground was used for storing barrels of wine, flour, salted fish, and other provisions that were needed to feed the castle garrison. Weapons might also be stored at this level, which might include a guard room as well. On the main level was the great hall—the center of castle life. Everyone took their meals in the hall, and many people slept on its floor after the trestle tables had been put away for the night. The lord of the castle performed acts of governance in the great hall, and all guests were entertained there. The upper stories were reserved for the lord and his family.

Recipe for a Cure

Herbal cures were common in the Middle Ages. Some could be grown at home, but others had to be purchased at an apothecary's shop. Herbs from the vessels on the shelves were mixed and ground in different proportions according to the patient's needs.

The following recipe, from a 15th-century English manuscript, gives instructions for servants to follow to cure their lord of illness.

A medicinal bath: "Boil together hollyhock, mallow, wall-pellitory and brown fennel, danewort, St. John's wort, centaury, ribwort and camomile, heyhove, heyriff, herb-bennet, bresewort, smallage, water speedwell, scabious, bugloss, and wild flax which is good for aches—boil withy leaves and green oats together with them and throw them hot into a vessel and put your lord over it and let him endure for a while as hot as he can, being covered over and closed on every side; and whatever disease, grievance or pain ye be vexed with, this medicine shall surely make you whole, as men say."

Life was fairly comfortable in castles. Drinking water came from wells. Water for washing came from a cistern, or retaining tank, on the roof that collected rain, and pipes provided a flow of water through spigots to washbasins, called lavatories, in the living quarters and the great hall. Latrines in the castles might feed into chutes within the walls, or they might be outside the keep (central tower and living quarters) and drop directly to the ground or into the moat. The problems with latrines were re-corded with some vividness by one English king when he implored the engineers, "for the love of God," to fix the latrines, since the cold updrafts and their odor in a castle that he frequently visited were intolerable.

The bailey area of the new stone castles was also more sophisticated. The bailey was defended by a gate that would serve as a first line of defense during an attack. The walls were punctuated with towers, and protected pathways ran around the walls so that the garrison could move around the castle to defend it. Within the bailey walls, the buildings were arranged for times of both war and peace. There were stables for animals and workshops for repairing armor and shoeing horses. The kitchen was often located in the bailey as well, to keep the heat generated during food preparation outside the main hall, particularly during the summer. In addition, there was room for storage barns for hay and straw. The gardens were the preserve of the lady of the castle, who grew herbs used to treat the various ailments and wounds that the garrison might suffer. Women generally were responsible for preparing herbal medicines and healing foods for the ill in their households.

Castles were, of course, primarily meant to be defensive structures rather than pleasant residences, so they were constructed to withstand a siege. Walls were thick, and the external windows were narrow, permitting arrows to be shot out but not in. A castle had to be well stocked with food, wine and beer, weapons and armor, firewood, timber, and other necessities. One of the most essential elements, however, was a source of water. Although water could be piped

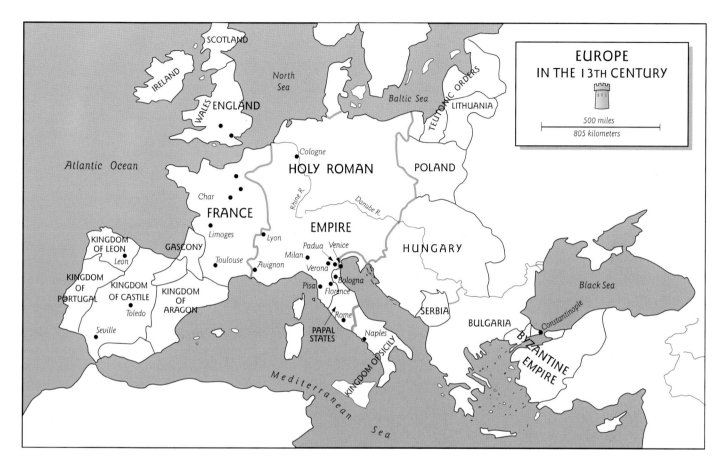

Map caption labels (as shown on the map):

EUROPE IN THE 13TH CENTURY

500 miles
805 kilometers

SCOTLAND · IRELAND · North Sea · WALES · ENGLAND · Baltic Sea · TEUTONIC ORDERS · LITHUANIA · Atlantic Ocean · Cologne · HOLY ROMAN · POLAND · Rhine R. · Char · FRANCE · Danube R. · EMPIRE · Limoges · Lyon · Padua · Venice · HUNGARY · KINGDOM OF LEON · GASCONY · Toulouse · Milan · Verona · Avignon · Bologna · Black Sea · Leon · KINGDOM OF PORTUGAL · KINGDOM OF CASTILE · KINGDOM OF ARAGON · Pisa · Florence · Toledo · Rome · Constantinople · Seville · PAPAL STATES · Naples · SERBIA · BULGARIA · BYZANTINE EMPIRE · KINGDOM OF SICILY · Mediterranean Sea

into a castle from outside its walls, relying on such a system was too dangerous. Besiegers could block the supply, and the castle's defendants would be "parched out"—that is, they would be threatened with dying of thirst. A castle, therefore, was best situated if it had a well within its walls. If a castle was built on a hill of rock, as many were in the Latin Kingdom of Jerusalem, the wells would be very deep.

Although castles were built as defensive structures, few experienced sieges. The most effective way to lay siege was to surround a castle and cut off its water and food supplies. This maneuver would eventually starve or parch out the defenders. With exposure to the more sophisticated siege strategies used during the Crusades, however, the use of various siege machines became more common. The weak point of a castle was the bailey gate, and a battering ram could be used to break it down. To scale walls, ladders and even wooden towers that could be rolled up the castle walls were popular. Finally, more accurate weapons, such as the trebuchet, were developed. A trebuchet was a type of catapult that could hurl stones repeatedly at one place in a castle wall and thus weaken it.

Perhaps one of the most effective siege tactics was to undermine or sap the castle walls. This process was similar to putting a mineshaft under the walls. A description of the attack of King John I of England on his barons, who had seized Rochester castle, gives a vivid account of the sapping process. King John hired miners to sink a shaft under the wall and build supports of dry wood. He then called for a dozen hogs that were too fat to be eaten. These he had killed and their lard rendered. The lard was spread over the wooden supports in the

The Krak des Chevaliers in Syria was built for defense against Turkish attack on the Latin kingdom of Jerusalem. The walls were extremely thick and a well was dug down through the rock so that the castle would have an internal water supply. The castle held out against attack until 1268.

shaft and set ablaze. The wall tumbled down as the supports burned.

Most castles were living quarters for noble families and their households. Children who grew up in castles were not necessarily raised by their parents in their early years, because their parents might be away at other castles, on crusade, or at the king's court. These children had nurses who fed and entertained them. But their lives were not lonely, because there were many adults in the castle as well as other children to play with. They rode horses, climbed around the battlements, went out into the countryside, and received some early instruction from a clergyman hired to teach them their letters. Parents customarily sent both boys and girls to another noble family of higher status when they reached the age of seven or eight. This practice was called fostering. There they learned the correct court manners from the lord and lady of the household. Both boys and girls learned to ride and hunt, to wash their hands before coming to the table, to eat properly with their fingers (they had

no forks), and to share their trencher (a piece of rough bread that served as a plate) with their dinner partner. Glasses were also shared, and the proper young courtier learned to wipe the glass after drinking so that the rim would be clean for his or her dinner partner. Dogs were not fed at the table for fear that they would fight over the bones. Young boys might also become pages (perhaps late Latin or German for "child") and serve their lord and lady and their guests at the table.

As children grew up, boys and girls were trained to take on different roles. Young women learned to sew and embroider. They spent most of their time with the other women of the household in the women's quarters. Here they might also learn to read romances and lyric poetry, play musical instruments and cards, and dance. Young men, on the other hand, became squires and learned to fight. They had to practice using a sword and lance while riding on a horse. Some young squires even accompanied their lords to battles or on crusades. The knighting ceremony, usually held when a man reached 21, ended his tenure as a squire.

Marriage was important for those noble children who would inherit their father's or mother's property. Usually, the older children in the family would marry, and the younger children might find careers in the administration of the Church or in monasteries. Parents or often a lord arranged the marriages. The Church taught that girls of 12 and boys of 14 were old enough to be married, but the age of marriage varied greatly depending on the couple's social class and the circumstances at the time. Among the nobility, girls were often mar-

ried at a young age because the marriages could create alliances of political or economic importance. They might have been heiresses with valuable land, or given in marriage to a former enemy of their father as a symbol of peace between two families. Their marriage partners could be as young as they were or as old as their fathers. A large age disparity between husband and wife was not uncommon.

Major negotiations took place between the families of the bride and groom. The bride's family provided a dowry that might include land, but could also be wealth in the form of jewels, serving vessels of gold and silver, war horses, armor, or fine clothing. Princess Philippa, the fiancée of the young man who became Edward III of England, was given a dowry of a fleet of boats and fighting men so that the groom's mother could invade England in his name.

The husband's family promised a dower (a benefit that a wife could collect on her husband's death) composed of a third of his lands and estates. She would have the use of this land for as long as she lived, then it would be inherited by the children of the marriage. Widows living on their dower lands were called dowagers. Practices varied from region to region. In Italy the dower disappeared, but in other areas both the dower and the dowry remained important parts of contracts for arranged marriages.

The marriages might be happy or at least acceptable to the married couples, or they could be miserable. Women were expected to produce children to carry on the family name, but their husbands might be away much of the time. One of the reasons that courtly love flourished was that ritualized

flirtations helped to pass the time and ease the loneliness of a loveless marriage. Castles always had a number of young fighting men around to sing, compose songs, and participate in tournaments for the entertainment of the women and girls who lived there.

The elaborate castles of the Middle Ages were also centers of government. From them, lords administered their estates, and kings administered their kingdoms.

In the 12th and 13th centuries throughout Europe, monarchs consolidated their power. To trace the development of the monarchies, it is necessary to go back a century to the time of Henry II's grandfather, Henry I (reigned 1100–1135). When William the Conqueror died in 1087, he had three sons—Robert, William, and Henry. Robert received Normandy, William got England, and young Henry was given a cash settlement. Henry was ambitious, and when William died from an arrow wound during a hunt, rumors spread that Henry was responsible. But Henry became king of England and, after Robert died, Duke of Normandy as well. In France the Capetians continued to rule from Paris. They tried to gain recognition from their wayward counts and dukes, among whom Henry I of England was the most troublesome. Henry controlled not only Normandy, but also Brittany and some of the territory along the Seine River. He consolidated his power in England, then began to extend his authority throughout the realm.

Henry I had misfortunes as well as successes. His two sons died crossing the English Channel, so as he approached death as an old man who had ruled for 35 years, his only heir was a daughter, Matilda. He took the

Thomas Becket (on horse at right) refused to agree to the demands of Henry II that members of the clergy be tried for any crimes in the king's court. When Henry enlisted the help of Louis VII (both at left), Becket went into exile to enlist the help of the pope.

best measures he could to assure his succession. Henry married her to his worst enemy—Geoffrey Plantagenet, the Count of Anjou—in the hope that this maneuver would protect her inheritance of Normandy and Brittany. He then persuaded the English and Norman vassals to accept her as queen. Before he died he had the satisfaction of knowing that she had a son who was named Henry.

But the barons of England refused to accept Matilda as their queen, partly because she was a woman and partly because she married the Count of Anjou, who was their enemy as well. They selected a grandson of William the Conqueror, Stephen of Blois, to become king. Civil war raged, and Matilda sometimes took to the saddle herself to lead her army against Stephen. Eventually a compromise was reached, and Henry II, son of Matilda and Geoffrey and grandson of Henry I, became king. His kingship marked the beginning of what is known as the Plantagenet dynasty. The

name derives from a type of heather flower that Geoffrey customarily wore. Henry Plantagenet, of course, added the Duchy of Aquitaine to his fiefs in France by marrying Eleanor in 1152, after her marriage to Louis VII of France was annulled. Historians have called this vast territory, which included half of France, the Angevin Empire.

Henry II set about reorganizing England so that he would be free to defend his fiefs in France. Since William the Conqueror, all the kings of England had regarded the realm as a convenient source of revenue, but not as a fit place for a French-speaking Norman to live. So Henry II followed his grandfather's example in making England's judicial system work very smoothly and for his own financial gain. He encouraged the lesser barons and freemen to purchase writs from the crown. Writs were legal instruments that allowed the free population to have the king's officials and judges try their cases. Henry not only made a profit on providing uniform legal standards to the English, but also won support for the idea that the king's law should prevail throughout the land.

When a dispute arose over who had the better claim to a piece of land, a writ empowered the king's judges to call a jury (from the Latin term *jurati,* or men serving on oath to tell the truth) of the best informed people from the surrounding country. The judges called on the oldest and wisest members of the community to serve on an inquest jury, and asked them to determine who had the best claim to the property. On the basis of their testimony and verdict (from the Latin word *veredictum,* or true statement), the judges settled land disputes, with the authority of the king backing up their decision. The system was very popular and in time England used juries to decide criminal matters as well.

For Henry the benefits were peace and increased profits. To keep track of the revenues that he received from England, he reinvigorated the Exchequer established by Henry I, which is still the chief cabinet office in charge of finances today. The Exchequer takes its name from a large tablecloth on which the accounts of the realm were calculated. On it was a series of columns, which were crossed by horizontal lines. The tablecloth was simply a large abacus that permitted calculation of sums owed without using cumbersome Roman numerals. The word "exchequer" derived from the Arabic word for the game of chess or checkers. The Exchequer usually met in Westminster (the royal palace located just west of London), and all county officials and royal justices rendered their accounts at this central location. All debtors, even if they were officials, were imprisoned until they paid the amount due to the king.

Henry was an energetic man. In fact, his courtiers complained that he exhausted them because he constantly administered, fought in tournaments and battles, hunted, and pursued his enemies with ruthlessness. Even during church services he had to have writing materials with him, or he would fidget. He was a redhead with a freckled face and a muscular physique. A fiery temperament accompanied his generally ruddy appearance. None felt the quick anger more than Thomas Becket, who became Archbishop of Canterbury. Becket, a London merchant's son, had served Henry as Chan-

cellor of the Exchequer. When the Archbishop of Canterbury died, Henry thought he could reward a loyal servant and have a subservient archbishop by appointing Becket.

But Becket seemed to have undergone a conversion when he was elevated to the archbishopric. He took the side of the Church against his old friend, Henry. The focus of their fight was the relations between the church courts and the royal courts. Henry wanted clergy who had committed crimes tried in the powerful royal courts, and Becket wanted them tried by their bishop. If the clerks were tried in royal courts, they would be hanged if convicted, but if they were found guilty in the bishop's court, they would only have to say prayers or go on a pilgrimage to atone for their wrongdoing. Henry exiled Becket, but the

The Exchequer, or treasury, took its name from the checkered table cloth, a type of abacus on which they tallied the fines they had collected for the king. Officials presented their accounts and the money that was due. The Chancellor of the Exchequer and his clerks kept a record of the accounts and imprisoned those who did not pay the full amount.

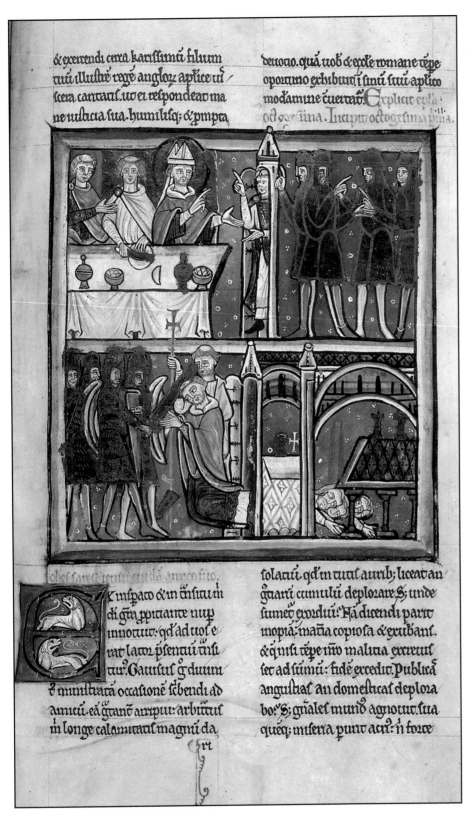

de exerendi entra karissimu filium
tuu illustre regë anglo; aplice tu
scera cantant. uo ei respondeat ma
ne iustitia sua. humilisq; & pmpta

deuotio. quá uos & ecclie romane tepe
oportuno exhibuit i sinu siui aplico
modamine tuerrabi. Explicit epla
octogesima. Incipit octogesima prima.

olosest careb tenti eiusdam amico suo.
xn inspato & in tristitiu
di gra pptiante nup
innotuit. qd ad uos e
rat lator psentiu tristi
tur. Gauisus q duum
s ministrata occasione scribendi ad
amicu ea gratia arripui: arbitrui
in longe calamitatis magnu da
rt

solatiu qd in titui aurib; liceat an
gratiu cumulu deplorare S; unde
sumet exordiu: Ná dicendi parsi
mopia: matia copiosa & exuberant.
& quisi tepe nro malitia excreui
ter ad summu: fide excedit. Publica
anguistias an domesticas deplora
bo; S; gnales mundi agnoscit. sua
queq; miseria punit acri: in force

The martyrdom of Thomas Becket at
the altar of his cathedral in Canterbury made him a saint almost
immediately. His fame spread rapidly
and illustrations of his martyrdom appeared quickly in England and as far
away as Spain.

move was so unpopular with both the pope and the laity that Henry had to reinstate him. When Becket came back to Canterbury and resumed the old fights, Henry allegedly remarked to four of his knights, "Will no one rid me of this troublesome priest?" His courtiers were all too willing.

They went to Canterbury and killed the archbishop as he was praying before an altar. Immediately, Becket became a martyr and saint. Henry was forced to confess that his short-tempered remark had led to the death of his archbishop, and was beaten to atone for his role in the death. The tomb of St. Thomas became the most popular place of pilgrimage in England, and figures in Chaucer's *Canterbury Tales,* written two centuries later.

Most of Henry's energy went into protecting his continental possessions from the French kings who kept up continual warfare and intrigues against him. Louis VII was an obvious enemy even before Henry married his ex-wife, but when Louis died, his son, Philip II Augustus, became a formidable foe. Philip even succeeded in getting Henry's heir, Henry "the Young King," and Eleanor to conspire against Henry. Henry then imprisoned Eleanor in a rather comfortable English castle, where she was separated from the court culture that she had created and the pleasantries of life in her own Aquitanian duchy. Young Henry died before his father, so Richard, Eleanor's favorite son, inherited all of the Angevin territory in France and the kingship of England.

Before his brother died, Richard was destined to become the Duke of Aquitaine and to follow in the footsteps of his great-grandfather: duke, fighter, troubadour, and chivalric figure. Richard carried out at least some of the roles. He sang and played musical instruments, but most of all, he was an ideal Christian knight who embraced the Third Crusade with zeal. The pope persuaded his archenemy, Philip II

Augustus of France, to crusade with him. Also entering into the scheme was Frederick I Barbarossa, emperor of Germany. Frederick had gained this name because of his large, red beard.

The Third Crusade took careful planning. Richard was the only enthusiastic participant, but Philip and Frederick joined because the Church and laity were concerned that the Turks had unified under their great leader, Saladin, and threatened to take over the entire Holy Land once again. Richard, imbued with the romances of his mother's court, flung himself wholeheartedly into the campaign. Indeed, his name became Richard the Lion-Hearted, or *Coeur de Lion* to his French-speaking subjects. According to myth, he fought single-handedly against Saladin. Whether or not this is true, he did in fact achieve major victories and succeeded in reaching a compromise with the Turkish leader, who agreed to give the Christians the port city of Acre and a corridor through which pilgrims could pass to worship in Jerusalem.

Frederick I Barbarossa never reached the Holy Land because he died while taking a swim. Philip II, on the other hand, hated fighting, disliked cooperating with the chivalric Richard, and decided to return to France to take advantage of Richard's absence by attacking his fiefs. On the way home from the Holy Land, Frederick's heir, Holy Roman Emperor Henry VI, took Richard prisoner and held him for ransom. While England and the Angevin territories in France scrambled to pay the ransom, Philip waged war against Richard's French fiefs. When Richard was released, he conducted campaigns against Philip, but

died at Chateau Gaillard from an infection resulting from an arrow wound.

Philip II Augustus was not as loved by his subjects as Richard had been in England and in his French possessions, yet he was a very successful monarch. Unlike his father, Louis VII, he was an intelligent politician. He expanded his kingdom north into Flanders through marriage and bided his time until he could challenge the English king. The opportunity came under Richard the Lion-Hearted's successor, his brother John. The youngest son of Henry II and Eleanor, John I had not been in line for the succession, and became king only because his older brothers had died without sons. John was groomed for a more comfortable life than defending his territories against a calculating enemy such as Philip. John made a fatal blunder in marrying a young woman, Isabelle of Angolême, who was engaged to one of King Philip's vassals. Invoking a feudal lord's right to protect his vassals' interests, Philip invaded Normandy, Anjou, and Poitou (the northern part of the Angevin Empire) to punish John. He met with little resistance. John earned the name "Lackland" because of his loss of territory.

The capture of Richard I in Germany was related to German political ambitions. Frederick Barbarossa (1152–1190) came to the throne with grand plans to restore the influence of the Holy Roman Empire by gaining power either in Germany itself or in Italy and Burgundy. But to consolidate power in Germany would involve protracted fights with relatives and other German nobles. Frederick acquired the duchy of Burgundy by marrying its heiress, but Italy was a more difficult problem.

Frederick I Barbarossa got his name from his red beard. His dream to restore power to the Holy Roman Empire would naturally interest his sons (depicted here giving their father advice), one of whom would inherit the throne.

At the coronation of John I, two arch-bishops anoint him with holy oil and place the crown on his head. Medieval kings claimed that this ceremony, based on the crowning of David in the Bible, gave them sacred powers that permitted them to challenge the ecclesiastical officials. The Church, however, disagreed.

Italian towns had entered a period of great prosperity, but they had also become independent of lay and church authority. Frederick either had to overwhelm the towns of northern Italy or win them to his side. Finally, only Milan withstood his siege. At the end of three years, when the irate Frederick finally captured it, he threatened to destroy Milan entirely and salt the earth so that nothing would grow there. He relented to his regret, because Milan soon led a coalition of cities, called the Lombard League, against him. Frederick was de-

feated at the battle of Legnano in 1176. Facing ultimate defeat in Italy and rebellion among his dukes in Germany, Frederick had no choice but to retreat to Germany and try to base his empire there.

Although Frederick I died in 1190 during the Third Crusade, his plans to unite Italy with Germany looked as if they could be realized through marriage rather than war. Frederick's able but ruthless son, Henry VI, detained Richard the Lion-Hearted simply because he needed a ready source of cash to unite his empire. Richard happened to be taking the land route home from crusading and was a convenient target. Henry pursued his father's Italian policy by marrying the heiress to the kingdoms of Naples and Sicily. Before he died at the young age of 32, his wife produced a son, Frederick II, who became one of the most remarkable figures in medieval history.

The Holy Roman Emperors' Italian ambitions were countered by popes, who remained strong advocates of papal independence. The Church continued building its political power in the 12th and early 13th centuries. Gregory VII and his successors had put the papacy in a good position to take control of its own bishops and abbots. Popes exercised greater power over the appointment of the bishops and kept in contact with their appointees. In this way, they directed both the spiritual and financial interests of the Church throughout Europe.

In Rome itself, they established a central bureaucracy to handle their far-flung interests. In addition to the College of Cardinals, the popes developed special bureaus that dealt with papal finances; a judicial branch that specialized in appeals to the pope for divorces, annulments of marriages, and other matters of spiritual guidance; and a chancery that handled diplomatic issues. The bureaucrats of the papal government also developed special ways of writing and special seals so that the directives and letters that came out of their offices could not be easily counterfeited. Papal bulls, as the official directives were called, had nothing to do with the male bovine, but rather took their name from the lead seal or *bulla* (a knob) that was attached to the documents to authenticate them.

The most notable pope of the late 12th and early 13th centuries was Innocent III. He represented a new type of clergyman. Innocent had studied theology at the University of Paris and church law at the University of Bologna. His legal training was very helpful to the Church, which was expanding its bureaucracy throughout Europe and entering into political fights with the European monarchs. After becoming pope at the comparatively young age of 37, he had the energy and intelligence to accomplish much during his papacy (1198–1216).

Among Innocent III's political goals was to ensure that the German emperor respected the pope's authority and left Rome in peace. He feared that an aggressive Holy Roman emperor could take control of the papacy because Henry VI's marriage gave the family domination over Germany to the north and Naples to the south. Citing the coronation of Charlemagne as emperor, Innocent claimed that as pope he had the authority to intervene in the election of the German emperor. He thought that

Frederick, Henry VI's young son, would bend to his guidance. By 1209, Frederick II was old enough to be made emperor, and Innocent extracted three promises from him: He would follow the spiritual direction of the pope; he would lead a crusade; and he would abdicate as king of Naples and Sicily and sever that territory from the Holy Roman Empire once he had gained control over his German possessions.

In England, Innocent played a more proactive role. John I had his own candidate for the position of Archbishop of Canterbury, but Innocent insisted on the appointment of Stephen Langton. Innocent excommunicated John and even threatened to encourage Philip II Augustus to invade England. John engaged in a series of unsuccessful campaigns to regain Normandy that proved very costly. In order to raise money for his battles, he forced

The Holy Roman Empire

The imperial title of the Carolingians was abandoned in 924, but was revived in 962 by the emperor of Germany, Otto the Great. His realm is known to historians as the Holy Roman Empire. Despite its name, the Holy Roman Empire had little in common with the Roman Empire. In fact, it was geographically located, for the most part, in an area that had included no Roman settlement.

As a political unit, the Holy Roman Empire survived until 1806. Its unity relied on the wealth and personality of the emperor rather than on common institutions or even common languages, since Slavs, Hungarians, Bohemians, and Italians were all part of the empire. Its governance was weak compared with that of England and France, and its inhabitants developed no sense of a collective identity. If the emperor was strong and aggressive, the empire played a prominent role in European politics, but if the emperor was involved in internal civil wars, it was not a great power. The German nobility continued to claim the right to elect the emperor, and they were often inclined to elect the weakest candidate that they could find from the royal family. Nonetheless, some notable figures held the title, including Frederick I and his grandson, Frederick II.

Frederick II, king of Sicily and emperor of Germany, was a threat to the power of Rome and the Papacy. He holds an orb, a symbol of the globe and the emperor's control over it.

the English nobility and townspeople to pay more taxes than they had ever paid before. When they refused, he used extortion. He insisted on turning a profit on every feudal right that he had over the nobility. For instance, he sold the right to marry noble widows. The right to marry went to the man who would pay the most money for the privilege of using the widow's dower (one-third of her former husband's property). For a fee, he also allowed guardians of noble orphans to keep an orphan's property beyond his or her 21st birthday, the age of legal maturity. But faced with the possibility of revolt and invasion from the French king, John agreed to become Innocent's vassal.

In 1214 John and one of the German princes, who was a contender for the title of emperor, joined forces against Philip II Augustus at the battle of Bouvines. Philip won once again, and John returned to England in disgrace. The English nobility was no longer willing to accept his government and, under the leadership of Archbishop Stephen Langton, the nobles, townsmen, and knights banded together and defeated John at the battle of Runnymede in 1215. They then drew up a series of demands that have become known as the Magna Carta, and they insisted that John sign the document.

The Magna Carta (literally, the "great charter") derived its name from the large piece of parchment on which it was written rather than from its historical significance. Most clauses of the Magna Carta dealt with John's abuses of his power over the nobility and of his feudal rights as king. It held, for instance, that the king could levy taxes if they were customary, but extra taxes required the consent of the kingdom. It also addressed abuses involving the remarriage of widows and the property of heirs and heiresses.

Although some nobles disliked the judicial reforms the Magna Carta embodied, they were very popular among the townspeople, lesser nobles, and knights. One of the clauses, for example, read that "all free men shall be tried by a jury of their peers." This provision ensured the continuance of the jury system. In a larger historical framework, the Magna Carta is seen as the beginning of the constitutional monarchy in England because it preserved the jury and stated that the king could not be above the laws of the land, but rather must abide by them. Various monarchs fought against this type of constitutional monarchy, but political events in the 13th and 14th centuries only made the principle more binding.

Pope Innocent defended his vassal against the English nobility, claiming that John had signed the Magna Carta under duress and therefore should not be bound by it. When he died a few years later from consuming too many fresh peaches with cider, John left a nine-year-old son, Henry III (1216–1272), as king. Because Henry was too young to rule, the nobility selected nobleman William Marshall to act as regent and formed a council that would rule according to the Magna Carta.

Pope Innocent, meanwhile, called a council of bishops and leading church figures to the Lateran Palace in Rome in 1215 to address reforms of church practices. Among the matters affecting the laity of Europe was the role of clergy in determin-

ing the guilt or innocence of those accused of crimes. Until the Lateran Council, the accused were subjected to ordeals by fire or water or trials of combat. In an ordeal by fire, the person on trial would walk through a fire or carry a hot iron object. In an ordeal by water, he or she was thrown into a body of water. Before the trial began, a priest blessed the fire or water and asked God to allow the innocent to go unscathed. If the person was innocent, he or she would not be burned by the fire or would sink in the water. The guilty would float, having been rejected by the blessed water. In trial by battle, the innocent man would win and the guilty man would lose, whatever the natural advantages of either fighter.

Pope Innocent and his advisers believed that the presence of priests gave credence to these superstitious procedures. Furthermore, the ordeals did not prove very much. In a well-known example from the First Crusade when the army was besieged in Antioch, a man was told in a dream that if he dug in

a certain place in a church, he would find the lance that had pierced Jesus' side. Not convinced that his dream was true, he told no one. But when he had the same dream three times, he consulted a priest. Together they dug as directed and found a lance. Many crusaders were skeptical about this "miracle," but their leaders were hard-pressed and decided to use the lance as a rallying symbol. Carrying it before them, they led a successful attack on the Turkish army outside the city walls. But the skeptics and the believers both wanted proof. The man who found it was to undergo the ordeal by fire. A hot bed of coals was prepared, and the lance was wrapped in cloth. The finder walked across the coals carrying the lance. Surely, the spectators reasoned, Jesus would protect the man if it was the true lance. But even when the poor man died, the sides were not reconciled. The skeptics believed that he died from his burns. But the believers argued that although he had made it across the coals safely

The Magna Carta is named for the size of the parchment it is written on rather than for its importance in constitutional history. Although considered the fundamental document of constitutionalism in the English-speaking world, it is really a reiteration of feudal rights and legal procedures that the barons forced John I to confirm.

The Inquisition: Notorious Secret Inquiries

The Inquisition proceeded in secrecy until it had either gotten a repentance from the person it was investigating or sufficient evidence to condemn the suspect.

Traditionally bishops had been charged with the spiritual correction of the laity, including dealing with heresy. In the 1230s, the papacy replaced the bishops with tribunals of judges. These tribunals, known as the Inquisition, were made up of well-educated churchmen who had taken religious vows (often in the Dominican order). They were given sweeping powers to question suspected heretics and witnesses. The Inquisition, which did not allow suspects to confront witnesses or obtain legal counsel, accepted the testimony of two witnesses as sufficient evidence for conviction. The inquisitors often used torture as a way of extracting a confession. Their goal was to save the souls of those who had been led astray by heresy. Therefore they sought confessions, so that they could bring heretics back into the fold of the Church where the salvation of their souls could be assured. Those who confessed were given penances or prison terms. Only when heretics refused to recant their beliefs were they burned at the stake or otherwise executed.

enough, the mobs had been so rough in their jubilation that he had died as they flocked around him to touch the true lance.

The Lateran council called for the exclusion of priests from ordeals and judicial combats. This policy forced monarchs to change the way they established guilt or innocence in criminal cases. No one was satisfied with ordeal, because the horror of it simply forced the accused and the accusers to reach an agreement. England had a tradition of using juries to settle land disputes and to decide if there was adequate evidence in a case to indict a person for a crime. Indictment meant that the known evidence strongly suggested that the person might be guilty and that he should therefore be tried in the king's court. The indictment jury eventually was named the grand (large) jury. To replace ordeals and combat, England created another jury, the petty (*petit* or small) jury, which rendered the verdict at the conclusion of a trial.

On the continent, a different model was selected. Instead of a jury, a board of magistrates or judges questioned the accusers and then, separately, questioned the accused. The two sides did not confront each other, which prevented the possibility of intimidation on either side. The justices then rendered a decision. Guilt in either system resulted in punishment by hanging. Fortunately, both systems were lenient, and only about a quarter of the accused were hanged.

The Church itself was having problems with a large minority of laity who held beliefs contrary to those of the official doctrine. In the urban centers of southern Europe, the population began to question the growing power of the clergy and the wealth of the Church. Several heresies disturbed Innocent and the Church, but the most alarming were the beliefs of the Cathari (the pure), also known as the Albigensians, a name derived from the town of Albi in southern France around which their movement was centered.

The Albigensians offered a coherent, distorted, and appealing alternative to the theology of the Church. Their theology might have had its origins in the Zoroastrian dualistic religion of Persia. Both recognized two gods: a god of good who represented the spirit and a god of evil who represented the world of matter or material life. Because the Old Testament contained the story of the creation of the material world, in their view it portrayed the god of evil. The New Testament, they believed, portrayed the god of good, for it dealt with salvation, souls, and resurrection. Because spirit was better than flesh, the Albigensians urged abstinence from worldly living, animal meat, and sex. In fact, only a few Albigensians, the *perfecti* or the perfect ones, were able to follow this severe regime. When Albigensians died, they requested one of the *perfecti* to be at their bedside to speed salvation.

By the beginning of the 13th century the Albigensians were attracting a large following, and Innocent III became alarmed. With no immediate weapon to combat them, he preached that a crusade should be undertaken against them in 1208. He promised the successful leader of the crusade the right to take over the Albigensians' property in southern France. The crusade was brutal, but not until 1229 was the heresy under control. Many

Albigensians were killed, and some returned to Christianity, but a determined group of believers practiced their religion secretly. To root out these secret groups of Albigensians, the Church resorted to the Inquisition, a tribunal for the discovery and punishment of heretics.

The Albigensian Crusade was not the first that Innocent had launched. In 1202 he persuaded some European noblemen to undertake the Fourth Crusade to liberate the Holy Land from the Turks. The crusaders contracted with the Venetians to take them there by boat, but when they were unable to pay, the Venetians suggested that, as part of their payment, they could recapture a trading port that had been claimed by the Hungarian king. When Innocent learned of this attack on a Christian king, he excommunicated the crusaders. Undaunted, they decided to proceed to Constantinople, where in 1204 they attacked and looted the capital and drove out the emperor. Their domination of the city lasted only 50 years, but those who participated in the crusade returned to Europe with immense wealth in gold and gems, as well as many religious relics.

Church councils and crusades were not the most effective way to confront and counter dissent. Instead, new religious orders sprang up to provide the laity with spiritual and intellectual guidance. Dominic (1170–1221), a Spaniard by birth, received an excellent education in the Hebrew/Arabic/Christian environment of his native country. In his mid-30s he traveled to Rome, where he met Innocent III. Innocent, worried about the Albigensian crisis, asked him to preach against the heretics in

Relics of saints, including their bones and clothing, played an important part in religious worship during the Middle Ages. People felt that saints could intervene to help cure them of diseases or ease other distress. The relics were housed in rich reliquaries and became part of a church's treasury. Pieces of the cross on which Jesus was executed, contained in this reliquary, were especially important.

Francis of Assisi's "Song of Brother Sun"

Francis of Assisi is frequently pictured preaching to birds. Also gathered around is a friendly lion and a member of the women's order founded by Clare, a follower of Francis.

Much of St. Francis's poetry praised nature as an example of God's greatness. St. Francis is frequently represented as preaching to animals.

Praise be to you, my Lord, for all your creatures,
Above all Brother Sun
Who brings us the day, and lends us his light;
Beautiful is he, radiant with great splendor,
And speaks to us of you, O most high.
Praise to you, my Lord, for Sister Moon and for the stars;
In heaven you have set them, clear and precious and fair.
Praise to you, my Lord, for Brother Wind,
For air and clouds, for calm and all weather
By which you support life in all your creatures.
Praise to you , my Lord, for Sister Water
Which is so helpful and humble, precious and pure.
Praise to you, my Lord, for Brother Fire,
By whom you light up the night;
and fair is he, and joyous, and mighty, and strong.
Praise to you, my Lord, for our sister, Mother Earth,
Who sustains and directs us,
And brings forth varied fruits, and plants,
and flowers bright.

southern France. Although Dominic brought to this calling a considerable reputation as a preacher and as a priest who led a humble, devout life, initially he won few converts. Realizing that he could make little impact alone, he organized volunteers to help him create an order whose mission would be to preach to heretics and unbelievers throughout the known world. Pope Innocent recognized the order in 1216. It was called the Order of the Friar Preachers, but it is still known also as the Dominicans.

Rather than retreating to monasteries as previous monastic orders had done, the Dominicans moved about in the world. They were an educated order who could preach to inquiring new urban dwellers, argue with heretics, and provide teachers for the new universities. They could also staff the Inquisition. Rather than living off the proceeds of manors that were given to monasteries, as other orders did, the Dominicans made their living by soliciting donations from the pious laity to support

their preaching. With their learning and their example of living in the poverty associated with Jesus' apostles, the Dominicans made converts among the Albigensians. Later they became missionaries in central Asia and even China.

A contemporary of Dominic, Francis of Assisi (1182–1226), earned the love and captured the imagination of the people of his time. As a young man he led the carefree life of a wealthy young Italian. His father was a cloth merchant in Assisi, in central Italy. Young Francis was not interested in business, being more inclined to imitate courtly manners and spend his time in revelry. In his early 20s he underwent a series of experiences that led to a profound religious conversion. The first incident occurred after a banquet that he had given for friends. The revelers moved into the street—singing and waving torches and flowers. Francis, however, separated from them and was later found in a religious trance. Continuing his religious commitment, he went

on pilgrimage to Rome, where he led a life of poverty. He exchanged clothing with a beggar and spent his days asking for alms. After returning to Assisi he continued to dress as a beggar and began giving away the family money. His father disinherited him to stop this erratic behavior. The action may have saved the family fortune, but Francis withdrew to the outskirts of Assisi, where he lived with the poor and ministered to the sick. He adopted a mission he had heard described in a sermon: "Cure the sick, raise the dead, cleanse the lepers, drive out devils. Carry neither gold not silver nor money in your belts or bag, nor two coats, nor sandals, nor staff, for the workman is worthy of his hire." So Francis took on these symbols of poverty and began preaching, even though he was a layman.

When Francis had about a dozen followers, he urged them to go to Rome and ask permission to preach with the pope's blessing. It was farsighted of Innocent to grant this request. He must have seen this completely pious young man as a valuable counter to the *perfecti* of the Albigensians. Even before Dominic had established his mendicant or begging order, Francis had organized his followers according to this model. As much as possible, they strove to imitate the life of Christ: They dressed as peasants, tended to the wants and ills of the urban poor, and preached to the uneducated with stories derived from folktales already familiar to their audiences.

Their very name, "Friars Minor," or "little brothers," indicated the cheerful humility that they preached as an ideal all over Europe. Some of Francis' old life as a troubadour reappeared in his hymns, which praised God through his creatures and his creation. Francis is associated with preaching the word of God even to animals. His order drew a vast following, including many women. Although it was acceptable for men to go begging, the Church certainly did not want women from respectable families to beg. Therefore, an enclosed female order was established by Francis's friend and follower, Clare. The Poor Clares worked among the poor.

But even the horde of men who followed the rule of Francis was too large to be supported by begging alone. They had to be organized into monastic institutions, and eventually they and the Dominicans came to resemble the older orders. Nonetheless, their monastic houses tended to be located in urban areas rather than in isolated regions like those of the Benedictines and the Cistercians.

The 12th and early 13th century was a period of enormous excitement. There was something to engage everyone's interest: campaigns, battles, revolts, high-stake politics between kings and popes, heresies, and new religious orders. Universities were being established at the same time that Francis and Dominic were preaching, and radical new intellectual debates caused as much chaos in the universities as the Albigensians did among the nobles and peasants of southern France. The English nobles continued their attempts to control their kings, resulting in the development of Parliament. Even the crusading ideal did not die. The great crusader and king of France, St. Louis, graced the 13th century with his presence. The next chapter will look at this exciting era from another perspective—that of the peasants. Faced with war, political troubles, and taxes, were they as thrilled as the nobles during this exuberant period?

Innocent III, flanked by two cardinals with their characteristic flat hats, recognizes the order of Francis of Assisi. His followers are shown with the traditional tonsure of monks and the simple garments of the order, including a rope belt holding together the brown robes.

Chapter 7

Communities and Their Members

Louis IX, or St. Louis (top right), was known for his pious life and his crusading. His mother, Blanche of Castile (top left), became regent for her son when he was abroad on crusades. The author dictating to the scribe (at bottom) indicates the intellectual excitement that characterized 13th century Paris.

During the Middle Ages, local communities were important to people's sense of belonging. If peasants were asked to identify themselves, they would not say that they were English, French, German, or Italian. They would say that they were the son or daughter of a certain man or woman. If pressed, they would explain that they were from a particular village. In international markets, a merchant from London, Florence, Milan, or Leipzig would identify himself by his town. People cared a great deal about the community from which they came. If pressed further they would identify themselves as Christians, but the idea of having a national identity such as English, French, German, or Italian would leave them perplexed. They might identify their king or emperor and agree they owed allegiance to that person, but being part of a nation had little meaning for them.

In the 13th and early 14th centuries, people organized their communities with rules and regulations that determined who belonged to the group and who was excluded from it. Rules of behavior and membership requirements regulated trade and production of goods, education of scholars, government by councils and assemblies (either with or without the king's approval), and establishment of everyday order in peasant communities. These groups went by different names, but they had much in common. *Universitas* was a Latin name that translated into "guild" in English. (It is also the root of the modern word "university.") In the Middle Ages, it applied to students and masters who organized into groups that regulated classes and examinations as well as to guilds that organized craftsmen and merchants, setting the standards for the quality of products that members produced and rules for permitting others to join the group as apprentices. Peasant communities developed mechanisms that regulated peacekeeping within villages. The representative units that advised the monarchs of Europe went by the generic name of council, but they were called Estates in France, Parliament in England, Cortes in Spain, and diets in Germany. They might consist of only nobles and higher clergy, but increasingly they included representatives from the urban populations and successful country gentle-

University students learned their lessons by listening to a passage from the text and then taking notes on the lecture.

A goliard was a glutton, but the name was applied to medieval students and a style of satiric poetry they wrote in both Latin and the vernacular. Some were love lyrics, others were drinking songs, and still others concerned nature. The poem below is a begging song, in which the student could insert the name of the patron to whom he was making his appeal in the last verse.

I, a wandering scholar lad,
Born for toil and sadness,
Oftentimes am driven by poverty
to madness.

Literature and knowledge I
Fain would still be earning,
Were it not that want of pelf
Makes me cease from learning.
These torn cloths that cover me
Are too thin and rotten;

Oft I have to suffer cold,
By the warmth forgotten.

Scarce I can attend at church,
Sing God's praises duly;
Mass and vespers both I miss
Though I love them truly.

Oh, though pride of [Normandy],
By thy worth I pray thee,
Give the suppliant help in need;
Heaven will sure repay thee.

men who had made their name as administrators of the king's justice.

The development of collective units was not sudden: All of them had their roots in a variety of institutions of earlier centuries. Universities, for instance, can be traced back to the days of Charlemagne, who felt so strongly about the need to educate clergy that he ordered his bishops to establish schools at their cathedrals. Scholarship remained centered at cathedrals, but by the early 12th century, scholars and professors had begun to move from place to place, giving lectures and charging students per lecture. Lectures were delivered in Latin, the universal language of the educated. (The name of the area in which students congregated on the left bank of the Seine in Paris is still known as the Latin Quarter.) By the early 13th century, universities were moving toward more formal structures as masters and students placed higher value on the knowledge and skills necessary to qualify for a degree. New careers in state and church bureaucracies and in business had opened for those with a university education.

Europe developed two major models for universities: the student-run professional schools such as the University of Bologna, and the master-dominated universities such as the one in Paris. By the 12th century Bologna was sufficiently famous for the study of law that Thomas Becket, the Archbishop of Canterbury who opposed Henry II, and the future Pope Innocent III went there for their legal training. Such students had clear career goals and wanted to ensure that the university prepared them for their chosen profession. They had already received instruction in Latin, reasoning, and mathematics but needed specific training in either canon or civil law—that is, in the law of the Church or in Roman law. Students of canon law studied the works of Gratian, a compilation of papal pronouncements. This law was very important because tradition made St. Peter and his successors (the popes) the keepers of the keys to heaven. Whatever laws they issued on earth, according to the Doctrine of Petrine Succession, would also be binding in heaven. Students of Roman law studied the *Codex Justinianus* and the *Digest*, which had been prepared by Justinian's jurists centuries earlier. Because much had changed in both canon and civil law since these works had been written, the lectures consisted of explanations (glosses) and updating of the texts.

In Bologna the students formed a *universitas* or guild that set the standards to which professors were to adhere. To this end, the students determined the length of time that professors must lecture and the amount of text they were to cover in each course of lectures, and demanded that courses meet a set number of hours during the term and that professors not leave town without their consent. In defense, the masters formed their own guild to regulate their status within the university. They set the requirements for the exams that qualified a person to become a master and teacher in his subjects, established fees for their lectures, regulated standards for degrees, and prescribed the dress and hoods that would distinguish them from the students.

At the University of Paris the masters' guild dominated the students. Most of the students at Paris were working for their bachelor of arts degrees (baccalaureates) and were very young, usually between 13 and 18. Without experience in organizing their lives for themselves, they got drunk, ate irregularly, and neglected their studies while pursuing the proverbial wine, women, and song. They also fought with the townspeople over a number of issues, including high rents, unpaid bills for food and drink, crimes and property damage caused by student rowdiness, and the hostilities of townspeople who felt imposed on by the rowdy young men. A series of riots finally forced the masters to take responsibility for their young students.

As was usual in university towns, including Bologna, students were both a blessing and a curse. Towns enjoyed profits from renting them rooms and providing them with food and drink; on the other hand, the students were disorderly. From the students' point of view, the townspeople charged too much for their provisions and brutalized them with threats of criminal action. Whereas the sober student guilds of Bologna negotiated such disputes by the

Lady Philosophy appears to Boethius in a dream in this 15th-century edition of Boethius's Consolation of Philosophy. *Adorning Lady Philosophy's gown are the seven liberal arts that formed the core curriculum for the bachelor of arts degree: arithmetic, music, geometry, astronomy, grammar, rhetoric, and logic.*

The Lecture Method of Odofredus

Odofredus, a law professor in Bologna, outlined his lecture method when he announced his plan to give a series of lectures on the *Old Digest* of Justinian: "For it is my purpose to teach you faithfully and in a kindly manner, in which instruction the following order has customarily been observed by the ancient and modern doctors and particularly by my master.... First, I shall give you the summaries of each title before I come to the text. Second, I shall put forth well and distinctly and in the best terms I can purport of each law. Third, I shall read the text [including all the glosses done before my time] in order to correct it. Fourth, I shall briefly restate the meaning. Fifth, I shall solve conflicts, adding general matters and subtle and useful distinctions and questions with solutions, so far as divine Providence shall assist me."

The medieval method of teaching was for the professor and students to read a text together. The professor then explained the meaning of the text.

in the courts of the city of Paris. All students became members of the clergy when they entered the university and were, therefore, eligible for prosecution in ecclesiastical courts. These courts tended to be somewhat more lenient: the punishments they meted out were penances (prayers, fasts, or pilgrimages) rather than hanging.

The masters were in rebellion against the bishop of Paris over their own organization and the curriculum. In 1215 Pope Innocent III, himself a graduate of the University of Paris, confirmed the academic freedom of the Parisian masters. His statutes established that a master of arts must be at least 21 years of age and have completed six years of academic work. Masters were to wear dark gowns reaching to their heels and to maintain sober behavior. Students were to enroll with a particular master, who undertook both to teach and discipline them. The faculty of arts, which granted the bachelor of arts degree, was the largest, but theology, law, and medicine were also taught at Paris.

Scholasticism dominated the study for advanced degrees. Put simply, scholasticism is a method of logical argument used for examining a variety of issues. The method derived first from the "old logic" used by the 12th-century philosopher Abelard, which was drawn from the portions of Aristotle's and Plato's works that were translated by Boethius. But in the 13th century the "new logic," based on the complete works of Aristotle, was introduced into Europe. The corpus (or body) of Aristotle's writing had come to Europe by a curious route. It was among the books that the Arabs found in Persia. They translated it, and their scholars brought it to Spain.

very real threat of simply moving the university out of town, the young, hotheaded Parisian students had violent clashes with the legal establishment in that city.

After a particularly serious riot in 1200, in which some people were killed, the masters took control and threatened to leave the city entirely unless the king offered redress. The king acted immediately. He granted a charter to the university, in which he allowed the students and masters to be tried in ecclesiastical courts rather than

Thomas Aquinas reconciled the philosophical logic of Aristotle with the teaching of the Church. His works are still studied and form the basis of much of Catholic theology.

There Hebrew scholars translated it, and finally it was translated into Latin. The reaction of European scholars to Aristotle was extreme excitement, but the Church was skeptical because his logic suggested that knowledge of God could be derived by reason rather than by faith or revelation. Part of the argument between the Church and the masters in Paris centered on the study and teaching of Aristotle. The Church could not ban his work, so instead it sought to integrate it into Christian teachings.

The man who accomplished this task was Thomas Aquinas. He was born near Naples in 1225 into a family related to Frederick II. His father, a count, was appalled when his brilliant younger son decided to become a Dominican. After all, he reasoned, no member of his family should belong to a begging, mendicant order. Thomas's father offered to buy the boy a bishopric if he was set on going into the Church. His mother pleaded tearfully with him not to become a friar and tried to kidnap him from the order. His six brothers thought that they could corrupt him and break his resolve by putting a prostitute in his bed. Thomas, however, would not be tempted. After finishing his studies at the University of Naples, he went to Paris, where he earned his doctorate in 1257. He then taught at the university, where he wrote the treatise *Summa Theologica* (the highest or most important theology), which applied Aristotle to all aspects of Christian teaching, including social and doctrinal matters. Thomas argued that revealed knowledge of the Bible and the truth that was arrived at by Aristotle's logic must agree because truth is truth—one could not be-lieve one thing on faith and another thing on reason.

To this end he applied the tools of logic, including logical proof for the existence of God. But he held that some concepts, such as the Trinity (God, Christ, and the Holy Ghost), could not be understood by human reason because they were infinite. Only God's reason, which was infinite, could understand such concepts, and faith would have to be humans' directive here. The Dominican order so revered Thomas that, when he died in 1274, they boiled his body so that they could extract his bones and keep them as relics. He was canonized as a saint shortly after his death.

The best medical school in the 12th and 13th centuries was in Salerno, Sicily. Sicily encompassed a remarkable mixture of cultures, unlike that in any other area of Christian Europe except for parts of Spain. In Sicily western Christians, Moslems, and Greeks had all lived together, bringing with them their intellectual texts, including the superior Greek and Arabic medical texts. At the University of Salerno students studied these texts and learned anatomy by dissecting human cadavers. In Paris the Church prohibited the dissection of human bodies, though it did allow pigs to be dissected. As a consequence, physicians with degrees from Salerno were the more learned and most valued.

Other universities were established throughout Europe, mostly modeled on the University of Paris. Another riot from 1229 to 1231 was partly responsible for the dispersion of the Parisian faculty across Europe. The masters had threatened to leave Paris entirely, and some indeed did move to the university in Oxford, which was established in the late 11th century, and to Cambridge, which traces its origins to the dispersion of faculty from both Oxford and Paris. Germany opened its first universities in the 14th century, and gradually towns in southern France, Austria, Bohemia, and Poland built universities as well. With Latin as the universal language of literacy and lecturing, all the universities were international. Both students and faculty often traveled from one university to another.

A series of examinations established a student's competency to teach. Students seeking the bachelor of arts degree were allowed to take the examinations after attending lectures for four years. The curriculum was divided into the *trivium* (grammar, rhetoric, and dialectic, or logical argumentation) and *quadrivium* (arithmetic, geometry, astronomy, and music). The *trivium,* from which the word "trivial" derives, would have been easy for a young man coming to school with a good background in reading and writing the Latin language and in presenting arguments, or logical proofs. The *quadrivium* was more difficult, involving as it did the study of mathematics and sciences; even the music

To treat a broken skull, medieval surgeons cut the head open and either put the pieces of bone back in place or extracted them. The patient in this illustration from a medical treatise looks remarkably placid about this operation, but the chances of surviving such radical surgery were poor.

portion focused on the study of harmony rather than on performance. Books for these subjects were expensive—some cost as much as £10 when a loaf of bread cost a penny—so students might rent books or try to learn the subject matter by taking lecture notes. The professor would read a selection of the text for the day and then explain or gloss its meaning for the students. Students used wax tablets and a stylus to take notes, which they later transferred to parchment.

When a student was at least 20 years old and felt ready to take the examination, the masters made up a committee that swore to examine him fairly and pass or fail him without prejudice. The student in turn swore not to contest the masters' decision. The student was required to wear proper attire, a gown with a hood and a cap (much like modern academic robes), and was forbidden from bringing a knife to the examination. The panel of examiners questioned the student, judged his success, and awarded a degree if he knew the material well. The student then invited the masters and other students to a feast at his expense, as custom dictated. Advanced degrees in law and theology took an additional five to seven years; candidates for the theology degree had to be at least 35 years old. The examination was similar, but the candidate also had to present a written thesis that he would be called upon to defend.

To pay for tuition, books, and room and board, a student had to have a patron—a member of the clergy or his family—or rely on alms. Students customarily spent their summer vacations begging for money to support them for the next year. Robert de Sorbonne, a theologian, found a solution to financing education, providing living expenses, and disciplining students with the establishment of a residential college in Paris in about 1258. His will included the building of quarters for students of theology, where they could live, dine, and study in a library under a master's supervision. The Sorbonne, now a part of the University of Paris, takes its name from this original foundation.

Founding colleges became a favorite form of charity for kings, queens, bishops, and other wealthy people. The colleges provided rooms, meals, libraries, lecture halls, and chapels for students and for the masters who supervised them. The college

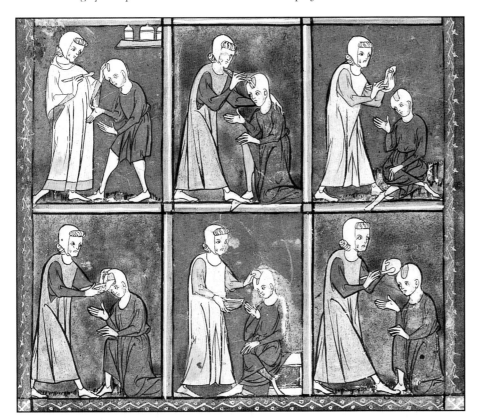

system still exists today and can best be observed at Oxford and Cambridge.

A number of options were open to boys preparing to enter university. Those from wealthy families had private tutors who taught them grammar and rhetoric (the *trivium*). Parish priests taught the children of their parish, and many cathedrals had choir schools in which boys were given lessons in theology in exchange for singing at services and funerals. Monasteries and nunneries also played a role in educating young men and women. By the late Middle Ages, the endowment of grammar schools had become as popular among the wealthy as the endowment of colleges. For instance, in the 15th century John Carpenter, a wealthy London merchant, founded a grammar school that still exists today. His will provided for the teaching and housing of boys called "Carpenter's Children," and gave them a master who in addition to giving lessons saw that they learned to shave, bathed frequently, and had clean clothes and adequate shoes.

A cardinal rule for the education of the young was that "to spare the rod was to spoil the child." If a boy did not know his lessons, he was beaten so that the next time he came to school he would be prepared. (The youth of Oxford must have enjoyed hearing that one of their masters fell into a river and drowned while gathering willow twigs to make a switch.) Children learned Latin from grammar books, used dictionaries to help them translate their vernacular language into Latin, practiced their sentences and Latin declensions on wax tablets, and recited famous passages in Latin to their teachers.

Women could not go to universities, because they were clerical establishments and women were excluded from any role in the Church except that of a nun. Some women, however, did learn to read and possibly to write. They sometimes gained a knowledge of Latin and classical works within nunneries. Hildegard of Bingen (1098–1179) composed a religious opera and hymns, wrote medical treatises, and made up a private alphabet of 23 letters and a language with 900 words. Traveling extensively, she talked to people of all walks of life about her religious visions. She was so famous in her day that even St. Bernard of Clairvaux consulted her.

A lay woman named Jacoba Felicie practiced medicine very successfully in Paris and its environs, until she ran afoul of the University of Paris because she did not have a university degree. In her defense, a number of men and women came forward to testify that she had succeeded in curing them after the "Doctors of the University" had failed. Jacoba probably had more immediate knowledge of the body and its parts and functions than did those who received medical degrees from Paris after studying the anatomy of pigs. Furthermore, she, like many women, knew much more about healing herbs than did the "doctors." Nevertheless, she lost her right to practice in the face of the university's monopoly on medical education.

The medieval universities established a college system to provide students with rooms, meals, books, and supervision by masters. Merton College at Oxford University still exists today. In the Middle Ages it was best known for its scientific and mathematical scholars. Now known as the "Merton Calculators," they worked on the earliest form of mathematical physics.

Hildegard, pictured in the left corner at her desk, wrote about medicine in her Book of Divine Works. *Like many other medical thinkers, she believed that cosmic forces such as planets and constellations influenced the body and health. The constellations and signs of the Zodiac surround the body in the center.*

The guilds and the cities of Europe regulated the price and quality of basic items such as bread and other foods, wine, beer, shoes, and clothing. Bakers were to make bread of good-quality grain rather than adding sawdust, the weight was specified, and the amount they could charge depended on the market price of grain. Those who sold inadequate bread were put on a hurdle behind horses with the bad bread tied around their necks, and were pulled through the streets to advertise to the population who sold bad bread.

Women tended to be more literate in the vernacular languages than men. Some probably also could read official documents in Latin on legal matters concerning land and divorce. Certainly, the 12th century produced authors such as Marie de France and literary patrons such as Eleanor of Aquitaine. Wills show that women bought and bequeathed to their daughters religious books, romances, and books on courtly behavior. In the art of the period, the Virgin Mary and other women were often depicted holding books, as opposed to men, who were shown clutching either swords or symbols of ecclesiastical office. Such images indicate how closely women were identified with reading.

In all probability, women were the first instructors of their male and female children. Whereas the boys went on to schools, the girls continued to learn in the home with tutors or were sent to nunneries for further training. But an education in reading and doing sums was a requirement mostly of the landed classes and the bourgeoisie. Women were often left in charge of estates and businesses either because their husbands were away at war or on business

or because they were widows. In any case, they needed to learn how to read household accounts, charters, and other official documents.

The demand for education spread throughout Europe as the legal, clerical, and judicial worlds became more complicated. Students needed to have the baccalaureate in order to receive more specialized training. With only two years of law school in continental Europe, a man could become a notary and make a very good living drawing up legal contracts. In England the baccalaureate degree was helpful in entering the Inns of Court, where students learned common law. Common law was based on precedents established in earlier cases or practice. Lawyers could work for the government as bureaucrats or for private clients as attorneys. Merchants who traded both locally and internationally needed to be able to read a contract in Latin. Increasingly, they required their apprentices to be literate before they could become masters in their vocation.

Controlling admittance into a guild or *universitas* was the practice not only of universities in the 13th and 14th centuries. In urban communities as well, craftsmen and merchants came together to keep the untrained out of their professions. The masters began by regulating themselves. They established the standards of quality necessary for their basic products and required anyone who wanted to be a master to demonstrate that he could produce a product of this standard. For example, a baker or a shoemaker had to prove to his guild that he could produce a fine quality basic loaf of daily wheat bread or a basic

shoe. Only after having done so could he become a master of his trade. Those who were not guild members could not trade. Those who allowed the quality of their wares to drop were punished by the guild and the city for selling false goods. A loaf of bread or a shoe, for instance, had to be made of high quality materials. Bread could not contain sawdust or rotted grain, and shoes had to be made of new, well-tanned leather. Punishments for selling false goods included fining members for a first offense. If a guildsman proved recalcitrant, city officials would have him paraded through the streets with musicians playing drums and beating on pans. The miscreant would be led to the public pillory with the offending item—his bad bread or his shoddy shoes—strung around his neck. His false goods would then be burned under his nose. Vintners who sold sour wine had to drink a draught of it, and the rest was poured over their heads. Guilds of merchants who dealt in banking and long-distance trade also regulated their members and fined them for false dealings.

Modern economists have criticized guilds because they limited outside competition and kept prices high as a consequence. Consumers, however, benefited under the guild system. With both guilds and the city governments regulating business, they could be sure that the city's banking and trade practices conformed to international business standards, and that the products they bought were of good quality. Weights and measures were carefully regulated by the city. Consumers had the satisfaction of seeing corrupt tradesmen paraded through the streets, a warning to all not to buy products from them. Those merchants and

artisans who persisted in their bad practices were expelled from the guild and the city, so they could no longer trade. The guild system also allowed tradesmen a margin of profit. Although the price of basic bread, shoes, or cloth was set, a guildsman could sell higher quality goods—such as fine cakes and pies, exquisite boots or court shoes, or beautifully woven velvets or brocades—for a great profit. Price controls affected only basic goods.

Like those of the universities, the urban guilds were controlled by masters, who undertook the training of apprentices. Apprentices wanted to learn particular trades so that they too could become masters. In the artisan guilds, most apprentices were peasants. But in the higher guilds—such as those of goldsmiths, bankers, overseas merchants, vintners, and clothiers—the apprentices came from urban families and were often the younger sons of knights. The family or friends of an apprentice agreed to pay a sum to his master to take in the young person for a set number of years, usually from 7 to 10, or sometimes even more. Apprenticeships began when a young man was about 14, old enough to be able to learn a trade. Parents or friends testified to the honesty and good upbringing of the young person, and the master agreed to provide clothing, a sleeping space, food, training, and a small salary as the apprentice became more skilled at the work. The apprentice could not spend the master's money on gambling or theater and could not marry during the course of apprenticeship. The apprentice moved into the home of the master and his family. He or she might be the only apprentice in the house-

Guilds identified themselves by their clothing and other symbols. Each guild wore specially colored robes in civic parades and at guild feasts. They also had coats of arms that indicated their trade.

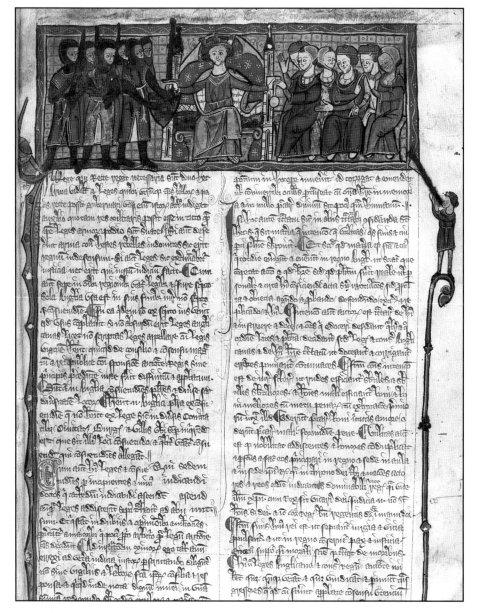

Tensions existed at all levels of village life. Because the strips in the open fields were not marked by fences, men argued over where one strip ended and another began. They claimed that their neighbors reaped their wheat or that another man's plow had encroached onto their strip. They also argued about when the village herds should be allowed to graze in the fields after the harvest and who among the villagers had gleaning rights—that is, the right to go into the fields after harvest and pick up the stray grain that had escaped harvesting.

The villagers found that having bylaws that regulated these petty encroachments and a system of fines that permitted them to punish offenders helped to keep the peace. For example, the bylaws established that only the very poor of the village would have gleaning rights both after the grain harvest and just before the pea and bean harvest. The period after the harvest during which animals could graze was mutually agreed upon. To define the boundaries dividing one village from another, villagers established a date when the whole village would turn out and walk around the boundaries—a custom called "beating the bounds."

The bylaws were enforced in the lord's manorial court. Every three weeks the lord's bailiff, or estate manager, held a court that recorded transfers of lands, inheritances, infractions of the rules of the manor, and so forth, and the dues and fines that were paid for these transactions and reprimands. The peasants used the same court to settle their private disputes and to enforce village peace. Thus two men who argued about encroachments on each other's strips could bring the dispute to court and ask a jury made up of their neighbors to declare

hold or there might be three or more, depending on the extent of the master's business.

Relationships between masters and apprentices varied considerably. Sometimes, they became extremely close, at other times, apprentices were badly abused. A male apprentice might be left his master's business and responsibility of rearing his minor children. On the other hand, apprentices sometimes needed to call in the guild and the urban officials to remove them from the starvation, poor training, and beatings received in the master's home. If all went according to plan, however, an apprentice could produce, at the end of the term, a fine loaf of ordinary bread or a very good shoe and qualify for membership in the appro-

priate guild. At first, apprentices might not have the capital to open their own business, but they could get work as day laborers, or journeymen, and make a living by working as skilled laborers.

In the 13th century, formal corporate movements were also organized in villages. While such movements might have existed before, it is only from this period that written records about how peasants organized their communities have survived. Peasant villages had anywhere from 50 to 800 residents. With such a small number of people living and working closely together, people were able to get to know everyone very well and to look after each other.

But sometimes villagers knew each other too well and got on each other's nerves.

who was at fault and fine the guilty party. People who disturbed the peace of the village by being noisy, argumentative, or abusive could be brought to court and fined. And those wealthy peasant women who went to the fields to glean when only poor women had that right were reported and fined in the manorial court.

Peasants became used to acting as a governing unit through their administration of the bylaws and participation in community policing. They learned to argue in courts; to recognize, even if they could not read, the various Latin documents from the king; and to understand the value of written records by having their own land transactions recorded in the manorial courts and by asking the bailiff to check these where disputes arose. Their cooperative action in village governance also led them to negotiate with their lords about changes in manorial rules.

The people's desire for self-government spilled over into the arena of the monarchies as well. In England John I was succeeded by his son, Henry III, who was a mere child. A coalition of nobles, churchmen, townsmen, and knights from the shires wanted to be sure that the provisions of Magna Carta would not be set aside. They had become accustomed to intervening in the royal government and formed a council to rule for the young king.

When the king came of age, he rebelled against the nobles and pursued his own policies. Throughout most of his long reign in the 13th century, he fought with his nobles, but particularly with Simon de Montfort, who organized resistance against him. Although there were several pitched battles, the most lasting effect of the struggle

The Memoirs of Jean, sire de Joinville

Jean de Joinville was a nobleman from Champagne who wrote a biography of King Louis IX of France. He accompanied Louis on his crusade to Egypt and on subsequent ones to Jerusalem and other points in the east. Joinville paid his own way on these expeditions, but at least once he received aid from Louis. Throughout his life he was an intimate of the king. After the king died and his grandson married the countess of Champagne, Joinville wrote his memoirs at her request.

Joinville completed his task in 1309. He lived 10 years more, dying at the fine old age of 95.

Although he wrote of events many years after they had taken place, his detailed stories, particularly those concerning battle such as the one depicted below, retain their sense of immediacy. Joinville's work is a testimony to the importance of the oral retelling of tales in the Middle Ages.

"On Christmas Day I and my knights were dining with Pierre d'Avallon. While we were at table the Saracens [Moslems] came spurring hotly up to our camp and killed several poor fellows who had gone for a stroll in the fields. We all went off to arm ourselves but, quick as we were, we did not return in time to rejoin our host; for he was already outside the camp and had gone to fight the Saracens. We spurred after him and rescued him from the enemy, who had thrown him to the ground."

Louis IX (in center of boat) and his knights set sail for one of his crusades. Joinville was his companion throughout his campaigns.

Edward I—flanked by the two arch-
bishops of England and the kings of
Scotland and Wales—convenes the
English Parliament in Westminster
Hall, which still stands. Churchmen
sit on the left and red-robed barons on
the right. The judges are seated on
woolsacks between them. Wool was
one of the most important products of
England, so it is fitting that it had a
place in Parliamentary ceremony.

arose from Simon's need to enlarge his
power base by asking representatives of the
counties and towns to support his rebellion.
These meetings of an expanded council
came to be called the Parliament.

When the representatives of the towns
and counties gathered in Westminster, they
met separately from the nobles and powerful bishops and abbots. Eventually these

two groups became known as the House of
Communes or communities ("commons"
in modern parlance) and the House of
Lords. Simon de Montfort called the representatives together largely for a show of
support for his policies. But the meetings
proved so useful that when Edward I came
to the throne on Henry's death, he continued to call two elected representatives from
each county and town on special occasions.
His parliament of 1295, during which the
representatives split into the two houses,
became the model for future parliaments.
Edward's main purpose in organizing the
parliaments was to inform the people of his
policies, including his wish to conquer
Wales. When Wales was finally defeated,
he called a parliament to announce his
victory and to consult with the representatives on whether David Llwellyn, the king
of the Welsh, should be hanged like a
common criminal or beheaded as befitted a
nobleman. The representatives were not
given the option of sparing Llwellyn's life,
nor did they have any say in the appropria-
tion of the title "Prince of Wales" for the
heir apparent to the English throne.

By the 14th century it had become
customary for the king to call Parliament
when he planned to impose a general tax on
the population. It was convenient to have
the House of Commons approve the tax,
because the king and his officials received
more cooperation from the people if the
parliamentary representatives returned to
the countryside and explained why the king
wanted taxes. Increasingly, however, the
subjects became more concerned about
how their money was being spent, and
instructed their parliamentary representatives to negotiate with the king and correct

Philip IV the Fair (seated, center) is surrounded by his children. The crowned queen is Isabelle, wife of Edward II and mother of Edward III. When Louis died his four sons inherited the throne in succession. Since none of them produced a male heir, Edward III, as the son of Isabelle, claimed the throne. This act of defiance was among the causes of the Hundred Years' War.

mistakes they believed he was making in government. For instance, the House of Commons would tell the king that it would grant a subsidy, but only on the condition that he make some changes in law enforcement that would get rid of criminal gangs and punish those who were disrupting daily life and trade. By the mid-14th century, the Commons had become critical of the king's free spending of money on warfare and wanted even more say in the way tax money was being spent. Thus, the House of Commons gradually became more powerful, and more inclined to intervene in royal government.

In France the development of representative institutions was largely at the local level, because the provincial structure of France remained strong. The defeat of John Lackland and the crusade against the Albigensians had brought much more French territory under the direct rule of the monarch. The French mode of ruling relied on a well-trained, university-educated class of professional lawyers and administrators. Royal officials administered the king's justice, collected his taxes, and carried out his policies. To keep them honest and loyal, they were paid a salary and were moved about every five years so that they did not build up a local patronage system. Furthermore, Louis IX (1226–70) increased surveillance of their work by sending out royal agents who traveled throughout the kingdom to hear complaints about his officials' administration. The French came to use the word *parlement* (meaning "a talk" or "a discussion") for a central court that tried cases from all over France.

France retained elements of the old system of government until the late 13th century. The contemporary biographer of Louis IX, Jean, sire de Joinville, wrote that his monarch sat on a rug under a tree, listening to cases his subjects brought to him and dispensing justice. Louis, however, spent little of his reign in France. His consuming passion was crusading, which earned him the title of "Saint Louis." Leaving the kingdom in the capable hands of his mother, Blanche of Castile, he set off with an inadequate army in 1248, hoping to capture Egypt and force the Moslems there to surrender Jerusalem. Joinville accompanied Louis and later described the king's great enthusiasm as the army began its first battle. Ignoring his advisors' warnings, Louis jumped into the sea in full armor with his lance and shield and waded ashore with the first wave of knights. Once in Egypt he entered into a prolonged fight, during which dysentery (a serious intestinal disorder) was more of a threat to his army than warfare. The king's own case was so bad that, according to Joinville, his undergarments were cut away so that he could have easier access to latrines. He and his army were captured, and only because he fell into the hands of superior Arab physicians did Louis survive the dysentery.

After paying ransoms for their freedom, the men returned to France but stayed only briefly. Soon they were off to the Holy Land on another crusade of hardship and defeat. Louis finally died in Tunisia, again on a crusade.

His grandson, Philip IV the Fair (1285–1314)—he was reputedly very handsome—was not the idealist that his grandfather had been. Pitting himself against a worthy adversary, Edward I of England, he carried on a series of skirmishes over the former Angevin possessions in France. For both Edward and Philip, carrying out warfare required first raising the money to finance it. Whereas the English became increasingly used to taxation, the French monarch looked elsewhere to raise his funds. Philip identified two potential sources of wealth that he might tap: the Jews and the clergy. In 1306 he expelled the Jews from France but seized their wealth before they left. Edward had already plundered and expelled the English Jews in 1292. The Jews went to the more tolerant new kingdoms and to the old Arab states in Spain.

Philip was aided in his maneuvers by the new class of university-trained lawyers, particularly his chief adviser, William de Nogaret. This man had mastered the most practical aspects of a university education, which included sophisticated argumentative styles and a good knowledge of canon and civil law. His rise to power was based on his good education, audacity, and loyalty to

his monarch. He organized an attack on the pope in order to gain control of the money that lay people paid to the clergy every year. The clergy in turn sent a portion to the pope in Rome. Tapping these funds would give the French king considerable income. But understanding this struggle for money requires a digression to Italy, to explain what was going on there at the time.

In the early 13th century, Italy was part of the Holy Roman Empire. The heir to the throne, Frederick II—son of Queen Constance of the Kingdoms of Naples and Sicily and Henry VI, Emperor of Germany—was the ward of Pope Innocent III. The pope insisted that Frederick agree to three conditions when he became emperor: He must be loyal to the pope, crusade against the Moslems in Jerusalem, and abandon control of Sicily and Italy while retaining an empire north of the Alps in Germany.

Frederick had the most unusual rearing and parentage of any European monarch. He was the grandson of Roger II of Sicily and had many of the Norman characteristics that had earned his predecessors names such as "the Fox." The grandson of Frederick I Barbarossa, he was also a German, although he did not visit Germany until 1211. Although a papal ward and heir to the German imperial title, he was reared in Sicily. He was endowed with a fine intelligence that permitted him to absorb the

learning of local Arabic, Greek, and Latin cultures. Unlike most people during the Middle Ages, he was comfortable dealing with people from all three cultures.

Frederick was always interested in scientific experiments and the observation of nature, and was fascinated with biology. He traveled with a menagerie that included ostriches, parrots, monkeys, leopards, panthers, lions, camels, a giraffe, and an elephant. He wrote a book, *On the Art of Hunting with Birds,* that contains a general sketch of ornithology (the study of birds), as well as information on hawks, falcons, eagles, and other hunting birds. The book is based on his own observations and is illustrated with accurate pictures that were drawn and colored under his personal direction. He also conducted a number of experiments. For instance, he had heard that in Norway certain geese hatched from barnacles. He sent for some of the barnacles and discovered for himself that they did not produce geese. He concluded that the myth had started because people did not know where the birds' nests were built. Frederick also experimented with how buzzards identified meat. He placed hoods over their eyes, and when they could not detect meat near them, he concluded that sight rather than smell facilitated their hunting. It was also said that he thought he could discover the language of Adam by raising two children

who would be nursed and cared for but would not be taught to speak. The children, however, died before they spoke.

Frederick applied his scientific reasoning to politics—a most unusual practice for a monarch of his day. At 18 he was already defying the new pope. He made it clear that he planned to concentrate his power in Sicily and Italy rather than in Germany by having his infant son made king of Germany and himself declared emperor. His empire was to include the wealthy states of southern Italy in addition to Milan and selected cities that surrounded Rome. The pope countered by reminding him of his oath to go on crusade. Frederick, whose first wife had already died, married the heiress to the Latin Kingdom of Jerusalem. He claimed to be eager to crusade, but only when the time was right—he was secretly negotiating with the Arabs to gain access to Jerusalem.

Under papal pressure, he finally embarked on a crusade but returned to port complaining that his army was sick and could not go to war. Suspecting that he was only malingering, the pope excommunicated him. Nevertheless, once Frederick had finished his negotiations he sailed triumphantly out of port as an excommunicated crusader. He concluded his mission by signing an agreement with the Moslems to give Jerusalem to the Christians and provide a corridor from the port of Acre to the holy city. All that the Moslems required in exchange was that they be permitted to worship in their mosques. Frederick, a man with a good understanding of Arab culture, had no hesitation in entering into an agreement with the "infidel" within a year of beginning the crusade. But the pope was very distrustful of any Christian, particularly Frederick II, who made deals with those who could not swear an oath that was binding with the Christian God. Several more years passed before he removed the ban of excommunication.

The pope was right to be suspicious of Frederick. He simply did not play by the rules of medieval feudal and Christian ethics. His kingdom and rule were more similar to those of an eastern despot or a Byzantine emperor than a king of England or France. After returning from his crusade, Frederick began to build an efficient state in Sicily. Sicily became a safe haven for shipping because his trade agreements with the Moslem states had removed much of the threat of piracy. Within Sicily Frederick encouraged the growth of new crops such as dates, sugar, and cotton. Under his guidance laws were codified; the economy prospered; and Moslems, Greeks, Jews, and Christians lived in harmony. He had vowed to the pope, however, that he would abandon Sicily in favor of Germany. Instead, he allowed the princes, prelates, and cities of the Holy Roman Empire to go their own way. Like his grandfather he tried to take control of the wealthy cities of northern Italy. A series of battles, in which the pope sided with the cities, remained inconclusive because Frederick died in 1250.

The 13th century saw a great number of changes in the politics of Europe that would have consequences for centuries to come. Henry III's weak rule in England and the death of Frederick II's sons meant that the Capetian dynasty in France became the most powerful monarchy in Europe. King Louis IX's younger brother, Charles of Anjou, was looking for projects and decided to take over Sicily and southern Italy. By good fortune and some maneuvering on the part of the Capetians, there was a French pope who welcomed a French initiative. Charles, however, did not take into consideration the local opposition in Sicily nor the power of King Peter of Aragon. Aragon had emerged as a powerful kingdom in Spain when its king married the heiress of the valuable province of Catalonia and gained a navy. With a power vacuum in Sicily, Peter of Aragon sent his fleet. His aggression coincided with the Sicilian Vespers of 1282. On Easter Monday, when the church bells rang to call the congregations to evening service, this prearranged insurrection led to the massacre of all Charles of Anjou's supporters. Peter of Aragon stepped into this civil revolt and claimed Sicily for himself. Some historians argue that the Mafia originated in the Sicilian Vespers.

Following the Sicilian Vespers, the College of Cardinals realized that it must elect an Italian pope rather than a French one and that he must be a person of outstanding character who could regain respect for the spiritual mission of the Church. The cardinals selected a pious monk from southern Italy, who became Celestine V. The cardinals hoped that Celestine would be a figurehead for spiritual matters and leave the papal bureaucracy to continue running financial and political affairs. But the more Celestine learned of the papal bureaucrats and their program the more worried he became. He felt that if he allowed the corruption he discovered to continue, his

Pope Boniface VIII argued strongly for papal supremacy. He quarreled with both Edward I of England and Philip IV of France to keep them from taxing the clergy in their countries. He died after being captured by agents of Philip IV.

Marco Polo

The caravan route across the vast internal land of Asia was known as the Great Silk Road. Marco Polo and his family took it to China. Silks, rugs, spices, precious gems, and other luxury goods were carried by camel. The merchants rode horses.

Marco Polo's father was a Venetian merchant named Niccolò. He and Marco's uncle had made a trip to China in 1260 when Marco was only six years old and returned with stories of the great wealth they had found there. On a second voyage in 1271 Marco went along, and he and his family spent 20 years traveling through India, southeast Asia, and China under the patronage of the Chinese emperor, Kublai Khan. Other Christians—including merchants, missionaries, and Byzantine immigrants—were also present in the Orient at the time.

Marco Polo wrote his memoirs after his return in 1292. He was then a prisoner in Genoa, where he met the romance writer Rustichello of Pisa. Polo's account indicates that both men wrote the memoirs. The book recounts the perils of the route and the customs Polo learnt along the way. For example, he described a drink he discovered in southern Asia: "In this country they make date wine with the addition of various spices, and very good it is. When it is drunk by men who are not used to it, it loosens the bowels and makes a thorough purge; but after that it does them good and makes them put on flesh." Not having seen coal before, he wrote: "Let me tell you next of stones that burn like logs. It is a fact that throughout the province in Cathay [China] there is a sort of black stone, which is dug out of veins in the hillsides and burns like logs. These stones keep a fire going better than wood."

The three Venetians spent 17 years in the service of the Khan and became immensely rich. They then wanted to return home, but the Khan was reluctant to let them go. Finally, however, he needed to transport a Chinese bride to the king of Persia by sea. Marco, his father, and his uncle undertook the task and from Persia made their way back to Venice.

---

immortal soul would be endangered. How could the successor of St. Peter rule over such covetousness? Celestine began to have dreams in which he heard a voice saying that it was the will of God that he resign. Later, detractors of his successor, Boniface VIII (1294–1303), suggested that he had actually rigged up a speaking tube into Celestine's chamber and intoned the words himself.

Boniface undertook to stop secular rulers from taxing the clergy by issuing a papal bull against the practice. Edward I of England responded by threatening to outlaw any subject who disobeyed him, and Philip

IV of France simply forbade any gold or silver to leave his domain, thereby effectively stopping the flow of money to the papacy. Not one to take defeat lightly, Boniface issued more bulls, which Philip took as insults to the French monarchy. In 1302 Philip called the first general meeting of the three estates: the nobility, the clergy, and the commons or third estate. The French king usually met these groups separately on a regional basis, but Philip brought together all representatives for what became known as the Estates General. At that first meeting, the king's adviser, William de Nogaret, twisted the content of the bulls to

make them seem even more insulting and persuaded the Estates General to back Philip. Undaunted, Boniface issued yet another bull, this time claiming that all Christians were his subjects. Philip IV's response was to send Nogaret to Italy to confront Boniface. Finding the pope at his vacation home in Anagni, he and some of the pope's enemies from Rome captured Boniface. Realizing that a captive pope was just an embarrassment to them, however, they let him go. Boniface died a month later.

It is a measure of the low prestige of the papacy that Philip suffered no reprisals for his attack on Boniface. When the cardinals elected the archbishop of Bordeaux, a subject of the king of England, as the next pope, people thought he would favor the English. In fact, he rescinded the bulls against Philip and forgave all those who had taken part in the attack at Anagni. Rather than moving to Rome, the new pope stayed in France, settling in the city of Avignon. This marked the beginning of the Avignon papacy; his successors also settling there.

The 13th century was a pivotal period in the political history of Europe. The organization of representative bodies was the first tentative step toward constitutional monarchy. Universities provided educated and trained people not only for the clergy, but also for secular governments and towns. The breakup of the Kingdom of the Two Sicilies and the disintegration of the Holy Roman Empire changed the political map of Europe for centuries. The island of Sicily remained under Aragon, but Naples became a separate city-state. The northern Italian towns also formed city-states that bickered and warred with each other. Italy would not be united into a single state until 1870. In Germany the tendency for the nobles, bishops, and towns to pursue their own policies gathered momentum with Frederick II's abandonment of interest in the empire. The princes of the Holy Roman Empire finally met in the late 13th century and elected Rudolph of Hapsburg (reigned 1273–1291), a minor noble from Alsace, as emperor. The Hapsburg dynasty became a major power in the 16th century through a series of marriages that brought Austria, Hungary, Bohemia, and even Burgundy and Spain under its control. But if the Hapsburgs gained a title, they lost con-

siderable territory. The Swiss formed a confederation and freed themselves from the Hapsburgs in 1291. Germany remained a loosely organized group of principalities, bishoprics, and towns under a Hapsburg emperor until Otto von Bismarck unified them in the late 19th century.

After the death of Frederick II and a period with no king, the German nobility elected Rudolf I of Hapsburg. He was not among the powerful nobles and the German nobility thought that he would be unable to create problems for them or involve them in struggles in Italy. However, the Hapsburgs were more successful than anticipated. Largely though a series of strategic marriages they became a dominant power in central Europe.

Chapter 8

The Four Horsemen of the Apocalypse

Francesco de Marco Datini, an Italian merchant from Prato, lived through the best and the worst of the late Middle Ages. He was only a child when the Black Death raged through Italy in 1348 and killed his parents. He had a small inheritance and was raised by a woman to whom he referred affectionately as a substitute mother; she signed her letters to him as "your mother in love." Francesco apprenticed himself to a merchant in Florence and learned to trade. Soon after his 15th birthday, he joined other merchants who were going to the rich papal city of Avignon. He prospered by importing Italian art and luxury items for the cardinals and other wealthy people who lived there. When Datini was more than 40, he returned to Prato and married Margherita, who was 25 years his junior. He was often away, and they exchanged letters weekly. All of these letters and many others are preserved in his house in Prato. Although he was successful in business, he shared the anxieties of many people in the late Middle Ages about visitations of the plague. When plague was raging in Prato, Datini, Margherita, and his illegitimate daughter set out by mule for Bologna

on June 17, 1400. One of his correspondents wrote from Florence, "I have seen two of my children die in my arms in a few hours." Datini himself lived another 10 years, dying peacefully in Prato in 1411.

People living during the 14th and 15th centuries often alluded to the Four Horsemen of the Apocalypse: famine, disease, war, and death or salvation. In northern Europe a prolonged shift in the weather patterns brought colder and wetter weather, which resulted in poor harvests and severe famines in the early 14th century. Disease, the second horseman, brought the Black Death in 1348, killing off a third to half of the population. War, never a stranger to Europe, took on a new and more deadly form in the late 14th and 15th centuries. Europe had settled down to organized warfare under monarchies. Battles were contained on battlefields and did not do much harm to the local populations. During the Hundred Years' War (1337–1453) between England and France, however, battles were infrequent. The real fighting was a war of attrition, in which France preyed on English shipping and invaded England's southern coast and English troops marauded the French country-

The mortality from the plague was so great in the late 14th and 15th centuries that death became a predominant theme in medieval art. Representations of death, such as the sarcophagus below the horseman, showed the ravages of decayed bodies. The armies of the dead, clothed in their shrouds, are led by Death, one of the four horsemen of the apocalypse. They easily defeat the living army and march toward a prosperous city.

side, where they destroyed vineyards and plundered livestock, valuables, and crops. The pope was still at Avignon, but the papacy was by now completely discredited by its continual search for new sources of money. Many people had begun to question the pope's authority, and new heresies—such as those of university professors John Wycliffe and Jan Hus—drew followers. With so much going wrong, people thought the end of the world was near.

But these two centuries also brought new ideas, new freedom, new piety, and a comfortable life for many who survived the calamities. Vernacular, as opposed to Latin, literature became popular. Dante Alighieri, Francesco Petrarch, Giovanni Boccaccio, Geoffrey Chaucer, and Christine de Pisan all contributed to the new literature. If the papacy was corrupt, the laity was becoming more pious and more intent on building their own parish churches and ensuring their own salvation. Luxuries of fine cloth, foods, larger homes, books, and art became more available as the population shrank. In the midst of death, therefore, new benefits arose for the living.

Famine devastated the poor of northern Europe during the Great Famine from 1315 to 1317 and again in the early 1320s. Contemporary accounts note that it rained so much in the summer of 1315 that the crops were ruined by the wet weather. The rain continued, making the fields too muddy for planting the winter wheat in the fall and the summer crops in the spring. The harvest was pitiful, and the grain that could be harvested had to be dried in ovens. And the rain continued into 1317. The cattle developed diseases due to the wet weather and lack of grain and died. The poor died of starvation in lanes and fields in the country and in alleys in the cities. Prisoners tore apart and ate new inmates who were put into their jails. At a distribution of alms in London, 60 men, women, and children were crushed to death as the crowd pushed forward to get pennies for food. Charities had no surplus food to distribute because crops grown at monasteries were also ruined. Importation of food in large quantities from southern Europe was not feasible. When the king of England sought such relief, pirates boarded the ships before they could reach port. The population had no sooner recovered than another famine hit in 1323.

The pope, comfortably resident in Avignon, suffered none of the deprivation of the faithful of northern Europe. Rome was in the hands of hostile families who engaged in fighting each other and opposing any candidate for pope that the other side proposed. Over time the popes purchased the town of Avignon (located in what is now southern France), which was surrounded by vineyards, orchards, and grain fields. They built a magnificent palace that still stands, and the cardinals built palaces for themselves in the town and surrounding countryside. The churchmen became patrons of artisans, artists, and writers, who were flourishing in the late 14th and 15th centuries. But the Avignon popes had some serious problems. They had the difficult task of defending their position as successors of St. Peter, founder of the Church of Rome, while living outside that city and never visiting it. They also had financial woes. All of the estates that Pope Gregory the Great had spent so much time organizing and administering and that subsequent popes had defended against such powerful monarchs as Frederick I and II were now in the hands of various factions, none of which wanted to contribute the usual amount to support the papacy. The papacy therefore had to look elsewhere for money. The pope had lost much of his power to tax the clergy because of fights with Edward I and Philip IV, so the papal courts became even more rapacious in collecting fines for divorces and annulments of marriages, and the popes sold bishoprics to the highest bidder. They also began an aggressive policy of selling indulgences, or the forgiveness of particular sins. Finally, they began to sell a plenary indulgence, which would forgive sins not yet committed. The theological presumption was that the sacrifice of Jesus at his crucifixion and the suffering of martyred saints had created a reservoir of goodness, similar to a bank deposit, that the faithful could draw upon for a price and avoid the torments of hell. The Franciscans and Dominicans participated in selling indulgences, thus alienating themselves from the inspiration of their founders. The orders had become so corrupt that they were little more than fund-raisers for themselves and the papacy. Other clergy were also willing to enter into money-making schemes for personal enrichment.

The lay response to churchmen using the money they raised to fund their own opulent lifestyles was twofold. Criticism of the lavish living mounted among the faithful, but some flocked to the papal court as purveyors of fine merchandise or as suitors for papal patronage. The correspondence of Francesco de Marco Datini provides an accurate picture of the luxury market and

the opportunities it presented to shrewd businessmen. His orders to his partners in Italy included "a panel of Our Lady on a background of fine gold with two doors, and a pedestal with ornaments and leaves, handsome and the wood well carved, making a fine show, with good and handsome figures by the best painter, with many figures." He was more of a merchant than an art critic, for he added, "Let there be in the center Our Lord on the Cross, or Our Lady, whomsoever you find—I care not, so that the figures be handsome and large, and best and finest you can purvey."

Others, such as Francesco Petrarch (1304–1374), came to sell their poetry and writing rather than goods. The son of a Florentine notary, Petrarch studied law at Montpellier and Bologna and then took holy orders, moving to Avignon. Putting aside his vocation as a priest, he wrote a series of love sonnets in Italian to a woman named Laura, who died in 1348, the plague year. Denied the patronage that he sought from Avignon, he became a severe critic of the town. He wrote that Avignon was a "fountain of anguish, the dwelling-place of

The Burgundian court played a leading role in politics and in setting aristocratic style in the 15th century. The marriage of Duke Philip the Good of Burgundy to Isabel of Portugal in 1430 was an occasion to display beautiful dress and fine foods. The wedding party was held outdoors and men and women even brought their falcons with them.

Separated from Rome and its regular income, the Avignon papacy began to sell indulgences, or forgiveness of sins. The assumption was that the sacrifice of Christ and the saints had built up a reservoir of salvation which the Church could dispense by selling it to the laity. One could buy forgiveness for a specific sin or get a plenary indulgence that would cover all possible sins. Even when the Church returned to Rome, it continued to sell indulgences, as this woodcut from the early 16th century indicates.

wrath, the school of errors, the temple of heresy, once Rome, now the false guilt-laden Babylon, the forge of lies, the horrible prison, the hell on earth."

Edward I of England and Philip IV of France had challenged the pope and taxed the clergy in order to carry on their political struggles against each other. Edward, of course, wanted to get back the French territory that John I had lost a century earlier, and Philip wanted to take from Edward the territory he still held in southern France. The two monarchs, however, did not engage in active warfare and, finally, Edward married his son, the future Edward II, to Isabelle, daughter of Philip.

War between the two countries did not break out until the reign of their son, Edward III (1327–1377). Edward III's ascent to the throne was surrounded by drama. His mother had taken him to France

to pay homage to the French king for the English territory in France. Traveling with young Edward and his mother was the English baron Roger Mortimer. The three of them made a plan to overthrow Edward II. Young Edward married the daughter of the count of Hainault, and, as a dowry, she brought military help for the invasion of England. Isabelle and Mortimer returned to England and had Edward II killed after a humiliating captivity. With the support of Parliament, they declared Edward III king and themselves as his regents. But Edward III was an energetic young man. Collecting a band of knights, he seized Isabelle and hunted down her lover in their bedchamber. He had Mortimer executed, but confined his mother to a comfortable royal castle far from the political scene.

Edward III embodied the ideals of medieval kingship. He was young, chivalrous, intelligent, and an excellent warrior. He fought in tournaments, sometimes anonymously, and he reestablished King Arthur's Round Table and a chivalric order, a group of nobles and knights selected by the king, called the Knights of the Garter. His love of warfare led him to pursue aggressive relations with France. The excuse for beginning what became known as the Hundred Years' War was that the Capetian line had failed to produce a male heir. Philip IV's sons inherited in succession, but they did not have male children. This meant that Edward, as the grandson of Philip through his mother, had a claim to the French throne. The French could not allow their ancient rival to take over the throne of France, so they selected another branch of the Capetian family, the

As a young man, Edward III of England paid homage to Philip IV of France for fiefs he held in France as a vassal of the French King. Edward wears a robe with the rampant lions symbolic of the English king, and Philip wears a robe with the fleur-de-lis that was the symbol of France.

Valois. Nonetheless, Edward made himself a new coat of arms by combining his arms (the rampant lions) with the lilies of France (fleurs de lys) and declared himself king of France as well as England.

Another dispute that led to the war involved the county of Flanders (part of modern Belgium), which the French kings claimed belonged to France. Flanders was one of the wealthiest cloth-manufacturing centers of Europe. Fine woolen cloth and tapestries were woven and dyed there by wage laborers who worked on heavy looms. The wool for the cloth came mainly from England, so the Flemish economy was dependent on English wool. Edward saw a way to get at the French by stirring up trouble in Flanders. He encouraged the Flemish weavers to revolt by withholding the English wool from their markets. The embargo worked, and the Flemish weavers sided with the English against the French. With trouble brewing in Flanders, Edward launched his first campaigns.

A Feast Fit For a King

Servants served food to the nobles, who sit with their trenchers before them and with spoons to eat with. Musicians created a lively party.

The dukes of Burgundy in the 15th century were renowned for their feasts in honor of the Order of the Golden Fleece. The hall in which the feasts were held measured 140 feet by 70 feet. The head table stood on a dais at one end of the hall, and two other tables ran lengthwise down the outside of the room, leaving the center free for performers who provided entertainment. A buffet displayed gold and silver plates and was used for serving food and dispensing wine.

By preference, guests sat on only one side of the u-shaped table to facilitate service and to allow each person to see and be seen by all. The order of seating was important, with each guest seated according to his or her rank. The highest-ranking sat at the head of the table. Sometimes the dukes of Burgundy ate from silver-gilt plates, but generally trenchers of whole-wheat bread that was several days old served as plates. Trenchers absorbed the sauces and juices from the meal and were distributed to the poor after the feast. The most prominent object on the table was the salt cellar. In addition to the trencher, each place was set with a drinking vessel, bowl, knife, and spoon. Until the 15th century when forks were introduced for upper-class use, guests ate delicately with their fingers.

A trumpet fanfare announced the beginning of the feast, with guests entering by rank to take part in the handwashing ceremony. They held their hands over a basin while a page poured herb-scented water over their hands and then offered them a linen napkin. The meals had a number of courses, called *mets*, and the activities between the courses were the *entremets*, or "sotelties" to the English. At one Burgundian feast, the *entremet* began with the presentation of 30 pies, each enclosed in a silk pavilion. When the pies were opened, birds popped out. They not only began to sing but also flew around the room to the delight of the guests. It is easy to see that the nursery song about four and twenty blackbirds baked in a pie refers to a medieval banquet.

Early in the Hundred Years' War the English established their supremacy on the seas at the Battle of Sulys. Here, Edward III's son lands in France. At the beginning of the war, Edward claimed his inheritance of the French throne and put the rampant lions of England with the French fleur-de-lis on his shield and banner. The English ships carry this banner.

In 1345 Edward landed an army in Normandy and marched north toward Flanders. The French king met Edward's army at Crécy in 1346 with a force that outnumbered the English by two to one. Fired with enthusiasm, the French attacked without resting from their march or waiting for their footsoldiers to arrive. Edward had the better position on a hilltop. He had his cavalry dismount, then grouped them on the crest of the hill. He flanked them with bowmen using the longbow, which had been extremely effective in the Welsh wars. The French army had to charge uphill against a shower of arrows that shot the horses out from under them. Edward won this glorious first battle, but all that he had to show for

a brilliant victory was the capture of the port city of Calais.

After a truce—the Hundred Years' War was not fought continuously—England launched another campaign in 1356. This time the leader was Edward's oldest son, who was known as Edward the Black Prince. At a famous battle at Poitiers, the English used a similar tactic, and the French suffered major losses. It was said at the time that the French lost 2,000 knights and that an equal number were captured and held for ransom. Among those captured on the battlefield was the French king, John. King John spent the rest of his life in comfortable imprisonment in England, while his aggressive heir dragged his feet about paying a ransom for the return of his father. Instead, the French prince took control of the kingdom and harassed the English territory in France.

These two major battles did little to determine the course of the war, but they did leave a legacy that marked a change in the nature of warfare. They showed that the heavily armed knight and pitched battles had become obsolete. The foot soldier armed with the English longbow, a crossbow, or a pike was the soldier of the future. The longbow was both accurate and easily reloaded, so it could be used to create raining volleys of arrows. The crossbow was so powerful that it could penetrate chain mail. To counter its force, armor was made of plates with convex surfaces to deflect arrows. Even horses were armored so that they could not be shot from under their riders.

Compared to foot soldiers, knights with such heavy armor lacked maneuverability

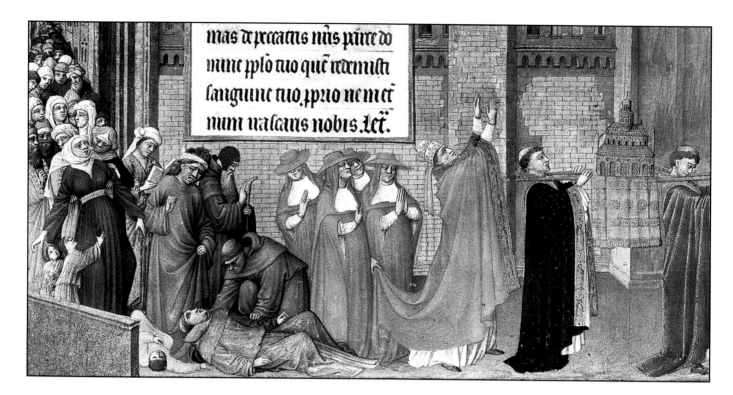

mas d pcatis nus punc do
mine ipsō tuo que reemisti
sanguine tuo, ipio ne mei
num valeans nobis. let.

on the battlefield. Crossbows had the disadvantage that their strings had to be cranked before an arrow could be released. At close quarters, foot soldiers with pikes were useful even against knights on horseback. A pike had a long shaft, a cutting blade like an ax, and a sharp knife like a spear on the end. In modern terms, they are sometimes referred to as "multipurpose can openers"—that is, they could be used to pull a knight off his horse, spear the knight or his horse from underneath, chop at a foe on the ground, or form a barricade of pointed and sharp surfaces to halt a cavalry charge.

The fact that foot soldiers rather than knights won battles had major consequences for social structure as well as for warfare. Foot soldiers were recruited from the peasantry and urban dwellers of Europe. They were often violent men who had committed crimes or impatient youths who wanted to make a quick fortune or who preferred excitement over the tedium of working as apprentices or plowmen. They were mercenaries—that is, soldiers of fortune who were paid to fight. When the pay ran out between campaigns, their commanders kept them together by having them pillage the countryside. France was devastated by these marauding mercenary armies. The English ones raided French territory, and the French

ones raided the English-held territory in France. When these resources were spent, the mercenaries hired themselves out for war in Spain or Italy.

The return of bubonic plague, absent from Europe since the reign of Justinian in the sixth century, devastated the population so thoroughly that warfare ceased. The path of the plague to Europe can be traced along the trade routes. In caravans carrying silk and spices out of the East, the plague-carrying fleas and their host rats (*ratus ratus* or the common house rat) came to the ports of the Black Sea. The cargoes were loaded onto an Italian boat bound for Venice in 1347. A terrible disease immediately began killing the sailors and merchants on board. Venice did not want the ship to land there, so it touched at various other ports in Italy, where the rats and fleas were unloaded along with the cargo. The disease spread rapidly to all of Italy and then proceeded along trade routes until it had infected most of Europe, both the urban and rural areas. The disease had a curious pattern. Some villages were decimated, whereas others had no sickness whatever. The entire region of Poland was skipped over in this visitation of plague.

Unlike famine, plague claimed victims of every social class. Peasants' thatched roofs,

With no idea of what caused the Black Death or how to cure it, religious processions praying to God for relief became common. But even the pope, lifting his hands in supplication, followed by his cardinals, could not prevent several members of the procession from falling to the ground from the illness.

The Battle of Poitiers was the second major defeat for the French in the Hundred Years' War. The English longbowmen attacked the French knights, first shooting horses out from under them and creating confusion on the field. The English knights then went in and won the battle, taking the French king and many French nobles captive.

urban dwellers' dirty ditches and streets, castles' moats and wells, and bishops' and cardinals' palaces all had rats, and the fleas that lived on these rats bit humans, spreading the bacterial infection. After an incubation period of about two weeks, the infected person suffered from buboes, or swellings of the lymph nodes, and blood collected and congealed under the skin, leaving black patches. These symptoms gave the disease its two names—bubonic plague and the Black Death. In some urban areas, such as Florence and London, about half of the population died. In Europe as a whole perhaps a third of the population succumbed.

This huge number of deaths occurred in only two years. As a result, all of the normal civilities and ceremonies for dealing with death and dying had to be put aside. Priests

and members of the clergy who aided the dying by giving them the rites of the Church had a higher mortality than anyone else. Doctors claimed that they could do nothing, and, indeed, about all they could do was pierce the buboes. Very few patients recovered. No one knew what caused the disease. (Not until the 19th century was the bacterium responsible for bubonic plague discovered.) Some thought that the air was heavy and polluted. Others believed that the plague was the result of generally sinful living, and therefore only prayers and mortification of the flesh would help. Among these people were the flagellants, who went about the countryside beating themselves. Still others concluded that the plague spread through contagion and tried to avoid infection by closing themselves in castles or, like

Francesco de Marco Datini and his family, fleeing from places that had plague. But cities became wise to this maneuver and refused entry to those coming from plague areas. Artistic representations tended to dwell on the death of the rich as well as the poor, on decay, and on the horrors of hell.

Giovanni Boccaccio (1313–1375), an Italian poet, wrote about a fictional group of Italian merchants and nobles who gathered in a castle to avoid contagion. They agreed to entertain each other by telling stories. Boccaccio's masterpiece, *Il Decameroné,* is a collection of wonderful medieval stories about love won and lost as recited by these fictional characters. At the beginning of the book, Boccaccio wrote a vivid account of the Black Death as it ravaged Florence:

The mortal pestilence then arrive[d] in the excellent city of Florence, which surpasses every other Italian city in nobility. Whether through the operations of the heavenly bodies, or sent upon us mortals through our wicked deeds by the just wrath of God for our correction, the plague had begun some years before in Eastern countries. . . . It did not work as it had in the East, where anyone who bled from the nose had a manifest sign of inevitable death. But in its early stages both men, and women too, acquired certain swellings, either in the groin or under the armpits. The swellings reached the size of a common apple and others were as big as an egg, some more or less. . . . Then the appearance of the disease began to change into black or livid blotches, which showed up in many on the arms or thighs and in every other part of the body. . . . The evil was still greater than this. Not only conversa-

tion and contact with the sick carried the illness to the healthy and was cause of their common death, but even to handle the clothing or other things touched or used by the sick seemed to carry with it that same disease. . . . Such events and many others similar to them . . . conjure up in those who remain healthy diverse fears and imaginings. . . . Almost all were inclined to a very cruel purpose, that is, to shun and to flee the sick and their belongings. . . . Others were of a contrary opinion. They affirmed that heavy drinking and enjoyment, making the rounds with singing and good cheer, the satisfaction of the appetite with everything one could, and the laughing and joking which derived from this, were the most effective for this great evil.

As the plague reappeared about every 20 years, people began to have theories about the disease, including the possibility that it was contagious. They concluded that one way to stop the disease was to remove the victims from the city—in this case, the walled Italian city of Sansepolero.

John Ball, a priest, was one of the leaders of the English peasant revolt of 1381. He preached a simple message of egalitarianism: "When Adam delved [dug] and Eve span, where then were all the gentleman." He asked why, if our first parents cultivated the earth and made cloth, some people should now claim to be above such work.

The Black Death had extraordinary social and economic effects on Europe, perhaps the most dramatic of which occurred in England. The peasants there realized that the decreased supply of labor and the increased demand for it allowed them to charge higher wages and to refuse the heavy work burdens imposed by the lords under the manorial system. The king and his nobles also saw the implications of a reduced workforce and passed the Ordinance of Laborers in 1349 (made into law as the Statute of Laborers in 1351 by the House of Commons) in an attempt to freeze the prices of labor and products at the 1347 level. Like all price and wage freezes, it did not work and caused a great deal of resentment among the laboring population.

Similarly, in other areas of Europe, peasants and laborers saw that they could charge more for their labor because there were fewer of them. But, as in England, when they tried to take advantage of the situation they discovered that the upper class had passed laws to keep them as serfs or poorly paid wage laborers. The possibility of freedom from serfdom played itself out differently from country to country. In France in 1358 the peasants and the urban inhabitants revolted against a tax on salt levied on every person to finance the war with England. Furthermore, their agriculture and trade were being devastated by the war of attrition. The peasant revolt was called the Jacquerie after the name Jacques, which was used as a generic term for all peasants. The peasants formed a coalition with the middle class of Paris and had a short-lived success, but the king defeated them. The bloody repression of the peasantry that followed discouraged revolt for centuries to come in France.

The Revolt of 1381 in England was equally ineffectual, but by that time changes in the relationship between the lords and the peasantry were already underway. Enforcement of the Statute of Laborers was impossible because peasants simply left their manors and sought wage-paying jobs elsewhere. But the cause of the revolt in England was similar to that of the Jacquerie in France. Earlier in the 14th century, the English had been paying taxes at irregular intervals on the value of their moveable goods such as plows, grain, and animals. Because the wealthy had more goods, they were taxed more heavily than the poor. But in the 1370s and 1380s taxes were due more frequently and were levied equally on everyone over the age of 14 in the form of a poll tax, or a tax paid by each person. This meant that the rich paid little tax but the poor were devastated by taxes.

When the king's tax collectors did not bring in enough money in 1380, they correctly suspected widespread evasion and started collecting taxes again in 1381. A group of peasants in Essex, a county just north of London, killed several of the collectors, and the revolt spread rapidly throughout England. Some of the peasants marched on London under the leadership of Wat Tyler, John Ball, and Jack Straw. There they killed the king's advisors and destroyed the palace of the king's uncle. Richard II, the grandson of Edward III and a boy of only 15 years, responded by agreeing to meet with the peasant leaders. Leading them outside the walls of London, he listened to their demands for an end to serfdom. When one of his followers drew a sword and killed Wat Tyler, Richard had the presence of mind to ride boldly forward and tell the rebels that he was their leader. He promised them charters of freedom if they would go back to their homes. Richard broke his promise of freedom and sent out his royal justices to round up the ringleaders of the revolt and hanged them.

The Revolt of 1381 had little impact on the gradual disappearance of serfdom in England. The peasants continued to pay rent for the land they cultivated, but they no longer paid for the marriage of their daughters, for their sons to leave the manor, or for doing work on the lord's property. These and all other fines and burdens that had been the mark of serf status were abolished.

But in Poland, Spain, and some other parts of Europe, the 15th century brought more repression rather than less. In these areas the response of lords to the decreased labor supply was to bind the peasants more closely to the manors and limit their freedom of movement. Peasants were, therefore, forced into more restrictive serfdom than they had known previously.

The disruption of plague and changes in the population also led urban workers to revolt. In Florence, which was a very important center for the production of luxury woolen cloth, the workers rose up in the Ciompi revolt of 1378 when manufacturers tried to lower their wages. Cloth workers also revolted in Flanders in the 14th century. But like the Revolt of 1381 and the Jacquerie, these revolts failed.

The 14th century was not, however, all famine, war, and disease. Some of the greatest authors of all time lived during this century. Vernacular literature—poetry and prose written in the common tongue rather than in Latin—became fashionable. More people, both men and women, learned to read in their own languages.

Dante Alighieri (1265-1321) was the great predecessor of Petrarch and Boccaccio in writing in Italian. He grew up in Florence, but was exiled when Boniface VIII stirred up a revolt there. Retiring to the countryside, he began to write poetry and essays. One of his essays dealt with the need for a literary Italian that would be equivalent to French, which had already been accepted as a language for literature. Dante proceeded to write poetry in the Italian that was close to his own Florentine dialect. His greatest work in Italian was the *Commedia*, or the *Divine Comedy*. It is an epic of a personal travel through the circles of hell that concludes with a beatific vision of God. Not surprisingly, devils eagerly awaited Boniface VIII in the lowest pit of hell, and

Dante, shown here with a laurel leaf crown in imitation of the Roman custom for heroes, was the first great writer in the Italian language. His most famous book is the Divine Comedy, *but he wrote essays on politics and language and other poems. He was politically active in Florence, taking the side of the emperor over that of the pope.*

Christine de Pisan wrote about the virtues of women in the late 14th and early 15th centuries. She argued against other authors of the time who claimed that women were inferior to men. She also translated one of the major ancient authorities on warfare. A manuscript illustration from one of her books shows two lords seated with their entourage.

dard English. Pronouncing the words aloud makes his language more comprehensible:

> Whan that Aprille with his shoures soote
> The droghte of March hath perced to
>   the roote,
> And bathed every veyne in swich licour,
> Of which vertu engendred is the flour ....

Chaucer served as a diplomat for King Richard II and traveled extensively on the Continent, where he became familiar with the works of French and Italian authors, particularly Boccaccio. Although Chaucer wrote many poems, his *Canterbury Tales* is certainly the best known. Using Boccaccio's device of having a group of storytellers link a series of tales together, Chaucer selected a cast of characters that included a knight and his son, a squire, a prioress, a monk, a friar, a student, and other clerical types, some urban dwellers and some country folk. The stories vary from highly edifying narratives to humorous tales of sex and scandal.

Christine de Pisan (1364–c.1440) was Chaucer's contemporary. Her father had come from Italy and served as a court astrologer. He educated his daughter in Latin as well as French. When her husband died, leaving her a young widow with children to raise, she turned to translating texts, including an ancient work on warfare, and writing poetry for patrons. Among her books was *The City of Ladies,* in which she discussed heroic and learned women from the past who could serve as role models for contemporary young women. It also showed that the prevalent view of both lay and clerical writers on the female nature was biased against women. The male au-

when Dante reached heaven, St. Peter encouraged him to speak about the degeneration of the papacy.

In England the greatest author was Geoffrey Chaucer (c. 1342–1400). Chaucer was born in London, and the English that he wrote reflects the rich mixture of Old English and French that was used in the capital and that became the basis for stan-

thors of the Middle Ages classified women as either resembling the Virgin Mary or Eve. Needless to say, most women were portrayed as Eve—given to lust and incapable of ruling themselves.

The production of art was also taking a new turn. Architecture, sculpture, and stained glass windows had previously been commissioned by the Church for public consumption. The miniatures that illustrated prayer books and other texts were the only works of art that were made solely for more private enjoyment. But in the 14th and 15th centuries, pious people began to commission works of art including illustrated books, altarpieces, and even portraits for their own use. Datini was typical of those who provided artwork for private consumption. He brought paintings and carvings from Italy to sell in Avignon.

During this period, Italian art was heading in new directions with the introduction of the technique of bronze casting. An early master of bronze sculpture, Donatello made an equerry statue of a Venetian general showing him fully armed as a Roman soldier sitting on a horse posed with one of its legs raised. But most striking in Italian art were the frescoes, or paintings on the plaster of church walls.

Paintings and sculptures also more realistically depicted their subjects. This movement toward realism predated the strong influence of classical art that characterized the Renaissance. In Flanders a northern European style became popular and spread to England, Norway, Sweden, and Germany. Jan van Eyck was noted for his realistic portraits, and a number of other artists contributed to a particular style of Flemish painting and carving.

Warfare did not interfere with the development of art, architecture, and literature. The Hundred Years' War was one of phases rather than continuous fighting. In the beginning of the 15th century, however, the war once again became a serious matter. Henry V (1387–1422) had dreams of repeating the glories of the battle of Crécy and the heroism of Edward III's reign. The king of France had bouts of insanity and could not control the factious nobles who divided the realm, presenting Henry with an opportunity to attack. When Henry landed with about 10,000 troops in Normandy, the French responded with the same tactics that they had used at Crécy, with the same disastrous results. Meeting the English at Agincourt in 1415, the French knights charged right into the volley of arrows from the English longbowmen and suffered defeat. The French, already politically divided, made a disadvantageous treaty with Henry at Troyes in 1420. Under this treaty the heir to the throne of France, the Dauphin (prince) Charles, was declared illegitimate and ineligible to inherit the throne. Henry married the Dauphin's sister Catherine, and the treaty stipulated that their child would inherit the thrones of both England and France. The dream of Edward III—who had decorated his shield with the lions of England and the fleurs-de-liys of France—became a reality when Henry VI (1421–1471) of England and France was born.

Holding on to the territory of France, however, was a problem. Henry V died young, when Henry VI was only an infant. An alliance between the English and the dukes of Burgundy, who now ruled Flanders, was met with deepening hostility among the French population. An amazing series of events ultimately drove the English from France. Dauphin Charles was only 15 when he fled south after the battle of Agincourt. In maturity he was a weak-willed man, who accepted the implications of the Treaty of Troyes that he was a bastard. A young peasant girl, Joan of Arc, is credited with giving him the courage to act as a real king of France. Although a woman and of peasant origins, she dressed in the armor of a knight and went to see Charles. His fortunes were so low that he was willing to listen to this strange girl who claimed to have heard the voices of saints telling her to rescue France. Under her guidance the course of the war changed. Orléans, one of France's major cities, was rescued from siege, and Charles was officially crowned king of the French. Joan, however, was captured and burned as a heretic in 1431. To King Charles's shame, he made no attempt to rescue his benefactress. The French, however, continued to fight the long battle to defeat the English. By 1453 the Hundred Year's War finally ended. Of the English Angevin Empire, only the port city of Calais was left.

By the time of the defeat, England was embroiled in civil wars, which have become known as the Wars of the Roses. Henry VI's insanity contributed to a dynastic fight among the descendants of Edward III and Philippa. The successive dukes of York, whose family badge was a white rose,

Joan of Arc: Peasant Girl Saves France

Much of what is known about Joan of Arc comes from her testimony at her trial for heresy in 1431. She was born in the village of Domrémy in eastern France. Her father was a well-to-do peasant, but she was not literate. Her early life included games, sewing, spinning, and prayers.

But this tranquil life was periodically interrupted by incursions of Burgundians who looted the countryside. During these attacks, the local people went to fortified cities for safety. According to her trial transcript, Joan began having visions that urged her to make an appeal to King Charles and rescue France from the Burgundians and the English: "Two or three times a week the voice said she must leave and go into France . . . she must raise the siege then being made of the city of Orléans." She persuaded one of the king's captains that she was serious, and he gave her a suit of

Joan of Arc favored armor and male attire, but medieval artists found this so repulsive that they represented her in female dress.

armor and an escort to Charles. She convinced him to give her troops to attack the city's besiegers. She herself did not fight, but she provided encouragement and the siege was relieved.

After this success in warfare, she encouraged Charles to go to Rheims and have himself properly crowned king as the French kings before him had done. The French gained new resolve from this move and continued to fight against the En-

glish and Burgundians. Joan was captured by the Burgundians and the English had her put on trial for witchcraft and heresy in a Burgundian church court. After a vigorous self-defense she finally confessed but took back her confession. She was burned in the public square in 1431. Charles did nothing to defend or rescue her. Although she immediately became the symbol of resistance for France, she was not made a saint until 1923.

claimed the throne by virtue of the third son of Edward III. The Lancastrians also maintained they had a right to the crown because they descended from the fourth son of Edward III and their line included Henry V and his son Henry VI. (Popular custom assigned the red rose to this party.) The wars were fought largely between contenders for the throne and their noble adherents. During their course, such notable characters as the Yorkist Richard III emerged as historical figures. His claim to the throne

was encumbered by two young nephews who were in direct succession before him. When they disappeared into the Tower of London, he was accused of having them murdered. Finally, in 1485 Henry Tudor defeated Richard at the battle of Bosworth Field. He became Henry VII, the founder of the Tudor dynasty. Richard fought gallantly to the end and died on the battlefield. In his play *Richard III,* Shakespeare was certainly wrong in portraying him as a coward who in his final moments called out, "A horse, a horse. My kingdom for a horse."

Throughout this period the Church provided little political or spiritual leadership. The popes continued to live in Avignon, but the critics of the papacy were becoming more and more insistent. Two women who eventually became saints, Brigitte of Sweden and Catherine of Siena, urged the popes to reform and return to Rome. Political theorists at universities were arguing that the Church should be governed by a council composed of laymen as well as clergy. They also maintained that the papacy should not be the dominant power in the religion or politics of Europe.

Even more serious were the attacks of John Wycliffe (c. 1330–1384), an ordained priest and professor at Oxford University. Increasingly, he argued that the papacy was corrupt and deviated from the early Church. He placed his belief in the authority of the Bible rather than the later pronouncements of popes, and he favored direct prayer rather than reliance on priests to intervene between Christ and Christians. His theology was so radical that he quickly came to be regarded as a heretic. Because he felt that the clergy should experience the poverty of the early apostles, he recommended the confiscation of church property. This position won favor at the English royal court, and he was protected from prosecution.

Wycliffe soon won followers in England, but more important were the students who brought his ideas from Oxford University to Prague University. In Prague Jan Hus, a young theologian, became attracted to Wycliffe's ideas and began to make them popular with the laity as well as the university community. His movement became tied up in politics and the revolt of the Bohemians (Czechs) against their German rulers.

While the theological attacks and popular lampoons against the papacy continued, the papacy became more and more mired in corruption. In 1378 Pope Gregory XI returned to Rome at the urging of Catherine of Siena, but he died that same year. Pressured by a Roman mob that broke into the voting chamber, the College of Cardinals selected an Italian pope. With the encouragement of the French king, the cardinals returned to Avignon and elected a French pope. Neither pope would abdicate, and the Great Schism began with a pope in Rome and a pope in Avignon. When these popes died, their respective Colleges of Cardinals selected another pope in each of their places.

Needless to say, the scandal of the Great Schism was immense. St. Peter could hardly have two voices on earth offering competing jurisdictions. The laity were concerned that since the schism no one had gone to heaven and baptisms were no longer removing original sin. With resources spread between the two popes, papal fundraising became even more voracious.

Finally, in 1409 a council was held in Pisa to resolve the schism. The council was intended to depose the two popes and elect a new one, but neither pope would abdicate. The third pope claimed that he was the only legitimate one because the Council of Pisa had elected him. With three popes and three colleges of cardinals, it was apparent that the Church could not reform itself. Emperor Sigismund of Germany called a council at Constance representing laity and clergy from all over Europe to resolve the schism, reform the Church, and get rid of heresy.

The Council of Constance managed to depose all three popes and elect an Italian pope who was acceptable to Rome and a newly formed College of Cardinals. The Council next turned to the question of Jan Hus. He was given safe conduct to Constance in order to defend his views. Thinking that he would receive a fair hearing because the Council was dedicated to reform, he came of his free will. Emperor Sigismund, however, had little sympathy for him because he had been at the heart of the Bohemian revolt. Hus was tried as a heretic and burned. Even Wycliffe was condemned, and his bones were dug up and burned. Having solved the two easier problems, the Council disbanded without taking up the larger problem of church reform.

One of the distinctive features of the earlier Church had been that new monastic movements took the lead in reforming the

Medieval urban residents often did not have a kitchen in their quarters and relied on the equivalent of "fast food." Two men moved an oven on a cart around the city and a woman made fresh bread and meat pies for customers. Other women sold prepared goods outside of shops. The shop sign shows that pretzels were available and the table indicates the availability of beer or wine (in the flask) and loaves of bread.

Catherine of Siena: The Saint who Confronted the Pope

Born in 1347, Catherine of Siena was the 24th child of a wool-dyer and his wife. Living just down the hill from a Dominican church, Catherine resisted all her parents' efforts to persuade her to lead a normal life and marry. Early on she instead embraced self-sacrifice in order to show her devotion to God. She scalded herself in hot baths, developed skin problems, and withdrew from her family. She fasted and rejected meat entirely. She was, perhaps, anorexic, because her biographer reported seeing her stuff twigs down her throat to bring up food. He wrote: "I myself saw it happen, not once, but again and again, that her emaciated body would be reduced to the last extremity, unable to take anything to restore its forces but a drink of cold water . . . and then suddenly she would seize . . . an opportunity of taking on some work for the honor of God's name or the good of souls, and like a flash, without the help of any other restorative [food] . . . all her forces would revive." She said in her letters that she was afflicted by God so that she would understand suffering and be purged of her gluttony.

Catherine kept a close association with the Dominicans all her life but did not become a nun. She preferred to go out into the world and work with the poor and sick. On one occasion she angered her father by giving away his best wine, but the cask was miraculously refilled. Catherine was educated and wrote extensively in Italian. Her works include 400 letters and a dialogue about her mystical experiences. In the dialogue God provided answers to a Christian soul about questions regarding reform of the Church and salvation of souls. In 1376 she went to Avignon and helped persuade the pope to return to Rome. Unfortunately, his return led to the Great Schism, which was in progress when in 1380 Catherine died from a stroke at the age of 33.

Church, but the 14th and 15th centuries saw no such internal reforms. The laity were no less religious than they had been in earlier centuries, but now they sought their salvation through personal spiritual exercises. They joined guilds in their parish that supported charity and funeral services for their members and said prayers for the souls of dead brothers and sisters. They also went on pilgrimages and followed personal devotions that imitated the life of Christ. While much of the wealth that people accumulated in the 15th century did go toward supporting religious projects, their funds were more likely to be given to a parish church and spent on personal devotions than offered to the papacy. Wycliffe and Hus had spoken for the larger laity when they suggested that the Bible rather the pope be a guide rather the pope.

By the 15th century the Bible had been translated into the vernacular languages. The invention of the printing press made the Bible even more available to an increasingly literate laity. The use of paper was perhaps as important as the invention of moveable, metal type. Parchment, a product made from sheepskin, was laborious to prepare and, therefore, very expensive. Paper, which was invented in China, decreased the costs of book production because even rags could be used to make it. The use of the printing press (whose design was derived from the wine press) and type also made books cheaper to produce. Johann Gutenberg published the Bible in about 1455 as one of the first printed books. As printing shops became common, translations of the Bible, grammar books, and works of literature soon became available throughout Europe.

Another invention, the cannon, played a decisive role in the fall of the last vestige of the old Roman Empire. In 1453 Constantinople fell to the Ottoman Turks. The Turks had surrounded the city after taking the territory of Asia Minor (modern Turkey) before moving into the Balkans and Greece. Finally, only the great walled city stood as a symbol of the power of the Roman Empire. Using cannons, which had first been experimented with during sieges in the Hundred Years' War, and other siege engines, the Turks forced the city to surrender, and Constantinople became the Moslem city of Istanbul. The fall of Constantinople seemed cataclysmic to Europeans, who had regarded themselves as part of the long continuum of Roman traditions and political life. Now this was broken, and a distant power, Muscovy, claimed to be the Third Rome. The new rulers called themselves caesars, or "tsars" in Russian. The patriarch of Moscow replaced the patriarch of Constantinople as the chief official of the Orthodox Church.

For all the major calamities, there was also an irrepressible feeling of opportunity during the 14th and 15th centuries. The vernacular languages made literature and learning available to a greater number of people, and the printing press allowed more people to own and read books. People exploited new ways of satisfying their desires—some by being more aggressive as traders, others by eating better because there were fewer mouths to feed, or by dressing in more luxurious cloth because it was more readily available. Still others built larger, more spacious homes.

The emphasis on individual salvation seemed to spill over into the possibilities of individual achievements. Inventions suggested new horizons. Perhaps even the fall of Constantinople suggested a new need to know what was beyond Europe in all directions. Befitting this climate of curiosity and optimism, the 15th century closed with the beginnings of an age of exploration, including Portuguese explorations around the coast of Africa and the discovery of the continents in the west (the Americas) by Christopher Columbus. Once again, Europe was expanding its horizons as it had done in the 11th century.

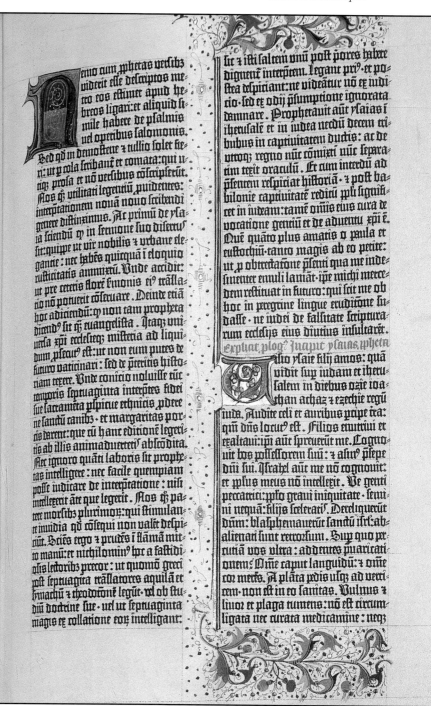

The Biblia Latina *was published about 1455 by Johann Gutenberg and Johan Fust in Mainz, Germany. Gutenberg was a goldsmith who experimented with moveable metal type and a printing press. This Latin Bible was printed on vellum (treated calfskin) rather than paper and was illuminated by hand in the manner of medieval manuscripts.*

Chronology

300
Franks and Alamans settle on the Rhine

303
Emperor Diocletian issues edict persecuting Christians

313
Emperor Constantine converts to Christianity at the Battle of Milvian Bridge and grants toleration to Christians

325
Council of Nicaea rejects Arianism and issues Nicene Creed

330
Emperor Constantine moves capital of Roman Empire to Constantinople (former site of Greek town of Byzantium)

342–348
Ulfilas translates the New Testament into Gothic and becomes a missionary; converts the Goths to the Arian heresy.

360
Huns invade Europe

364
The Roman Empire is divided along the Danube into western and eastern halves

378
Visigoths, settled within borders of Eastern Empire, defeat the Byzantine army

386–420
St. Jerome translates the Bible into Latin

400 and thereafter
Franks, Alamans, Burgundians and Vandals cross Rhine into Gaul; Vandals move on to Spain

401
Visigoths, under leadership of Alaric, invade Italy

406
Burgundians found kingdom on the Rhone

410
Visigoths sack Rome
Roman legions withdraw from England

416
Visigoths invade Spain

c. 420
St. Augustine writes *The City of God*

433–453
Attila leads the Huns in their attacks on Europe

440–461
Pope Leo I persuades Attila not to attack Rome

c. 450
Saxons, Angles, and Jutes invade Britain

455
Vandals sack Rome

c. 471–526
Theodoric reigns as king of the Ostrogoths and invades Italy in 488

476
The Western Roman Empire comes to an end

480–524
Boethius, a Roman in the service of Theodoric, writes *The Consolation of Philosophy* in prison before his execution

c. 475
Apollinaris Sidonius, a Roman bishop, writes letters to his fellow Romans in Gaul

510
Clovis, king of the Franks, converts to Christianity

511
Clovis dies and the Merovingian kingdom in France is divided among his sons

527–565
Justinian I, the Great, and his wife Theodora (d. 548) rule the Byzantine Empire, commission the *Codex Justinianus*, build Hagia Sophia, and finance military campaigns to regain the Western Empire

529
St. Benedict founds monastery at Mt. Cassino in Italy

537
Arthur, semi-legendary king of the Britons, killed in battle

539–562
War between Persia and the Byzantine Empire ends in victory for the Byzantines

540
Cassiodorus founds a monastery to copy manuscripts

542
Plague in the western Europe and the Byzantine Empire

568–572
Lombards invade and conquer northern Italy

596
Pope Gregory I, the Great, dispatches missionaries to England

610–632
Muhammad hears the word of God and recounts it to his followers; Islam is born

622
Muhammad emigrates to Medina (the Hegira), marking the advent of the Islamic calendar

624
Muhammad's followers defeat Meccans. Arabs unify under Islam

632
Arabic expansion into the Byzantine Empire begins

643–711
Arabs take possession of North Africa

664
Synod of Whitby unites Christians of England under the Pope, ending the strong Irish influence

714
Charles Martel becomes mayor of the palace under the Merovingians

717–18
Constantinople repulses major Arabic attack

730
Venerable Bede completes ecclesiastical history of England

732
Charles Martel stops Arabic expansion in the west at the Battle of Tours and Poitiers

751
Pépin the Short becomes king of the Franks (first of the Carolingian dynasty)

768
Charles the Great becomes king of the Franks

790
Alcuin becomes head of the Frankish court school

Golden period of Arabic learning in Baghdad during reign of Harun al-Rashid

787
Vikings begin their attacks on England

787
Vikings attack monastery of Lindisfarne

800
Pope Leo III crowns Charlemagne emperor

Irene rules in Byzantium

Harun al-Rashid sends an embassy to court of Charlemagne

Development of "Carolingian" minuscule writing

814
Charlemagne dies and his son, Louis the Pious, becomes king

825
Swedish Vikings establish bases on the Volga and Dnieper rivers in Russia and trade with Constantinople

835
Danes begin their attacks on England

840
Louis the Pious dies and divides his empire among his three sons: Lothair, Louis the German, and Charles the Bald

840
Norwegians attack Ireland and found Dublin

842
Louis the German and Charles the Bald swear oath in each other's language: first written example of German and French

843
Treaty of Verdun divides the Carolingian Empire among Lothair (middle kingdom and title of emperor), Louis the German (eastern, German speaking part), and Charles the Bald (western, French speaking part)

846
Arabs sack Rome and pillage southern coast of France

860
Danes invade England and France

862
Rus state is established at Novgorod

863
The missionary Cyril develops Cyrilic alphabet

874
Alfred becomes king of Wessex

874
Vikings occupy Iceland

886
Alfred defeats Danes and recognizes boundary of Danelaw

Vikings attack Paris

c. 890
Magyars attack Central Europe

900
Feudal system begins to develop

910
Duke of Aquitaine establishes monastery of Cluny

911
Carolingian line ends in Germany; Carolingian king in France gives Danes the province of Normandy

c. 937
Roswitha of Gandersheim (Germany) is born; becomes nun and playwright

962
Otto I, the Great, revives the empire in Germany, crowned emperor by pope

987
Last Carolingian on French throne is succeeded by Hugh Capet, first of the Capetian dynasty

988
Vladimir of Kiev marries a Byzantine princess and converts to Christianity

999
Gerbert of Aurillac becomes Pope Sylvester II

c. 1000
Norwegian Vikings reach North American coast

1016
Danish conqueror Canute becomes king of England and Norway

1020
Venice, Genoa, and Pisa emerge as powerful cities in Italy

c. 1025
Romanesque architecture reaches its height

1035
William the Bastard becomes duke of Normandy

1054
Great Schism occurs between Rome and Constantinople.

1059
A papal decree announces that all future popes will be elected by the College of Cardinals

1065
Henry IV of Germany becomes king

1066
Edward, king of England, dies; William of Normandy launches successful invasion of England, becoming king

1073
Gregory VII (the monk Hildebrand) becomes pope

1076
Gregory VII excommunicates Henry IV

1077
Henry IV travels to Canossa as a penitent

1091
Normans conquer Sicily

1095
Pope Urban II preaches the First Crusade

1096
First Crusade begins

1099
Crusaders take Jerusalem and establish the Latin Kingdom of Jersualem

1100
William Rufus dies and Henry I becomes king of England

1115
St. Bernard founds Clairvaux monastery

1119
Bologna University is established

1120
Scholastic philosophy becomes fully developed

Troubadour poetry and music develop

1122
Concordat of Worms settles the Investiture Controversy

1137
Louis VII of France ascends the throne

1142
Peter Abelard, scholastic philosopher, who wrote letters to Héloïse, *Sic et Non*, and *The History of My Misfortunes*, dies

1147-1149
Second Crusade fails

1150
University of Paris is established

1152
Louis VII and Eleanor of Aquitaine divorce and she marries Henry (II) of England

1154
Henry II ascends throne of England

1160
Vernacular literature develops

1162
Frederick I Barbarossa destroys Milan

1167
Frederick I Barbarossa is crowned emperor

1170
Thomas Becket, archbishop of Canterbury, is murdered by knights of Henry II

1173
Waldensian movement begins in Lyons

1179
Hildegard of Bingen, writer of music, medical tracts, and mystical works, dies

1189–1192
Richard I of England, Philip II Augustus of France, and Frederick I Barbarossa of Germany lead the Third Crusade

1198–1216
Pontificate of Innocent III marks height of medieval papacy

1202–04
Crusaders defeats Byzantine Empire and take Constantinople in Fourth Crusade

1207–08
Order of St. Francis is formed

1208–29
Crusade against the Albigensian heretics

1209
Cambridge University is founded

1215
King John I of England is defeated at the Battle of Runnymede and signs the Magna Carta

Innocent III calls the Fourth Lateran Council to reform the Church

1217–54
St. Louis leads unsuccessful crusades

1220
Frederick II is crowned Emperor of Germany; he is also king of Sicily

1228
Frederick II makes treaty with Moslems on a crusade in Holy Land

1233
Pope Gregory IX begins Inquisition for trial of Albigensian heretics

1265
Simon de Montfort calls Parliament in England: first time representatives of lords, knights and burgesses meet in two houses

1273
Thomas Aquinas writes *Summa Theologica*

Rudolph of Hapsburg is elected Emperor of Germany

1282
Sicilians revolt against Charles of Anjou in the Sicilian Vespers

1291
Swiss cantons form Swiss Confederation

1292
Marco Polo returns to Italy from China

1302
Philip IV the Fair convenes first Estates General in France at which all three estates (nobility, clergy, and commoners) are represented

Boniface VIII fights with Edward I of England and Philip IV over taxing clergy

1305
Clement V becomes pope and moves the papacy to Avignon

c. 1321
Dante completes the *Divine Comedy*

1337
Outbreak of the Hundred Years' War between England and France

1348–53
Boccaccio writes *The Decameron*

1348–50
Black Death or bubonic plague peaks

1358
Revolt of French peasants, the Jacquerie

1378
Great Schism in papacy begins with two popes

1381
Peasants' Revolt in England

c. 1387
Chaucer begins *The Canterbury Tales*

1414–18
Council of Constance ends Great Schism and pope returns to Rome

Jan Hus is burned as a heretic

1415
Henry V defeats French at Agincourt

1431
Joan of Arc is burned at Rouen

c. 1450
Invention of printing and moveable type

1453
Hundred Years' War ends
Constantinople falls to Turks

1485
Henry Tudor defeats Richard III at Battle of Bosworth Field and starts the Tudor line as Henry VII

1492
Ferdinand and Isabella of Spain finance the voyage of Christopher Columbus

Glossary

archbishop—a bishop in charge of a province that includes a number of bishops and their dioceses. He also exercises ecclesiastical law and authority in his own diocese.

Arianism—the belief that Christ was of a different substance from God and that they should not be worshiped as equal. Based on the teachings of Arius, a priest in Alexandria, the Arianist movement of the late 3rd and 4th centuries gained a considerable following. Arianism was declared a heresy at the Council of Nicaea in 325.

Black Death—the bubonic plague that appeared in the 6th and the 14th centuries in Europe. This bacterial disease was spread by the bite of a flea that lived on the common house rat. The signs of the disease were swellings (bubos) and the clotting of blood under the skin, giving the appearance of black blotches and hence the name, Black Death. (There was also a pneumonic variety of the disease.)

baptism—a cleansing ritual that among Christians symbolizes the washing away of the original sin of Adam and Eve in their defiance of God's commands. John the Baptist is traditionally credited with having baptized Jesus. In the Middle Ages, infant baptism was most common, but during the period of conversions, Clovis, King of the Franks, and many other converts received baptism as adults.

canon law—laws or rules regarding ecclesiastical doctrine and practice. In the Middle Ages, it was based on scripture, church councils, rules of religious orders, and, in the Roman Catholic Church, papal decrees. The body of canon law was organized and collected by Gratian (who died in 140), an Italian legal scholar whose work is known as the *Decretum*.

Catholic, catholic—with a capital *C,* the word refers to the Roman Catholic Church; with a lowercase *c,* it refers to something universal or general. The Roman Catholic Church used *catholic* and the Eastern Orthodox Church used *orthodox* to refer to the universality of their religious doctrines and to their religious correctness.

cathedral—the main church of a diocese; the church of a bishop or archbishop. Cathedrals tended to be larger than other churches and are some of the most famous architectural remains of the Middle Ages. The cathedra was the bishop's chair.

Codex Justianus—a collection of Roman laws and decrees that governed commercial transactions, criminal law, and the relationship of the emperor to the people. The *Codex Justianus,* properly called the *Corpus Juris Civilis,* was commissioned by the Byzantine emperor Justinian in the 6th century. It formed the basis of western European commercial law when it was brought west and widely studied in the 12th century. In addition to the *Codex,* Justinian's jurists also compiled a book of jurisprudence called the *Digest*.

commitatus—the fighting unit of the Germanic tribes described by Roman historian Tacitus in the first century A.D. Each commitatus had a leader who, because of his success in battle, was able to surround himself with armed fighters. They were loyal to him and did not leave the field as long as he was alive. In return, the leader provided them with spoils of war, including weapons and horses.

crucifixion—a common mode of execution in the Roman Empire. In a crucifixion, the hands and feet of a criminal were nailed or tied to a cross, and the offender was left to die in public view. According to the Gospels, Jesus was executed in this manner.

diocese—an administrative unit or a province in the Roman Empire. The Church adopted the term, and it became associated with a bishop. The diocese was a geographical area over which a bishop had jurisdiction. His responsibilities there included the ordaining of priests, administration of canon law, and oversight of monasteries. The symbols of the bishop's office were a ring and a staff (crozier) in the shape of a shepherd's crook, which indicated his care for all Christians in his "flock."

Doctors of the Church—early theologians of Christianity—such as Augustine of Hippo, Ambrose of Milan, Jerome, and Gregory the Great—who made essential contributions to the formulation of Christian thought.

Eucharist—the chief sacrament among Christians, which commemorates the last supper Jesus had with the apostles before his arrest and crucifixion. Derived from the Greek word for "thanksgiving," the Eucharist is also known as communion.

Germanic tribes—a group of loosely knit tribes—including the Anglo-Saxons, Franks, Burgundians, Alamani, and Swabians—who spoke languages in what is now known as the Germanic linguistic group and also shared customs, modes of warfare, economic systems, and religious beliefs. These peoples lived on the borders of the Roman Empire in the first century A.D., when Roman historian Tacitus wrote of them in a book titled *Germania*. They invaded the western Roman Empire in the late fourth and fifth centuries.

Gospels—the first four books of the New Testament, whose authors are traditionally believed to be the disciples Matthew, Mark, Luke, and John. The Gospels provide information on Jesus' life and spiritual teachings.

Gothic tribes—a group of loosely knit tribes—including the Vandals, Visigoths (west Goths), and Ostrogoths (east Goths)—who had their origins in Scandinavia and spoke a language in what is now known as the Germanic linguistic group. They swept east through central Europe and were forced into the western Roman Empire by the advance of the Huns in the 5th century.

heresy—the adoption of a set of principles at variance with those established or generally accepted. In the Middle Ages, people who accepted views that were contrary to those of the established church were regarded as heretics and their views as heretical. Among the largest groups of heretics were the Arians, Cathars, and Lollards (the followers of John Wycliffe).

Huns—a nomadic group from central Asia that was driven west by famines and forced the Goths into the Roman Empire. They entered the empire themselves under the leadership of Attila the Hun in the fifth century.

Koran—the religious book of Islam, which consists of the teachings of Muhammad and parts of the Old and New Testament. It is the moral and religious guide for the followers of Allah, or Muslims.

monastery—a house for religious seclusion whose residents withdraw from the world in order to concentrate on prayer and devotion. In the Middle Ages, monasteries contained religious communities whose members observed set rules and lived, worked, and prayed together. The Rule of St. Benedict was the most common monastic rule in the western medieval Church. The Rule of St. Basil was more common in the Eastern Orthodox Church. Monasteries were also known as abbeys, priories, nunneries, and convents. The head of these establishments was an abbot, an abbess, a prior or a prioress.

Mythras—a semi-divine figure who was the inspiration for the mystery cult of Mythracism. The cult flourished in the Roman Empire in the 2nd and 3rd centuries. Mythras symbolized the god of the sun, and the cult offered ethical precepts for living, the idea that Mythras was resurrected, baptism with bulls' blood, and salvation and eternal life for his followers.

Nicaean Creed or Nicene Creed—a creed repeated in many Christian churches that states that Christ, God, and the Holy Ghost are all of one substance and are all divine. It emerged from the Council of Nicaea of 325, during which a group of bishops led by Emperor Constantine examined Arianism and the disputes it had caused over the relationship of Christ to God. The council formulated the concept of the Holy Trinity and determined that Arianism, which held that Christ and God could not both be divine, was a heresy.

Orthodox, orthodox—with a capital *O*, the word refers to the Eastern Orthodox Church; with a lowercase *o*, it refers to the approved and generally accepted religious beliefs or doctrines of faith. The term Eastern Orthodox Church came into use in the 8th century to describe the Byzantine and Slavic churches. Although its beliefs were very close to the western version of Christianity, the Eastern Orthodox Church did not accept the authority of the Roman popes.

pagan—a heathen, or one who worships idols and false gods. In the Middle Ages, Christians considered as pagans those who worshiped either the Roman or Greek pantheon of Gods—including Jupiter, Mars, and Venus—or the Germanic gods, such as Woden, Thor, and Tiu.

plebeians—the common people or lower ranks of ancient and imperial Rome. The plebeians were free citizens who were not patricians (senators). Their representatives met as an assembly, whereas those of the patricians met in the senate.

rhetoric—the art of effective argument in prose, verse, or oratory. Knowledge of rhetoric was regarded as essential training in the Greek, Roman, and medieval periods, during which oral and written arguments were considered equally important.

Romance languages—those languages that are based on Latin, such as Italian, French, Spanish, and Romanian. English is a combination of Germanic and French roots.

senator—a title held by upper-class Romans that gave them considerable control over the army, government, and economy of ancient Rome and the Roman Empire.

Further Reading

General History and References

Barraclough, G. *The Origins of Modern Germany*. New York: Norton, 1984.

Bunson, Matthew. *Encyclopedia of the Middle Ages*. New York: Facts on File, 1995.

Collins, Roger. *Early Medieval Europe, 300–1000*. New York: St. Martin's, 1991.

Duby, Georges. *France in the Middle Ages, 987–1460*. Translated by Juliet Vale. Cambridge, Mass.: Blackwell, 1991.

Hollister, C. Warren. *The Making of England, 55 B.C. to 1399*. 6th ed. Lexington, Mass.: D.C. Heath, 1992.

Hyde, J. K. *Society and Politics in Medieval Italy*. New York: St. Martin's, 1973.

Jordan, William Chester, ed. *The Middle Ages: An Encyclopedia for Children*. New York: Scribner, 1996.

Kibler, William W., et al., eds. *Medieval France: An Encyclopedia*. New York: Garland, 1995.

Le Goff, Jacques. *Medieval Civilization, 400–1500*. Translated by Julia Barrow. New York: Blackwell, 1988.

Nicholas, David. *The Evolution of the Medieval World: Society, Government, and Thought in Europe, 312–1500*. New York: Longman, 1992.

———. *Medieval Flanders*. New York: Longman, 1992.

O'Callaghan, Joseph F. *A History of Medieval Spain*. Ithaca: Cornell University Press, 1975.

Power, Eileen. *Medieval People*. New York: Harper & Row, 1963.

Pulsiano, Phillip, et al., eds. *Medieval Scandinavia: An Encyclopedia*. New York: Garland, 1993

Riché, Pierre. *Daily Life in the World of Charlemagne*. Translated by Jo Ann McNamara. Philadelphia: University of Pennsylvania Press, 1978.

Strayer, Joseph R., ed. *Dictionary of the Middle Ages*. New York: Scribner, 1982–89.

Szarmach, Paul E., M. Teresa Tavormina, and Joel T. Rosenthal. *Medieval England: An Encyclopedia*. New York: Garland, 1998.

Primary Sources

Alfred the Great. Translated and introduced by Simon Keynes and Michael Lapidge. New York: Penguin, 1983.

Augustine, bishop of Hippo. *City of God*. Translated by Marcus Dods. New York: The Modern Library, 1950.

———. *Confessions*. Translated by Henry Chadwick. New York: Oxford University Press, 1991.

Bede, the Venerable. *A History of the English Church and People*. Translated by Leo Sherley-Price. Harmondsworth: Penguin, 1968.

Comnena, Anna. *The Alexiad of Anna Comnena*. Translated and Introduced by E. R. A. Sewter. New York: Penguin, 1969.

Einhard and Notker the Stammerer. *Two Lives of Charlemagne*. Translated by Lewis Thorpe. London: Penguin, 1969.

Eusebius. *The History of the Church from Christ to Constantine*. Translated by G. A. Williamson. New York: Penguin, 1989.

Francis of Assisi. *Francis and Clare: The Complete Works*. Translated and introduced by Regis J. Armstrong and Ignatius C. Brady. New York: Paulist Press, 1982.

Froissart, Jean. *Chronicles*. Translated by Geoffrey Brereton. Baltimore: Penguin, 1978.

Gregory the Great. *Dialogues*. New York: Fathers of the Church, 1959.

Gregory of Tours. *History of the Franks*. Translated by Lewis Thorpe. New York: Penguin Books, 1974.

Joinville and Villehardouin. *Chronicle of the Crusades*. Baltimore: Penguin, 1963.

The Letters of Abelard and Heloise. Translated by Betty Radice. New York: Viking Penguin, 1974.

The Book of Margery Kempe. Translated by B. A. Windeatt. New York: Viking Penguin, 1985.

Polo, Marco. *The Travels*. Translated and introduced by Ronald Latham. Baltimore: Penguin, 1958.

Stenton, Frank, et al. *The Bayeux Tapestry: A Comprehensive Survey*. New York: Phaidon, 1957.

Sturluson, Snorri. *King Harald's Saga: Harald Hardradi of Norway*. Translated by Magnus Magnusson and Hermann Pálsson. Harmondsworth: Penguin, 1966.

Suger, Abbot. *The Deeds of Louis the Fat*. Translated by Richard Cusimano and John Moorhead. Washington, D.C.: Catholic University of America Press, 1992.

Tacitus, Cornelius. *The Histories*. Translated by Kenneth Wellesley. Baltimore: Penguin, 1975.

Teresa of Avila. *The Life of Saint Teresa of Avila by Herself*. Translated and Introduced by J. M. Cohen. New York: Penguin, 1988.

Germanic Tribes

Burns, Thomas. *A History of the Ostrogoths*. Bloomington: Indiana University Press, 1984.

Campbell, James, ed. *The Anglo-Saxons*. Ithaca: Cornell University Press, 1982.

Christie, Neil. *The Lombards*. Cambridge, Mass.: Blackwell, 1995.

Heather, Peter. *The Goths*. Cambridge, Mass.: Blackwell, 1996.

James, Edward. *The Franks*. Cambridge, Mass.: Blackwell, 1991.

Jones, Gwyn. *A History of the Vikings*. New York: Oxford University Press, 1984.

Manchen-Helfen, J. O. *The World of the Huns*. Berkeley: University of California Press, 1973.

Thompson, E. A. *The Goths in Spain*. Oxford: Clarendon Press, 1969.

Todd, Malcolm. *The Early Germans*. Cambridge, Mass.: Blackwell, 1992.

Wolfram, Herwig. *History of the Goths*. Translated by Thomas J. Dunlap. Berkeley: University of California Press, 1979.

Monarchies

Bisson, Thomas N. *The Medieval Crown of Aragon*. Oxford: Clarendon Press, 1986.

Duckett, Eleanor Shipley. *Carolingian Portraits: A Study in the Ninth Century*. Ann Arbor: University of Michigan Press, 1962.

Fawtier, Robert. *The Capetian Kings of France*. New York: St. Martin's, 1960.

Gillingham, John. *The Angevin Empire*. New York: Holmes & Meier, 1984.

Riché, Pierre. *The Carolingians: A Family Who Forged Europe*. Philadelphia: University of Pennsylvania Press, 1993.

Wallace-Hadrill, J. M. *Early Germanic Kingship in England and on the Continent*. Oxford: Clarendon Press, 1971.

Religion

Brooke, Rosalind, and Christopher Brooke. *Popular Religion in the Middle Ages*. London: Thames & Hudson, 1985.

Brown, Peter. *Augustine of Hippo: A Biography*. Berkeley: University of California Press, 1967.

Bynum, Caroline Walker. *Holy Feast and Holy Fast: The Religious Significance of Food to Medieval Women*. Berkeley: University of California Press, 1987.

————. *Jesus as Mother: Studies in the Spirituality of the High Middle Ages*. Berkeley: University of California Press, 1982.

Duckett, Eleanor. *The Wandering Saints of the Early Middle Ages*. New York: Norton, 1959.

Ferguson, Everett, ed. *Encyclopedia of Early Christianity*. New York: Garland, 1990.

Hamilton, Bernard. *Religion in the Medieval West*. London: Edward Arnold, 1986.

Hilgarth, J. N., ed. *Christianity and Paganism, 350–750: The Conversion of Western Europe*. Philadelphia: University of Pennsylvania Press, 1986.

Jones, A. H. M. *Constantine and the Conversion of Europe*. New York: Collier Books, 1962.

Lambert, Malcolm. *Medieval Heresy: Popular Movements from the Gregorian Reform to the Reformation*. 2nd ed. Cambridge, Mass.: Blackwell, 1992.

Lawrence, C. H. *The Friars: The Impact of the Early Mendicant Movement on Western Society*. New York: Longman, 1994.

Lynch, Joseph H. *The Medieval Church: A Brief History*. New York: Longman, 1992.

Oakley, Francis. *The Western Church in the Later Middle Ages*. Ithaca: Cornell University Press, 1979.

Southern, R. W. *Western Society and the Church in the Middle Ages*. New York: Penguin, 1977.

Ward, Benedicta. *Miracles and the Medieval Mind*. Philadelphia: University of Pennsylvania Press, 1982.

The Crusades

Mayer, H. E. *The Crusades*. Translated by J. Gillingham. Oxford: Clarendon Press, 1978.

Riley-Smith, Jonathan. *The Crusades: A Short History*. New Haven: Yale University Press, 1987.

Unstead, R. J. *Living in a Crusader Land*. Illustrated by Victor Ambrus. Reading, Mass.: Addison-Wesley, 1971.

Architecture and Art

Binski, Paul. *Painters. Medieval Craftsmen series*. Toronto: University of Toronto Press, 1991.

Brown, Michelle P. *Understanding Illuminated Manuscripts: A Guide to Technical Terms*. Malibu, Calif.: J. Paul Getty Museum, 1994.

Brown, Sarah, and David O'Connor. *Glass-Painters. Medieval Craftsmen series*. Toronto: University of Toronto Press, 1991.

Coldstream, Nicola. *Masons and Sculptors. Medieval Craftsmen series*. Toronto: University of Toronto Press, 1991.

Eames, Elizabeth. *English Tilers. Medieval Craftsmen series*. Toronto: University of Toronto Press, 1991.

Gimpel, Jean. *The Cathedral Builders*. Translated by C. F. Barnes, Jr. New York: Grove Press, 1961.

Hamel, Christopher de. *Scribes and Illuminators. Medieval Craftsmen series*. Toronto: University of Toronto Press, 1991.

Staniland, Kay. *Embroiderers. Medieval Craftsmen series*. Toronto: University of Toronto Press, 1991.

Swaan, Wim. *The Late Middles Ages: Art and Architecture from 1350 to the Advent of the Renaissance*. Ithaca: Cornell University Press, 1977.

Literature

Alighieri, Dante. *The Divine Comedy*. Translated by C.H. Sisson. New York: Oxford University Press, 1995.

André le Chapelain. *The Art of Courtly Love*. New York: F. Ungar, 1959.

Beowulf. Translated by Michael Alexander. Harmondsworth: Penguin, 1973.

Boccaccio, Giovanni. *The Decameron*. Translated by G. H. McWilliam. New York: Penguin, 1995.

Chaucer, Geoffrey. *The Canterbury Tales*. New York: Knopf, 1992.

Chrétien de Troyes. *Arthurian Romances*. New York: Dutton, 1975.

Christine de Pisan. *The Treasure of the City of Ladies, or, The Book of the Three Virtues*. Translated by Sarah Lawson. New York: Penguin, 1985.

Geoffrey of Monmouth. *The History of the Kings of Britain*. Translated by Lewis Thorpe. Baltimore: Penguin, 1966.

The Lais of Marie de France. Translated by Glyn S. Burgess and Keith Busby. New York: Penguin, 1986.

Langland, William. *Piers the Ploughman*. Translated by J. F. Goodridge. New York: Penguin, 1968.

The Song of Roland. Translated by Glyn Burgess. New York: Penguin, 1983.

Von Strassburg, Gottfried. *Tristan*. New York: Penguin, 1967.

Feudalism

Bloch, Marc. *Feudal Society*. 2 vols. Chicago: University of Chicago Press, 1961.

Herlihy, David. *The History of Feudalism*. Atlantic Highlands, N.J.: Humanities Press, 1971.

Poly, J. P., and Eric Bournazel. *The Feudal Transformation, 900–1200*. New York: Holmes & Meier, 1991.

Chivalry and Courtly Love

Barber, Richard. *The Knight and Chivalry*. New York: Harper & Row, 1970.

Bumke, Joachim. *Courtly Culture: Literature and Society in the High Middle Ages*. Translated by Thomas Dunlap. Berkeley: University of California Press, 1991.

Keen, Maurice. *Chivalry*. New Haven: Yale University Press, 1984.

Painter, Sidney. *French Chivalry*. Ithaca: Cornell University Press, 1957.

Castles

Biesty, Stephen, and Richard Platt. *Castle*. Illustrated by Stephen Biesty. Boston: Houghton Mifflin, 1994.

Burke, John. *Life in the Castle in Medieval England*. London: B. T. Batsford, 1978.

Gies, Joseph, and Frances Gies. *Life in a Medieval Castle*. New York: Harper & Row, 1974.

Gregor, Hugh. *Castles: A Guide for Young People*. London: Her Majesty's Stationery Office, 1977.

Oakeshott, R. Ewart. *A Knight and His Castle*. Illustrated by R. Ewart Oakeshott. London: Lutterworth, 1965.

Unstead, R. J. *Living in a Castle*. Illustrated by Victor Ambrus. Reading, Mass.: Addison-Wesley, 1971.

Warner, Philip. *The Medieval Castle: Life in a Fortress in Peace and War*. New York: Taplinger, 1971.

Armor and Weapons

Ashdown, Charles Henry. *European Arms and Armour*. New York: Barnes & Noble, 1995.

Borg, Alan. *Arms and Armour in Britain*. London: Her Majesty's Stationery Office, 1979.

DeVries, Kelly. *Medieval Military Technology*. Lewiston, N.Y.: Broadview Press, 1992.

Glubock, Shirley. *Knights in Armor*. New York: Harper & Row, 1969.

Nicolle, David. *Arms and Armour of the Crusading Era, 1050–1350*. White Plains, N.Y.: Kraus International Publications, 1988.

Pfaffenbichler, Matthias. *Amourers. Medieval Craftsmen series*. Toronto: University of Toronto Press, 1991.

Peasant Life and Manors

Bennett, H. S. *Life on the English Manor*. Wolfeboro, N.H.: A. Sutton, 1989.

Chapelot, Jean and Robert Fossier. *The Village and House in the Middle Ages.* Translated by Henry Cleere. Berkeley: University of Califoia Press, 1985.

Fossier, Robert. *Peasant Life in the Medieval West.* New York: Blackwell, 1988.

Genicot, Leopold. *Rural Communities in the Medieval World.* Baltimore: Johns Hopkins University Press, 1990.

Gies, Frances, and Joseph Gies. *Life in a Medieval Village.* New York: Harper & Row, 1990.

Hanawalt, Barbara A. *The Ties That Bound: Peasant Families in Medieval England.* New York: Oxford University Press, 1986.

Morgan, Gwyneth. *Life in a Medieval Village.* New York: Cambridge University Press, 1975.

Trade and Towns

Cherry, John. *Goldsmiths. Medieval Craftsmen series.* Toronto: University of Toronto Press, 1991.

Ennen, Edith. *The Medieval Town.* New York: North-Holland, 1979.

Gies, Joseph, and Frances Gies. *Life in a Medieval City.* New York: Harper & Row, 1973.

Nicholas, David. *The Growth of the Medieval City: From Late Antiquity to the Early Fourteenth Century.* New York: Longman, 1997.

————. *The Later Medieval City, 1300–1500.* New York: Longman, 1997.

Rörig, Fritz. *The Medieval Town.* Berkeley: University of California Press, 1967.

Thrupp, Sylvia. *Merchant Class of Medieval London.* Ann Arbor: University of Michigan Press, 1968.

The Plague

Hatcher, John. *Plague, Population and the English Economy, 1348–1530.* London: Macmillan, 1977.

McNeill, W. H. *Plagues and People.* New York: Anchor Press, 1976.

Platt, Colin. *King Death: The Black Death and Its Aftermath in Late-Medieval England.* Toronto, University of Toronto Press, 1996.

Ziegler, Philip. *The Black Death.* New York: John Day, 1969.

Family Life

Duby, Georges. *The Knight, the Lady, and the Priest: The Making of Modern Marriage in Medieval France.* New York: Pantheon Books, 1983.

Hanawalt, Barbara A. *Growing Up in Medieval London: The Experience of Childhood in History.* New York: Oxford University Press, 1993.

Herlihy, David. *Medieval Households.* Cambridge, Mass.: Harvard University Press, 1985.

Parsons, John Carmi, and Bonnie Wheeler, eds. *Medieval Mothering.* New York: Garland, 1996.

Shahar, Shulasmith. *Childhood in the Middle Ages.* New York: Routledge, 1990.

Women in the Middle Ages

Ennen, Edith. *The Medieval Woman.* Oxford: Basil Blackwell, 1989.

Klapisch-Zuber, Christiane. *A History of Women in the West. Silences of the Middle Ages.* Cambridge, Mass: Belknap Press, 1992.

Labarge, M. W. *A Small Sound of the Trumpet: Women in Medieval Life.* Boston: Beacon Press, 1986.

McNamara, Jo Ann. *A New Song: Celibate Women in the First Three Christian Centuries.* New York: Haworth Press, 1983.

Power, Eileen. *Medieval Women.* New York: Cambridge University Press, 1975.

Shahar, Shulasmith. *The Fourth Estate: A History of Women in the Middle Ages.* Translated by C. Galai. New York: Methuen, 1983

Wemple, Suzanne Fonay. *Women in Frankish Society: Marriage and the Cloister, 500 to 900.* Philadelphia: University of Pennsylvania Press, 1981.

Food and Cooking

Adamson, Melitta Weiss, ed. *Food in the Middle Ages: A Book of Essays.* New York: Garland, 1995.

Arn, Mary-Jo, ed. *Medieval Food and Drink.* Binghamton, N.Y.: Center for Medieval and Early Renaissance Studies, 1995.

Black, Maggie. *The Medieval Cookbook.* New York: Thames & Hudson, 1992.

Cosman, Madeleine Pelner. *Fabulous Feasts: Medieval Cookery and Ceremony.* New York: Braziller, 1976.

Hieatt, Constance B., Brenda M. Hosington, and Sharon Butler. *Pleyn Delit: Medieval Cookery for Modern Cooks.* Toronto: University of Toronto Press, 1996.

Scully, D. Eleanor. *Early French Cookery: Sources, History, Original Recipes and Modern Adaptations.* Ann Arbor: University of Michigan Press, 1995.

Scully, Terence. *The Art of Cookery in the Middle Ages.* Rochester, N.Y.: Boydell Press, 1995.

Index

References to illustrations are indicated by page numbers in *italics*

Picture Credits

About the Author

Barbara A. Hanawalt is the George III Professor of British History at Ohio State University. She was previously professor of history at the University of Minnesota and the director of its Medieval Studies Center. Her most recent books include *Growing Up in Medieval London: The Experience of Childhood in History*, *The Ties that Bound: Peasant Families in Medieval England*, and *'Of Good and Ill Repute': Gender and Social Control in Medieval England*.